Michael Dummett

Bernhard Weiss

PRINCETON UNIVERSITY PRESS
PRINCETON AND OXFORD

Published in North and South America by
Princeton University Press, 41 William Street,
Princeton, New Jersey 08540. All rights reserved.

First published in 2002 by Acumen
Acumen Publishing Limited
15a Lewins Yard
East Street
Chesham
Bucks HP5 1HQ, UK

Library of Congress Control Number 2002107391

ISBN 0-691-11329-7 (hardcover)
ISBN 0-691-11330-0 (paperback)

Designed and typeset in Century Schoolbook
by Kate Williams, Abergavenny.
Printed and bound by Biddles Ltd., Guildford and King's Lynn.

www.pupress.princeton.edu

10   9   8   7   6   5   4   3   2   1

Contents

Acknowledgements

My thanks to David Cockburn, R. Rockingham-Gill and Christine Jacobsen for useful discussions. Three referees, Sanford Shieh, Peter Milne and Peter Sullivan, and Nils Kurbis read a complete draft of the book. I am very grateful to them for their detailed and helpful comments. For a spell during this project I corresponded with and then visited Michael Dummett. I am extremely grateful to him for his time, his philosophical inspiration and for his encouragement. I can only hope that my efforts here are fitting thanks.

Christine has suffered my irritability and raised my spirits; I know how lucky I am. My parents deserve special thanks for their robust, unwavering, thoroughly unphilosophical, support.

Bernhard Weiss

Abbreviations

FPL   *Frege: Philosophy of Language*. London: Duckworth, 1973 (2nd edition 1981).

EoI   *Elements of Intuitionism*. Oxford: Oxford University Press, 1977 (2nd edition 2000).

T&OE   *Truth and Other Enigmas*. London: Duckworth, 1978.

IFP   *The Interpretation of Frege's Philosophy*. London: Duckworth, 1981.

LBoM   *The Logical Basis of Metaphysics*. London: Duckworth, 1991.

F&OP   *Frege and Other Philosophers*. Oxford: Oxford University Press, 1991.

FPM   *Frege: Philosophy of Mathematics*. London: Duckworth, 1991.

SoL   *The Seas of Language*. Oxford: Oxford University Press, 1993.

OoAP   *Origins of Analytical Philosophy*. London: Duckworth, 1993.

Introduction

Born in 1925, Professor Sir Michael Dummett has, since the middle 1950s, exerted a dominant influence on British philosophy and, partly through important dialogues with the likes of Quine, Goodman, Putnam and Davidson, his sway has left its considerable mark on American philosophy too. After completing his military service Dummett went to the University of Oxford as a student where his main teachers were Urmson and Anscombe, the latter exerting the greater influence. He began his professional career with a year spent lecturing at the University of Birmingham. After that he returned to Oxford where, apart from visiting appointments at some American institutions and a year spent at the University of Ghana, he has spent the balance of his career. He was appointed to the Wykeham Chair of Logic at the University of Oxford in 1979, a position that he held until his retirement in 1992. He was knighted in 1999.

His writings are voluminous and are not confined to philosophy. His philosophical writings alone run to nine substantial books and numerous papers. In addition he has also written books on voting procedures, grammar and writing style, and the game of Tarot. His enthusiasm for Tarot has spawned two books (a third is in preparation); they are, I think, a testament both to his intellectual curiosity and to his sense of responsibility towards knowledge and its preservation. His work against racism is both long-standing and passionate. It led him, among other things, to act as chairman in two unofficial committees of inquiry (one into Southall, 23 April 1979,[1] and the other into the Blair Peach affair[2]). Philosophers will have come to know about this aspect of Dummett's life through the preface to the first edition of *Frege: Philosophy of Language*. This ends with

1

Dummett poignantly coming to terms with the fact that Frege, a philosopher whom he profoundly admires, held some extremely racist views. Speaking of discovering these views in one of Frege's diaries, Dummett says:

> When I first read that diary, many years ago, I was deeply shocked, because I had revered Frege as an absolutely rational man, if, perhaps, not a very likeable one. I regret that the editors of Frege's Nachlass chose to suppress that particular item. From it I learned something about human beings which I should be sorry not to know; perhaps something about Europe, also.
>
> (1981: xii)

Without doubt the major influence on Dummett's philosophy is his reading of Frege. Four of his books are explicit studies of him,[3] a fifth is substantially devoted to him[4] and even when Frege is not the object of discussion Fregean ideas and issues permeate Dummett's writings. Dummett places himself firmly within (his conception of) the analytical tradition in philosophy and hails Frege as the founder of that tradition. According to Dummett the distinguishing feature of the analytic tradition is a focus on analysing and explicating language, which become the method of philosophy. As he says,

> [First,] the goal of philosophy is the analysis of the structure of *thought*; secondly, the study of *thought* is to be sharply distinguished from the study of the psychological process of *thinking*; and, finally, . . . the only proper method for analysing thought consists in the analysis of *language*.
>
> (T&OE: 458, original emphasis)

He credits Frege with these insights, as he takes them to be. One might well debate whether these theses are distinctive of the analytic tradition; certainly it is easy to come up with examples of philosophers firmly embedded in that tradition who would question some or all of these claims. However that wouldn't, in itself, refute Dummett's contention since what characterizes a philosopher's place in a tradition is not simply a question of what tenets she cleaves to but is equally a matter of the body of literature which she examines and to which she reacts. So, for instance, Gareth Evans, who repudiated the third of these theses, would still count as an analytic philosopher because his philosophy was developed by rebelling against and adapting ideas which were present in that tradition. But let us leave that debate for another occasion; our focus here is Dummett and his conception of philosophy.

A consequence of the three theses is that the philosophy of language occupies a central and a fundamental role. Dummett, however, wants to distance the character of his concern with language from that of others', in particular from those of ordinary language philosophers and the logical positivists. Ordinary language philosophy had been the dominant philosophical school at Oxford when Dummett arrived there in the late 1940s. Its methodology consists in resolving philosophical problems by acute and sensitive observation of the way language is actually used. Dummett rejects the particularism of such an account, noting that the ordinary language philosophers found themselves formulating concepts which apply generally and which are systematically related to one another: their practice belies their espoused methodology. However, perhaps more profound than this perceived fault in ordinary language philosophy, Dummett sees language as a phenomenon which, through its intrinsic nature, calls for systematic study. Evidently we see language and linguistic mastery as a complex of interrelated features (we master language in its complexity by internalizing principles governing its use). Now Dummett insists that these features should be capable of being systematically represented. For, in providing a systematic representation of language, its complexity is thereby *explained*. So Dummett thinks that philosophy has an explanatory role, which it fulfils through being systematic.

The logical positivists too concerned themselves, after a fashion, with language. But they were never interested in the philosophy of language as such. Rather they deployed an inchoate conception of the nature of meaningfulness in constructing a methodology whose aim was to eradicate philosophical questions or to bring out their scientific character. Dummett should be carefully distinguished from these verificationists. First, as we shall see, though he is exercised by the apparent fruitlessness of many metaphysical debates, in contrast to the logical positivists, he doesn't see in this an indication of their vacuity. Instead he thinks we need to work somewhat harder in characterizing the nature of the debates and the respective content of the opposing positions *before* we set about trying to resolve them. Secondly, Dummett is not revisionary in the manner of the logical positivists who felt they were in possession of a criterion for determining whether or not any given putative proposition was genuine. Dummett never questions the meaningfulness of our statements; rather he wants to find the correct characterization of their meaning. So where he recommends a change in linguistic practice he does so, not because he thinks that we have a case in which we have falsely attributed content to a claim, but because we have grafted a use onto an expression which is justified only by a misconstrual of the nature of our understanding of it. In other words, he thinks that certain uses of an expression may be justifiable only on a mistaken view of the nature of the expression's meaning. Once that is seen aright we shall modify our use accordingly. His philosophy is sometimes confused with that of the logical positivists because he, like them, is interested in providing accounts of the meaning of statements in terms of what constitutes a verification of them. But, whereas for the logical positivists possession of a means of verification was a criterion of meaningfulness for statements, for Dummett it is only a criterion for legitimating the assumption that the statement has a determinate truth-value (see Chapters 3 and 4).

Dummett pursues his interest in the philosophy of language by thinking about the theory of meaning. A theory of meaning for a language will provide a way of generating specifications of the meaning of every expression in the language on the basis of specifications of the meanings of primitive expressions in the language. This way of pursuing the philosophy of language owes itself to an American influence and to that of Davidson in particular. Though as a matter of exegesis it is controversial, Dummett would claim that Frege himself took the most important steps in this direction. So the recent flowering of the approach is, in many ways, the yield of a rediscovery.

After Frege, Dummett's next most important intellectual debt is to Wittgenstein. But although he draws many important lessons from Wittgenstein's discussion of meaning and understanding, Dummett is fundamentally opposed to Wittgenstein's philosophical method. Whereas Wittgenstein puts forward a view according to which we cannot advance philosophical theses and must instead defuse philosophical questions by means of a kind of philosophical therapy, Dummett sees philosophy as part of the search for truth and as attempting to find answers to (well-put) philosophical questions. There is, he claims, no need for us to relinquish these ambitions and, in the face of no decisive evidence against their feasibility, every motive to cling to them. Thus Wittgenstein for Dummett is a brilliant thinker who provided a corrective to many Fregean misconceptions. Whereas Frege provided an account of meaning that is essentially Platonistic (since his only way of securing objectivity of meaning was via reification), Wittgenstein emphasizes the intersubjective realm and the role of language in communication and in human life in general.

But Frege provided the basic framework for conceptualizing how language functions; Wittgenstein (intentionally) provided no framework and cannot be seen as a model for how to practise philosophy.

Why exactly does Dummett repudiate what he sees as Wittgenstein's supposed philosophical vision and thus reject a Wittgensteinian influence in philosophy? He takes it that Wittgenstein thought that we should not attempt to provide solutions to philosophical problems but that we should instead try to unpick the confusions which led to our posing of the philosophical questions in the first place. Philosophical questions call not for responses but for defusion; attempting to answer philosophical problems is a part of the very same syndrome which led to us to ask them. Philosophical confusions are assuaged by returning us to ordinary language,[5] by seeing facets of our use of language aright despite our temptation to misconstrue that use by, for instance, mistaking analogies between different regions of language.[6] Such an approach makes impossible the search for a systematic theory of meaning and, conversely, Dummett claims, can be arrived at only by taking the impossibility of a systematic theory as a premise. So the upshot of this view of Wittgenstein is that Dummett is left wondering what the argument against the systematic approach is. To be sure, although *Philosophical Investigations* raises difficulties for the systematic approach no conclusive argument against it can be found.

The most eloquent of Wittgenstein's interpreters on this theme is, perhaps, Cora Diamond. On her reading, Wittgenstein is concerned to move us away from imposing philosophical *requirements*. For, in doing so, we move ourselves away from our practices and thus leave aspects of ourselves behind when we come to do philosophy. And those aspects might be just what we need in order to resolve or dispel our philosophical perplexity. So according to Diamond the main upshot of the Wittgensteinian perspective is that we cease to restrict the character and form in which philosophical illumination might come. We might achieve illumination by offering a conventional argument but we might achieve it too by means of a parable, joke or riddle.

Let's try to say something positive here without fully engaging in this debate. I am not sure what exactly a philosophical requirement is, nor am I quite sure why imposing such a thing is to be treated with such suspicion. But in any case it's quite clear that if there are philosophical requirements Dummett asks us to insist on one. For he thinks that language should admit of explanation by means of a systematic theory of meaning and, as we shall see, he takes those elements of our practice which fail to admit of such an explanation to stand in need of revision. So here without doubt we have a forthright and (relatively) clear philosophical requirement. Should we object to it because it is a philosophical requirement? Should we object to it because it restricts the mode in which we offer ourselves illumination? I don't see that any of this follows. Dummett is perfectly clear about the nature of his requirement and clear too about its motivation. So if it is well motivated he is right to restrict his attention to the search for a certain sort of account. True, in doing so we leave aspects of ourselves behind, or set them aside for certain purposes. But that we are doing so and the reason why we are doing so are both quite explicit in Dummett's writings. We don't have any potential source of confusion here. The Wittgensteinian has only two options. First, she can engage with Dummett, in which case we need an argument against the feasibility or, perhaps, against the potential interest of his approach and, lacking this, we would be right to stick with that approach as a matter of methodology; insight is sought through either the eventual success of the project or through its failure and the reasons for its failure. Secondly, she can simply revert to a blanket suspicion of "philosophical requirements". Apart from a bad inductive argument from past cases of imposing philosophical requirements, I cannot think why we should take such a crude view seriously.[7]

Dummett's philosophy is programmatic; accordingly we attempt to construct a systematic theory of meaning *and* the method of construction will be dictated by procedures of enquiry upon which we can agree: we search for a theory whose truth is definitive and conclusive. Thus he conceives of philosophy in conventional terms; philosophy is part of the search for truth: we aim at achieving philosophical knowledge. Our methods of enquiry are distinct from those both of science and of mathematics. But there is such a method; it is the method discovered by Frege. That discovery was hard won and came comparatively late in philosophy's history. It may not, in fact, be the true method, indeed there may not be such a thing, but we do philosophy and ourselves no service by turning our backs on it prematurely. Frege's work, viewed through Dummettian spectacles, constitutes a refreshingly forthright and positive philosophical vision.

The overarching theme of this book is Dummett's discussion of realism: his characterization of realism, his attack on realism and his invention and exploration of the anti-realist position. We begin, however, with an examination of some of his views about language. Only against that setting can one fully appreciate, not perhaps the content, but certainly the point of his characterization of realism. Having arrived at an understanding of Dummett's conception of realism, we return to his views about the nature of meaning and understanding to develop an argument against realism. If that argument is successful we shall be forced to adopt a position that refuses to endorse realism; that is, we shall be anti-realists. The nature of that position is then examined in the remainder of the book: first in very general terms; then its revisionary consequences are investigated; and, finally, two hard and revealing cases for the anti-realist – the past and mathematics – are discussed.

I haven't tried to present Dummett as a historical figure (we are still far too close to him to attempt that) nor have I been at pains to trace the shifts and developments in his views. Rather I've attempted to engage with, what I take to be, some of his most important ideas and arguments. It is worth stating at the outset that I am strongly sympathetic to much of Dummett's thinking. In particular, I think that his characterization of realism is a brilliant philosophical crystallization of a crucial but largely elusive set of metaphysical intuitions. His ingenious meaning-theoretic argument against realism is, at the very least, a way of focusing a set of fascinating questions about the nature of the relation between the world and our representations of it. And his conception of the theory of meaning embodies a lucid vision of the nature of language and of the business of philosophy. None of these elements in his thinking is unproblematic or completely clear. So I am critical about aspects of his thought and have used secondary sources to raise other criticisms of it. My aim here has not been to object at every conceivable stage but to use criticism to help to elucidate the character of Dummett's positions and to see how those positions might be developed. At some points I've offered my own responses to some of Dummett's critics. In many cases I am doubtful whether Dummett would agree with my suggestions and in some cases I know he wouldn't. Never mind. The best way of understanding a philosopher – as Dummett exemplifies in his study of Frege – is to engage with his thought. Here I've attempted to engage with Dummett's writings and my hope is that this will aid the reader in her own engagement with his thinking. This book should carry the following warning: reading it is no substitute for reading Dummett himself. If successful, it may be an aid and, perhaps, a spur to the latter.

Chapter 1

What is a theory of meaning?

The central task of the philosophy of language is to illuminate or explain the concept of meaning as it applies to language. One way in which we might do this is to reflect on and possibly offer an analysis of our concept of linguistic meaning. Another is to reflect on our use of the term "meaning" in application to linguistic items. Dummett's recommendation (and he takes himself to be following Davidson here) is that we do best to examine the concept by trying to get clear about the form that a theory of meaning for a particular language, a meaning-theory,[1] should take. We'll need to probe in much more detail Dummett's ideas about the nature of a meaning-theory. However, for the moment, let's characterize a theory in terms of what it should achieve. A theory of meaning for a particular language will provide the means systematically to generate specifications (or characterizations) of the meaning of each expression in the language. Our only model of how such specifications might be systematically generated as part of a theory is to conceive of the theory as a deductively connected set of propositions; axioms will provide the basis of the process of generation and the specifications will emerge as theorems of the theory. In other words, we shall have a basic set of truths about the language, truths which capture the meanings of primitive expressions and which explain how the meanings of complex expressions depend upon the meanings of their components. Given some expression of the language we shall then be able to infer the specific theorem which relates to its meaning. This sketchy characterization of a meaning-theory doesn't, of course, tell us very much about the nature of such a theory but it provides a sufficient contrast with other approaches for us to begin to weigh them up.

Let us contrast the case of knowledge with that of meaning, as Dummett does. Questions concerning the nature of knowledge can be pursued by asking questions about ascriptions of knowledge: when are these justified and what content do they have? But questions about meaning cannot be focused in this way. We cannot examine the nature of linguistic meaning merely by confining our attention to sentences of the forms: x means that y; or, x means the same as y. There are, it seems to me, two reasons for this. The first is that it is contentious that direct specifications of meaning (specifications of the first form) will, in general, be a possibility or that specifications of sameness of meaning provide all we want to capture in an explanation of meaning. Secondly, even if these queries could be quelled, what we are interested in is generally applicable conditions for determining the correctness of specifications of meaning. That is, we don't actually want to possess a set of clauses specifying meaning; we already understand our own language and are not engaged in the business of translating a foreign language. Rather we want to know how these clauses would be generated and what ratifies them as correct. So what we are interested in is something general, namely, a method for producing specifications of meaning and for testing the acceptability of the results. But now we seem to have regenerated Dummett's approach. For these constraints will be given content in terms of how they govern the form taken by a meaning-theory: that is, a general specification of meanings.[2]

An additional point is that the nature of an expression's meaning is at least as much a function of the sorts of explanation we use to teach its use and of features of that use, as it is a function of our use of the expression in contexts involving explicit discussion of meaning. So were we to focus on speakers' use of the term "meaning" we might be ignoring substantial information about the concept, information which would form part of the data for a meaning-theory. Conversely, it seems that speakers of a language lacking in vocabulary for talk of meaning would nevertheless possess that concept (otherwise they couldn't communicate or succeed in teaching language). Thus it seems that our concept of meaning is illuminated more thoroughly by reference to relevant uses of language rather than by the explicit use of the concept itself. The way to get round the potentially impoverished use of the term "meaning" is to think about how the concept *would* feature in an attempt, quite generally, to specify the meanings of expressions, that is, to investigate the form of a meaning-theory.

The subject matter of a meaning-theory

How would one set about constructing a meaning-theory? Clearly the
theory will begin with linguistic behaviour and so, in some sense, will
have to fit with it. So, on the one hand, we shall talk of ascending
from facts about linguistic behaviour to the mechanics of the theory
and, on the other, of descending from the inner workings of the theory
to an account of linguistic behaviour. However, the terms in which
linguistic behaviour is given to us, and the nature of the fit between
that and the theory, need to be explained. That explanation will depend on what we want the theory for and what sort of theory we think
it is possible to construct.

Dummett is quite clear that we don't want an empirical theory
that will enable us to predict linguistic behaviour. Predictive success
is neither necessary nor sufficient. It is not sufficient since a theorist
equipped only with a predictively successful theory would not be able
to exploit the knowledge she thereby possesses in order to pursue her
own ends in conversation. She may be able to pass unnoticed in the
community but she could only exploit her knowledge of the theory to
do such things as to express her view or ask for information if she
conjoined that knowledge with an antecedent grasp of the significance of certain sorts of linguistic acts. But then that knowledge
should properly be articulated in the theory. Predictive success is not
necessary since a theorist might have all the abilities just mentioned
and have them in virtue of her knowledge of the theory yet be unable
to predict linguistic behaviour in the way a good empirical theory
might. A theory of this sort would convey all the knowledge necessary
to illuminate the concept of meaning; it would be a meaning-theory.
So we don't want a theory that accounts for linguistic behaviour from
an external point of view (and which is thus constrained only by
predictive success), we want a meaning-theory that makes explicit
the *knowledge* implicated in linguistic behaviour. Thus a theory of
meaning is a theory of understanding. The connection between the
knowledge thus articulated by the theory (the knowledge possessed
by the theorist) and the knowledge possessed by actual speakers will
emerge as a delicate matter to be tackled below.

Systematicity, compositionality and meaning-theories

The meaning of an utterance is a product of that of its component words and the way in which they are combined in the utterance. This apparent platitude would appear to explain a speaker's capacity to understand novel utterances: the utterance is understood by deploying one's grasp of the meanings of the component words and of the effect of the manner in which they are combined in the utterance. Since words and modes of combination make repeatable contributions to the meanings of utterances, the meaning of an utterance is determined systematically by that of its parts and their mode of combination. An adequate portrayal of the meanings of utterances will exhibit these systematic dependencies; an account of meaning will be systematic and so will deserve the accolade "meaning-theory".

What assumptions – what views of language – are implicated in this, not unnatural, train of thought? What shape would a systematic account of meaning take? What relation would it bear to speakers' understanding of language? What is the relation between the (supposed) systematicity of the meaning-theory and the (supposed) compositionality of language? What justification is there for insisting either on systematicity or on compositionality? This and the next chapter attempt to make some progress on Dummett's answers to these questions. I begin with a contrast between two conceptions of language.

Interpretation and convention

Suppose someone makes an utterance. To an appropriately qualified audience the utterance has a certain significance. It may convey information about the world, about the speaker's state of mind or about what the speaker requires of the hearer, and may convey mixtures of these sorts of thing. Linguistic meaning might be seen as a product of the process of interpretation whereby the hearer attaches a certain significance to the utterance. On the other hand, linguistic meaning might be seen as a resource exploited in the process of interpretation. Davidson exemplifies the former, interpretivist outlook. In contrast, Dummett argues that linguistic meanings are products of conventions that enable interpretation (where necessary) to take place. The basis of systematicity in the theory of meaning is intimately connected with the rejection of the interpretivist in favour of the conventionalist approach. The debate between Dummett and Davidson is very illuminating here.

An utterance, a speech act, may be – to give an inexhaustive list – an assertion, a command or an enquiry. That is, utterances come in a number of varieties depending on what the speaker is attempting to achieve by means of the utterance: whether she is trying to convey information, request information, require that something be done. Utterances can be distinguished by what, following Frege, has come to be called the *force* that attaches to them. As social creatures we are adept at picking out the force with which an utterance is made, and doing so is an essential element in communication: one couldn't learn language if one failed to be sensitive to the force of an utterance, and a translation manual would be little help in communicating with a foreign people were one blind to matters to do with force. So, to be a competent speaker, one must be sensitive to the force of utterances, but the constitution of this sensitivity needs to be explained.

Force then is a property of utterances. But utterances involve the use of sentences, and sentences themselves come in a number of forms. Depending on word order, punctuation and so on, a sentence might be indicative, imperative, optative or interrogative. Consider "The apple is peeled", "Peel the apple", "Would that the apple were peeled" and "Is the apple peeled?". That is, a sentence might have one or another *mood*.

Now one way of explaining a speaker's sensitivity to force would be to reduce it to a sensitivity to mood. If, say, an assertion is an utterance of an indicative sentence then a sensitivity to the mood of the sentence will deliver a sensitivity to the force of the utterance (and similarly for the other moods and forces). In "Moods and Performances" Davidson (1984) puts this simplistic scenario under stress and thus questions the underlying thought, namely that a sensitivity to force is based on a sensitivity to mood. If I read him aright his thought is to reverse the direction of dependency here: mood is a product of a theory of interpretation whose object is the interpretation of utterances.[3] So interpreting an utterance as having a certain force is conceptually prior to the assignment of moods to sentences. The point relates to the issue between the interpretivist and conventionalist. For, if mood is prior to force, it is plausible to think of hearers interpreting speakers by availing themselves of conventions governing the use of sentences. Conversely, if force is prior to mood, then the assignment of a certain significance to utterances of sentences of a certain form will purely be a product of the process of interpretation.[4]

Dummett concedes that Davidson's argument shows there is no simple connection between the force of an utterance and the mood of a sentence. However, he thinks that each type of force must be explained by reference to a given practice. The mood of a sentence then may fit it for inclusion in one or another such practice, so it may have one or another force. But the force that an utterance possesses will be (very largely) determined by conventions governing the use of sentences in appropriate moods. So although mood does not determine force, force is determined by a certain conventional use being made of a sentence in a given mood. The *point* of making such an utterance will then determine answers to further questions – those questions that most occupy Davidson – about the role of the utterance.

I am here less interested in trying to decide between these points of view than in exhibiting the consequences each has for systematicity in the theory of meaning. Since Dummett distinguishes between what is said by means of an utterance and the point of saying it he can relegate the latter to an account of the general manner in which we set about estimating the intentions of others. This is not an essentially linguistic process and so does not fall within the scope of a meaning-theory for a language. If one refuses to acknowledge Dummett's distinction (as Davidson does) then the nature, and thus significance, of an utterance will not be a matter of convention. Linguistic meaning then will not be construed simply as a product of convention but will always be, in part, a product of a speaker's purposes and intentions. So the subject matter for a systematic theory of meaning vanishes. In contrast, Dummett's distinction combined with the further thought that what is said is determined by (linguistic) conventions allows for the systematic portrayal of these conventions in a meaning-theory. So the Dummettian perspective is a prerequisite for systematicity in the theory of meaning.

This may appear to be an odd claim given Davidson's predilection for a theory of meaning as a systematic theory of truth. But there is really no tension here since for Davidson the object of the meaning-theory is not a public language such as English or a dialect thereof. Rather a hearer will construct a meaning-theory in an effort to make sense of a speaker's utterances (on a given occasion). The theory is subservient to the process of interpreting the speaker; it is an instrument in this process. So, for our purposes, it is irrelevant that Davidson thinks that the most efficient way of engaging in this process of interpretation is via the construction of a systematic theory of a certain form. The main point is that he eschews a systematic meaning-theory for a language in favour of a notion of interpretation. Indeed, in denying that languages, as conceived of by philosophers and linguists, exist, Davidson precisely denies the object of such theories.

Sense and force

If we accept Dummett's view then the difference between mood and force becomes less important. I want now to discuss the relation between the sense of an utterance and its force. What drives the idea that there is a common element between, say, the utterances of "The window is closed", "Is the window closed?" and "Close the window", that this common element is a shared content or sense and, finally, that each of these utterances attaches a different force to the same content? In other words, what, if anything, inclines one to the view that an utterance can be dissected into a sense used with a certain force? What would be the consequence of noting that these sentences have very different uses and thus of being sceptical that there is a general and systematic set of relationships here to be described? That is, how essential is the common content view to an insistence on systematicity in the theory of meaning?

There is an intuitive plausibility to the common content view. It does appear that our three sentences above share a content and that the first puts this content forward as true, the second asks whether it is true and the third commands that it be made true. English clearly includes a procedure by which indicatives, quite generally, can be transformed into interrogatives and imperatives (by means of changes in word order and punctuation). Moreover it seems that an understanding of this procedure combined with a general grasp of the practice of using commands allows one to move from an assertion that one understands to a command that one understands (and vice versa, with similar remarks applying for the other sorts of force). But this last point about understanding is an addition to the banal observation about English. There is nothing surprising or thought-provoking in the idea that we can manufacture an imperative from an indicative and vice versa. What should give us some cause for thought is the idea that in doing so we are performing an operation on a given content (which is preserved). The additional thought about understanding goes hand in hand with this about content. For if the content of an imperative as used in a command can be seen as a product of an operation on the content of an indicative as used in an assertion then a grasp of the significance of the operation together with a grasp of the content of the indicative will deliver a grasp of the content of the imperative. Conversely, if an understanding of the imperative can be derived from a grasp of the significance of the grammatical transformation, indicative to imperative, and an understanding of the corresponding indicative then the content of the imperative is a function of the content of the indicative. So far we have a point about the structure of understanding. Given that structure, one might then think that there is a further question about the relative priorities of elements in that structure: should we see grasp of an imperative as *derived from* a grasp of the indicative or vice versa?

The following line of thought not merely supplies a reason for the claim about the structure of understanding but does so by addressing the question of priority. An imperative requires a certain action of its addressee. To understand the imperative is to know what sort of action is required, what constitutes compliance with the command. Now commands, like those issued on parade grounds – those that require very specific actions in their fulfilment – are surely rare and, indeed, exceptional. In general, there will be better and worse ways of fulfilling the requirements of a command but no specific course of action will be required. I may choose to comply with the command "Close the door" by setting off a controlled explosion. This would obviously be perverse but would comply with the command and, indeed, in sufficiently outlandish circumstances it might be the most appropriate way of complying. For another instance, my boss might command me to make the books balance, in bewilderment and horror I ask her how, only to be told that she doesn't know or care how. So the content of the command may well be completely clear even though the course of action it requires in given circumstances may be thoroughly obscure to both parties. And, in very many cases, it is a far from trivial question how best to carry out the command; so how it is to be carried out is not part of the content of the command. Thus one understands the command just when one knows what state of affairs it requires to be brought about and it is this knowledge which guides one's actions in an attempt to comply. But this state of affairs is precisely that described in the corresponding indicative. So grasp of the meaning of the indicative would deliver a grasp of the meaning of the imperative: they have a common content.

The thoughts just sketched argue not for a fundamental role for indicatives (and thus for assertion) but for the centrality of the notion of truth. They show that it would be wrong to think that the practice of a primitive language-game (such as that of Wittgenstein's builders) which only includes commands could adequately be described without presupposing a notion of truth, that is, an understanding of the conditions in which a command is fulfilled. To be sure, once we've recognized the centrality of truth it is tempting, in a language such as ours, which includes assertions, to take assertion as basic because the correctness of an assertion is so closely tied to its being true. We'll move on shortly to the question of whether we should yield to this temptation.[5]

The possibility of a systematic meaning-theory depends on a distinction between sense and force, for a systematic meaning-theory attempts to portray the meaning of a sentence as a function of the meaning of its component words. If there is no sense–force distinction then, in grasping the meaning of a sentence, a speaker grasps every aspect of its use. Or, better, there will be no generally applicable way of deriving certain aspects of the use of a sentence from a distinguished meaning-determining or canonical set of uses. Rather an understanding of the sentence will consist in an undifferentiated competence with all aspects of its use. So, if there's no sense–force distinction, then the meaning of any *utterance* must be a function of the meaning of its components. However, the force of an utterance is not a component of the utterance since, as Davidson makes clear, a prankster, joker, liar, faker or insinuator may appropriate any conventional indicator of force to her own ends. So the relation of the meaning of an utterance to that of its components is not functional. A systematic theory of meaning thus cannot be constructed in a framework that denies the sense–force distinction.

In contrast, if we retain the distinction then the meaning of a sentence can be given in terms of that of its components and we can then explain the meaning of an utterance in terms of the conventionally assigned significance of using a sentence with a certain content in an utterance with a certain force. So the shape of a systematic theory of meaning becomes apparent. At its core will be a systematic account of the meanings of sentences, each explained as a function of the meanings of its components and their mode of combination. The sentences will thus be seen as possessing a certain content which is thus placed at the disposal of the various types of force to effect utterances of one or another significance. The significance of the force of an utterance will be determined by convention.

Michael Dummett

Sense and reference

Thus far then the picture is as follows. As we work upwards from linguistic behaviour to the inner articulation of the theory, we need to distinguish a theory of force which gives a general characterization of the conventional significance of the various sorts of linguistic acts that can be performed and a theory of sense which accounts for the contents that the language makes available for use in those acts. We now need to consider the nature of a theory of sense.

The goal of a theory of sense is an account of the content common to sentences such as "Close the window", "Is the window closed?" and "The window is closed". As we noted above, that content appears to be intimately related with the notion of truth. In fact it seems that a certain truth-condition is, in turn, being commanded that it be brought about, enquired whether it obtains and asserted to obtain. So a natural thought is that the theory of sense should characterize the truth-condition of the relevant sentence in terms of the meanings of its component words. And for this task a theory of truth based on notions of reference and satisfaction seems ideally suited. The ultimate core of the theory of meaning will consist in a recursive characterization of the truth-conditions of (indicative) sentences in the language given recursive specifications of the references of sub-sentential expressions. The technical machinery involved in this generation of truth-conditions is well known to us from Tarski's work in giving a truth definition for formal languages. Davidson recommends that we exploit such a theory of truth for a natural language to yield a theory of meaning. The idea is familiar enough: a short reminder is relegated to Appendix 2.

It is crucial to note, however, that the theory of sense cannot be reduced to a theory of reference. We owe this point and the consequent distinction to Frege. The aim of the theory is to make explicit the knowledge possessed by a subject in virtue of being a speaker of the language. As Frege argues, we cannot attribute knowledge of reference to speakers for this misconstrues the nature of a speaker's capacities. The point is not merely that a speaker may fully understand an expression without knowing its reference but that a bare knowledge of reference is the wrong sort of knowledge to attribute to a speaker. Speakers' knowledge is both more fine-grained than could be accounted for in terms of knowledge of reference and need not extend as far as knowledge of reference. Speakers' knowledge cannot in general include knowledge of reference for then a speaker would know the truth-value of all identity, indeed, of all atomic statements expressible in the language simply on the basis of her understanding of the language. But speakers' knowledge cannot consist merely of knowledge of reference for then there would be no difference in cognitive value (or information content) between sentences involving co-referring terms. True identity statements are the paradigm here: "Hesperus is Hesperus" and "Hesperus is Phosphorus" would, on this misconstrual of understanding, convey the same information.

The argument is well known. But Dummett's discussion[6] and endorsement of it amply merit our attention. He finds two arguments. The first begins from the question of whether there can be bare knowledge of the reference of a word. We distinguish first between predicative knowledge and propositional knowledge. Predicative knowledge has the following form: S knows, of a, that it is F – for instance, Ludwig Wittgenstein knows, of Arkle, that "Arkle" refers to him. Propositional knowledge has the form S knows that P – for instance, Ludwig Wittgenstein knows that "Arkle" refers to Arkle. Now the premises of the argument are: (i) that predicative knowledge is based on propositional knowledge; and (ii) that there is never a single piece of propositional knowledge on which a given piece of predicative knowledge must be based: many cases of propositional knowledge will each give rise to a given piece of predicative knowledge.

The argument then proceeds as follows. Knowledge of the reference of a word is predicative knowledge. But, given (i), this must be based on propositional knowledge. However, given (ii), the characterization of this knowledge can be further refined by stating the precise piece of propositional knowledge that constitutes the predicative knowledge. This further characterization shows that there is always something more to be said about how a speaker knows the reference of a term. There cannot be a case of bare knowledge of reference.

Dummett takes the first premise to be "certainly true" and offers no argument for it. But why should we accept the second premise? If the second premise were false (or, at least, if it failed to apply in the cases in which we are interested) then there would be a unique piece of propositional knowledge constituting the predicative knowledge that, say, S knows, of Arkle, that "Arkle" refers to him. A plausible candidate would be, S knows that "Arkle" refers to Arkle. But if we ascribe propositional knowledge to a subject we must be able to say what this knowledge consists in, that is, we must be able to say what shows that the subject possesses this knowledge.[7] Now, where we can credit a subject with knowledge of language and thus with an ability to express her propositional knowledge, this is not problematic. But we cannot assume this in the present case where what we are concerned with is the basis of a speaker's knowledge of language. So here we shall need to think of the knowledge as manifested in an ability to recognize the object as the bearer of the name when *appropriately* presented with it. So we shall need an account both of how the object is to be presented and of the speaker's capacity to recognize it, that is, to re-identify it and to discriminate it from others. But this means that there is more to be said about S's knowledge than simply that S knows, of Arkle, that "Arkle" refers to him.

Dummett's thought here seems to be that, once we light on a likely candidate for the unique piece of propositional knowledge that must form the base of a piece of predicative knowledge, then there will be more to say about what this knowledge consists in, and that in spelling out this story we shall characterize the sense which a speaker attaches to a term. Two strands of thought appear to be involved here. One is that *many* pieces of propositional knowledge can constitute a given piece of predicative knowledge. So having specified the predicative knowledge there is an additional task of specifying the precise piece of propositional knowledge on which the former is based. The second, surely independent, line of thought is that *even if* a unique piece of propositional knowledge can be fixed upon then there is the additional task of specifying what manifestation of that propositional knowledge consists in. In any case we need to ascribe more than a bare knowledge of reference.

Even if we are persuaded by the thrust of the argument it is not clear that we have established a notion of sense. What we must concede is that there is no bare knowledge of reference. So there is always an additional task beyond specification of predicative knowledge. But it may be that, *qua speaker*, a specification of predicative knowledge suffices. Predicative knowledge is exhaustive of that knowledge which comprises understanding but that knowledge must be based on a further bit of knowledge that might vary from speaker to speaker and so is not part of what, as a speaker, one knows. Dummett and Frege would, however, reject this claim. For them understanding must include the second piece of knowledge also. To make this issue more than a terminological one about demarcations of the limits of understanding we need to invoke considerations about the content of sentences. This leads us to the second argument.

Let us suppose that "a" and "b" are co-referring terms. Suppose also that knowledge of the reference is part of knowledge of the meaning. Meaning is transparent in the sense that, if two terms share an ingredient of meaning, then anyone who understands the meaning of those terms knows (or can come to know on reflection on those meanings) that they share that ingredient. Thus, applying this to our case, "*a* is the same as *b*" is known to be true (or can be known to be true, on reflection) by anyone who understands "*a*" and "*b*". That, however, denies the a posteriori character of our knowledge of many identity statements. So a bare knowledge of reference is not an ingredient of understanding and, conversely, there must be a piece of knowledge that is both part of knowledge of meaning – understanding – and explains the cognitive value of identity statements. Another way of putting this point is as follows. Let's suppose that a bare knowledge of reference is necessary for understanding. That is, if *S* understands "*a*" then *S* knows, of *u*, that it is the referent of "*a*". Further, suppose that these predicative characterizations of *S*'s knowledge are complete. Then it follows that if *S* understands "*a*" and "*b*" then *S* knows, of *u*, that it is the referent of "*a*" and of "*b*", which is absurd. The only way to resist this conclusion is to offer a further characterization of *S*'s knowledge of the reference of a term. For then and only then shall we be able to say what knowledge *S* needs to gain in order to learn that "*a*" and "*b*" co-refer. Thus there must be more to be said about the nature of *S*'s knowledge *and* this knowledge is an ingredient of understanding.

Both arguments support the notion that there must be an ingredient of knowledge of meaning that is distinct from bare knowledge of reference. Neither, however, argues for a notion of sense properly so-called since neither argues that the relevant feature of meaning determines reference, as sense is supposed so to do. Both arguments begin from a position which attempts to characterize understanding in terms of predicative knowledge of reference and so neither says anything about a position which accepts that a bare knowledge of reference is not part of understanding but which holds that knowledge of meaning (understanding) fails to determine reference.[8]

If we set aside this question about whether or not sense determines reference, then the moral of the story is that we need to associate something other than a term's referent with it: a meaningful term has a sense and, possibly, a reference. The sense is part of the meaning of the term; it is part of what a speaker knows when she understands the term. But now, if understanding is (in part) knowledge of (a theory of) sense, then what is sense? And, what is the relation between a theory of sense and a theory of reference? These are large questions to which we will return below. Here, let us simply apply this lesson to our discussion of a theory of meaning construed as a theory of truth.

Take a sample clause from the theory of truth, for example:

"Fred" denotes Fred.

It might seem, from what has just been said, that the knowledge articulated in the clause is a knowledge of reference (since the clause specifies the reference of "Fred") and thus cannot form part of an articulation of the sense of the term. But this is false. The argument in favour of a notion of sense applies quite generally so it applies to the clause itself; the term "Fred" is *used* to give the reference of "Fred" with due sensitivity to its sense. And, although the truth of the clause would be preserved if a co-referring term were to replace this use of "Fred", the information content would not. So the clause can be taken to express a piece of knowledge that a speaker of the language possesses. The theory attributes to a speaker knowledge that "Fred" denotes Fred, not the knowledge of Fred that he is the denotation of "Fred". Thus knowledge of sense can, consistently with Frege's arguments, be seen in terms of knowledge of an appropriate theory of reference.[9] The upshot of the discussion is therefore that if a theory of reference is taken to be the core of a theory of meaning then this theory must deliver a theory of sense. For it to do so – and this is a crucial point in Dummett's thought – we must justify attributing knowledge of it to speakers. Also, so conceived, the theory of sense determines the theory of reference or, more succinctly, sense determines reference. Dummett accepts this last point as a general constraint: any theory of reference must mesh with a credible theory of sense. (This point will emerge as of some importance in Chapter 4.)

However, a theory of sense need not take this truth-conditional form (convincing though it seems to be *if* we credit ourselves with grasp of the appropriate notion of truth). An alternative possibility is that we characterize the meaning of a sentence by focusing on (an aspect of) its use. So, to explicate matters at the level of sense, we may concentrate on the conditions governing utterance of the sentence with a given force. The most plausible candidates for such an account of sense focus on conditions governing the making of assertions. For example one might argue that the meaning of a sentence is given by conditions warranting its assertion. The sense of a sub-sentential expression would then be given as its systematic contribution to determining the assertion-conditions of sentences in which it occurs.

Knowing the sense of a sentence would then be a matter of knowing its assertion-conditions. We shall discuss theories of this form in much more detail in Chapter 5. For the moment let me conclude this section by noting that even within such an account one might insist that sense determines reference and, as we shall see, given this insistence interesting consequences for the semantic concepts used in the theory of reference follow. Finally note that, although we might preserve this relation between the theories of reference and of sense, the direction of dependence has been reversed: the theory of sense delivers a theory of reference.

Summary

We began this chapter by thinking about how, as philosophers of language, we should seek for an account of the nature of linguistic meaning. Dummett's answer is that rather than focus on the functioning of the word "meaning" (and its cognates) in language we should think about the form that a theory of meaning for an entire language would take. This approach doesn't neglect our pre-theoretic concept of meaning but it recognizes that the best way of exploring that notion is through a sufficiently encompassing investigation of the meanings of our terms; that is, if we are to be ambitious, through construction of a meaning-theory. In addition, since a theory of meaning attempts to generate clauses which characterize the meanings of all terms in the language, it fully recognizes the truth in Frege's claim that the meaning of a word is its contribution to the meaning of sentences in which it occurs and Wittgenstein's claim that to understand a sentence is to understand a language: the theory embeds its account of the meanings of linguistic elements in a general account of the meanings expressible in the language.[10] So, in constructing the theory, we don't assume that it is possible to provide clauses of the form "*x* means that . . .". Rather we will have characterized the meaning of a term once we have characterized its contribution to the meaning of more complex expressions in which it occurs.

However, the meaning-theoretic approach to the question of meaning is not itself presuppositionless. A meaning-theory attempts to give a *systematic* characterization of the meanings of terms in the language and we noted that it is doubtful whether a systematic theory of meaning can be constructed unless we adopt a distinction between sense and force, that is, crudely, between the content of the

23

utterance and the conventional significance of the utterance. For a systematic theory of meaning will want to see the overall set of uses of a set of words as emerging systematically from an account of the content expressible using those words and a general account of the sorts of thing a speaker is, by convention, able to do with a given content. If we cannot do this then it is hard to see those uses as emerging systematically at all.

Having established this presupposition at the first stage in working upwards from speakers' use of language to the inner articulation of the theory, we then thought about how the theory should articulate the account of content. Frege's argument for a distinction between sense and reference was rehearsed through Dummettian spectacles. We noted that an upshot of this argument is not that a theory of reference (and truth) cannot be a basis for a theory of meaning. Rather the argument for the notion of sense simply claims that if it is to be so used we must be able to ascribe knowledge of the theory of reference to speakers.

Chapter 2 develops this theme of the role of the notion of knowledge in the theory of meaning. The investigation reveals important elements that are quite distinctive of Dummett's conception of the form that a meaning-theory must assume.

Chapter 2

Knowledge of the meaning-theory

Chapter 1 ended by noting that a meaning-theory must be a theory of understanding in the sense that, if the clauses of the core of the theory aren't already specifications of speakers' knowledge, then we must be able to ascribe knowledge of them to speakers. In this chapter we investigate Dummett's views on three issues – manifestation, modesty and molecularity – whose combined weight largely determines the role of knowledge in a meaning-theory. The first issue – manifestation – concerns the justification for ascribing a piece of knowledge – in particular for ascribing knowledge of meanings, as described by our preferred theory – to a speaker. The second issue – modesty versus full-bloodedness – concerns the terms in which we characterize knowledge of meanings. And the last issue – molecularity versus holism – takes up the question of whether knowledge of the theory is to be ascribed *en bloc* or in "small chunks".

Manifestation

Frege takes one important step in introducing the notion of knowledge into the theory of meaning: it won't do simply to discuss meaning in terms of reference; we need to be able to attribute knowledge of (the content of) the clauses of a theory of reference to speakers. Dummett recommends that this step should be followed by another: we cannot simply attribute such knowledge; we need to justify such attributions by explaining how possession of such knowledge is manifested.

There are a number of thoughts running through Dummett's insistence on manifestation. The simplest line of thinking is that it makes no sense to ascribe knowledge unless one thereby marks a distinction between someone who possesses the knowledge and someone who lacks it. If there is nothing that a subject is able to do which demonstrates her possession of a certain piece of knowledge then ascribing that knowledge is vacuous. Now, when we move to consider knowledge of the theory of meaning, there will be cases in which knowledge of the clauses of the theory is manifested by an ability to articulate them, that is, the clauses are explicitly known. But plainly knowledge of the theory cannot consist entirely of explicit knowledge since then speakers would, on the basis of the simplest reflection, be able to furnish a theory of meaning for their own language. Our present obscurity obviously belies that suggestion. Secondly, if the theory is meant to articulate the knowledge underpinning or comprising linguistic competence then it cannot in general be explicit knowledge without presupposing what we are intending to explain, namely, an understanding of language. So at various crucial points the knowledge of a theory of meaning will consist in implicit knowledge. Though it is trivial to say what constitutes a manifestation of explicit knowledge, it is a substantial task to explain what constitutes manifestation of implicit knowledge. On this reading the manifestation requirement often seems to be motivated by thoughts about the nature of knowledge and its ascription.

Another, rather more complex, line of thinking focuses on meaning and, in particular, on what is now seen as a Wittgensteinian lesson about the nature of language. The thought is that meanings must be public and that to insist on this is to insist that knowledge of meaning – understanding – must be (publicly) manifestable. To be sure, this thought fits in with Fregean thinking, though his attempt to guarantee the publicity of meaning simply consists in an insistence on the objectivity of senses. Having rejected Frege's reification of senses Dummett finds an alternative means of guaranteeing publicity by insisting on manifestability.

Why are meanings public? And, indeed, what is meant by "publicity"? Publicity seems to take its cue from ideas that take the meaning of a term to be exhausted by the use that is made of it, or by its role in communication or by what is made available to learners in explanations and demonstrations of meaning. Acceptance of these ideas leads, supposedly, to an acceptance of some version of the manifestation constraint. For, if meaning is exhaustively displayed in use, then an ingredient of understanding that is incapable of being manifested is an ingredient that transcends use and thus must be fictional. Similarly, there would be no way in which this ingredient could be guaranteed to be shared. So no way in which it forms part of the communicative role of language. And finally, it would be an ingredient of meaning that was not made available in the usual ways to learners of the language. But underlying these thoughts is a deeper one, one which rejects privacy in matters of meaning. If this further idea were absent then the insistence on communicativity and learnability would be unmotivated and the terms in which use is given would be underdescribed. The lack of motivation arises because many have thought and do think that language performs roles other than that of an instrument of communication. To many, language's role in thinking appears alluringly to be fundamental, while to others its relation to the world appears to be basic. The underdescription arises because one might suppose that use exhausts meaning but insist that the relevant notion of use be one that is responsive to privately available circumstances. Thus the underlying thought here is that there can be no purely private ingredient of understanding.

Although Dummett endorses Wittgenstein's argument against the possibility of a private ostensive definition – the, so-called, private language argument – he doesn't seem to make this a base for his requirement of publicity. Wittgenstein's argument is complex and appears to be intimately related to the notion of a standard of correctness and (consequently) to his views about following a rule.[1] Now although Dummett is arguing for a similar conclusion his arguments are brief and direct. He argues as follows. If there is an ingredient of meaning which transcends use then that meaning is incommunicable: we cannot guarantee that any two individuals, both participating happily within the practice, attach the same meaning to their terms. Meaning, so conceived, becomes irrelevant to the nature of the practice (T&OE: 218). At another point he argues, in a similar vein, that if private ostensive definition was the (ultimate) basis for conferrals of meaning then, on the one hand, the practice would be unaltered were the object of ostension misidentified or, indeed, if it were entirely lacking, or, on the other hand, the criterion for a misidentification would be a deviation from the practice. In the latter case the nature of use within the practice would be determinative of meaning, while in the former case the hypothesis of a private ostensive definition would fail to explain the nature of the practice: it would be explanatorily vacuous (SoL: 113, 102).

One worry here might take issue with Dummett's assimilation of the notion of meaning to an explanatory concept. However, more importantly, the arguments appear to beg the question. For they assume that the only acceptable notion of meaning is one whose entire content is given through being "relevant" to or explanatory of the nature of the practice. But why should we assume that, unless we had already granted that agreement in use constitutes agreement in meaning, that is, unless we had already granted what was to be shown?[2]

Implicit knowledge

Dummett thinks we must ascribe, at least, implicit knowledge of a theory of meaning to speakers. Alternatively, he sees the philosophical task as one of supplying a systematic representation of the knowledge underpinning speakers' ability to use the language. Ascription of knowledge only makes sense where possession of that knowledge can be manifested. So we need an account of what constitutes speakers' manifestation of their implicit knowledge of the theory of meaning.[3]

In his earliest formulations of the position Dummett takes the ability to speak a language as essentially a practical capacity or complex of practical capacities. The theory of meaning is intended to provide a propositional representation of these practical capacities. So part of the enterprise must involve detailing the practical capacities which constitute knowledge of the propositions of the theory of meaning. Despite this, in one of Dummett's first attempts to come to grips with the manifestation of implicit knowledge[4] his claim is that someone who possesses implicit knowledge need not, of course, be able to formulate the content of the knowledge but will be able to recognize as correct an apt formulation of it when presented with one. There is something a little odd about this position since this conception of implicit knowledge seems to suffer from some of the same difficulties in seeing speakers' knowledge of the theory of meaning as fully explicit. One problem with that view was that explicit knowledge presupposes linguistic competence and so cannot, on pain of vicious regress, be conceived of as the form of knowledge that delivers linguistic competence. Now, although the mooted conception of implicit knowledge explains our inability trivially to furnish a meaning-theory for our own language, it doesn't offer a conception of the sort of knowledge which feeds into or underwrites linguistic competence: it makes nothing of the practical aspect of that knowledge.[5] Conversely, one might well have a practical capacity yet be quite lacking in implicit knowledge of this form. On reflection, it emerges that talk of aspects is particularly moot here for the knowledge must be conceived of as having a practical aspect but cannot be conceived of as having only a practical aspect. It seems to possess a dual aspect.

Why can we not conceive of the knowledge purely under its practical aspect? Dummett points to a number of disanalogies between knowledge of a language and paradigm examples of practical capacities, pure cases of knowledge-how. There are two crucial points. The first is that the ability to speak a language, to make utterances of various sorts, is a rational activity. As it is a rational activity, individual utterances are subject to appraisal in terms of underlying motives and intentions. We couldn't thus appraise linguistic acts were we unable to ascribe knowledge of meaning to speakers; appraisal of this form demands not only that subjects possess a practical capacity but that an aspect of this knowledge has a theoretical cast. There would be no similar need to appraise cycling skills in this way and, consequently, no need to ascribe knowledge of the mechanics of cycling to proficient cyclists. Secondly, knowledge-how is knowledge of which we can have a perfectly adequate conception before we acquire the relevant capacities. We may have an adequate conception of what it is to swim before acquiring the capacity but we only acquire a conception of what it is to speak a particular language on learning to speak it. A further point is that we can imagine being born with a given practical capacity but speaking a language prior to instruction in it seems to be an entirely magical happening.[6]

There seem to be two major messages from these considerations. First, possession of linguistic competence involves some measure of self-consciousness. The competence is not purely practical since speakers must be seen as *guided by* and not merely as subject to the constraints of correct usage. The character of one's competence must, in some sense, make itself available to one. In a similar fashion being able to play a game such as chess might accrue without explicit introduction to the rules. But a criterion for successfully having mastered the game is that one should be able to recognize apt formulations of the rules. Otherwise we couldn't see the trainee's play as being informed by, rather than merely coinciding with, the rules. However, it is by no means clear that implicit knowledge, thus construed, is necessary for rule-guidedness. One might make sense of a piece of behaviour as rule-guided, not because of an ability to recognize a formulation of the rule, but because one engages in "normative behaviour" in connection with the rule, namely, making and accepting corrections.

The second point is that an implicit knowledge (in the sense of being able to recognize a correct formulation) cannot be had independently of the practical aspect of that knowledge. This may be either because the theoretical formulation makes no sense in the absence of the practical aspect of the knowledge or because (in suitable circumstances, such as the learning of a second language) implicit knowledge of this form might enable the practical capacity.

The resulting position is thus that a speaker's implicit knowledge must be capable of being fully manifested in the use she makes of language. Only if we construe the knowledge in this fashion can we do justice to the practical (and public) aspect of knowledge of a language. But we should not see this as reason for relocating the aim of a meaning-theory; we should not eschew the notion of knowledge and attempt simply to give an account of use. The reasons for this last point have just been rehearsed: we must cling to the notion of knowledge as long as we want to see linguistic behaviour as guided by established or conventional rules for correct use, that is, as long as we want to see speakers as rationally exploiting and so, in some sense, as being aware of these rules. Of course there may here be cases and cases. For it may be that one's mastery of some portions of language – for example, that of syntax – can be explained adequately without appeal to the notion of knowledge. The argument has been focused on the primary target of a theory of meaning: knowledge of meaning.

Dummett's ruminations here are inconclusive. He is adamant that a theory of meaning (in the sense in which philosophers should be interested in such a beast) must make use of the notion of knowledge. But he is far from clear about how the right notion of knowledge should be characterized. It is not a pure practical capacity but neither is it (except perhaps in some relatively rare cases) pure theoretical knowledge. Rather the requisite notion shares aspects of both sorts of knowledge.[7] Of course this leaves the question of the relation of the theory of meaning to speakers' knowledge of meaning somewhat vexed. The theory will naturally take the form of a deductively connected set of propositions. Speakers will be credited with knowledge of these propositions on the basis of supplementary clauses that explain what manifests knowledge of them. The nature of those supplementary clauses is, however, still far from clear.

Even accepting this unclarity, we can still ask a number of pertinent questions. First, will the supplementary clauses relate knowledge of the propositions of the theory to what counts as manifestation of that knowledge individually, in "small blocks" or *en masse*? This is the issue of whether we should be, respectively, atomists, molecular-ists or holists in the theory of meaning. Dummett advocates molecularism (see below). Another question concerns whether or not we can presuppose grasp of a certain base class of concepts in the account of speakers' knowledge of language. That is, would it do to offer an account of the capacities that constitute knowledge of some of the clauses in terms that presuppose some conceptual competence? This is the issue of full-bloodedness versus modesty in a theory of meaning. A full-blooded[8] theory of meaning offers an account of what it is to grasp every concept expressible in the language in terms that don't involve any competence with those concepts. A modest theory of meaning only gives an account of what it is to grasp complex concepts expressible in the language in terms of a grasp of a set of concepts expressible in some basic vocabulary. Dummett advocates full-bloodedness. I turn to this issue presently but as a prelude to this discussion we need to discuss Dummett's anti-psychologism and his rejection of the code conception of meaning.

Anti-psychologism

Language is prior to thought in the sense that we cannot make use of the nature of thought in giving an account of linguistic meaning (see F&OP: essay 15; SoL: essays 4, 7). To think otherwise is to think of language as, in some sense, a code for thought. And this, Dummett insists, is seriously confused. A first reason for this insistence is that it is mistaken to suppose that in most of the interesting cases we can give an account of what it is to have a thought, of what it is to grasp a certain concept without appealing to the subject's ability to use language appropriately. How, for instance, would we be able to ascribe complex expectations without appealing to an ability to use language? To reinforce this point Dummett is wont to make use of Wittgenstein's observation that we might say a dog is expecting his master to come home but not that the dog is expecting his master to come home next week. It makes no sense to ascribe the latter expec-tation to a languageless creature.

However the primary reason for rejecting this "code conception" of language is that it presupposes a notion of associating a word or expression with a concept and this notion of association is doubly mysterious, since it is unclear both in what the act of association consists and how we are to bring the concept to mind in order to make this association. To amplify the latter first, it seems that if we are to bring a concept to mind then we must be able to form a representation of the concept to ourselves. But what, one would then want to know, is such a representation like and what makes it a representation of *that* particular concept? Answers to these questions seem entirely lacking or appeal once again to a process of association thus launching a regress. Secondly, even if there is a mental bringing together of the word with the concept we still need an explanation of how this confers a meaning on the expression, how a use of the expression is thereby determined. If the association can "drift free" of use then it's not clear that speakers who use an expression in the same way share their understanding of the expression. And this subverts the role of language in communication. Conversely if agreement in use is the criterion for having agreed in the process of association the latter drops out of the picture in terms of performing any useful work; we might as well concentrate on explaining meaning in terms of the use to which speakers put expressions.

Modesty and full-bloodedness

A speaker must be capable of fully manifesting her understanding of any expression. And a theory of meaning must give an account of what constitutes a full manifestation of a speaker's understanding. Dummett rejects any requirement weaker than that of *full* manifestation as lapsing into psychologism and privacy. Here privacy essentially comes to the idea that it is, at best, a hypothesis that we share meanings. For instance it won't do simply to require that any difference in understanding be capable of being revealed in use since then it might still be the case that an actual agreement in use could, at most, constitute good grounds for supposing an agreement about meanings (this perhaps being the simplest hypothesis that would explain the evidence). If two speakers agreed precisely in their understanding of an expression then, according to the suggestion, they might never be in a position conclusively to determine this fact. So at no point would it then be possible for the one speaker to have communicated her understanding to the other. The supposition that, nonetheless, she possesses a perfectly determinate understanding is one that makes meaning essentially private.

So Dummett demands both an account of understanding that uniquely characterizes a speaker's understanding in terms of her manifestable behaviour and an account of what manifests understanding in terms that don't presuppose any conceptual competence. One might well wonder whether these two requirements can both be satisfied. For, if we describe a speaker's (necessarily finite segment of) behaviour in the requisite manner, then it just seems clear that there will be too many consistent attributions of understanding.

McDowell (in two papers: 1987, 1997) attempts to put Dummett's thought under some stress here. He applauds Dummett's insistence on manifestation (or publicity) as a rejection of psychologist accounts of meaning. Similarly he applauds Dummett's insistence that the theory of meaning describes language use as a rational activity and the consequent rejection of behaviourism. But McDowell insists that the correct way of satisfying these demands precisely presupposes rejecting full-bloodedness and embracing modesty in a theory of meaning. An insistence on full-bloodedness in the face of publicity risks a collapse into behaviourism – an inability to see the mindedness of linguistic behaviour. On the other hand modesty might seem like intellectual shirking. But it only seems so as long as full-bloodedness appears to be a viable proposition. Once we appreciate that the full-bloodedness is not, in fact, viable the taint of shirking is expunged.

Let us first consider Dummett's reasons for thinking that, though a full-blooded theory of meaning will offer a reductive account of what it is to possess a concept, it will not court a behaviouristic elimination of the mental. Dummett's point here is that the sort of account we are seeking is not one which is predictive but one which makes sense of use of language as a rational activity (or, as Dummett says, "*the* rational activity *par excellence*" (SoL: 104)). We constantly appraise one another's linguistic acts to determine the speaker's intentions in making a given utterance. A theory of meaning thus must situate language use within this background activity but, since this activity is not peculiar to language – it permeates through most of our interactions with one another – the theory need not itself include a description of it.

An adequate theory of meaning must allow for this process of estimating a speaker's intentions, but it should not incorporate a description of it. The process is in no way special to the particular language; it is based upon an understanding of language, but does not involve anything that has to be learned in learning that language rather than any other. Save for its subject matter, it involves nothing special to language as such: we estimate the intentions and motives underlying other people's utterances by the same general means as we estimate those underlying their non-linguistic actions.   (Taylor 1987: 261)

Dummett's thought seems to be that we have a certain architecture of concepts by means of which we take and appraise the doings of another as those of a rational agent. We can and do apply this architecture to other people's linguistic doings. The assumption might then appear to be that the architecture can be applied to those doings when described in content-free terms, that is, in terms that don't presuppose concept possession. If he is right here then the account is indeed full-blooded but still sees linguistic behaviour as minded precisely because it fits into the architecture of rational appraisal.

McDowell's one worry precisely takes issue with this apparent assumption. He finds it impossible to envisage that doings described in content-free terms are sufficiently rich for the imposition of the architecture: there is no appraising a linguistic act for its underlying intention unless it is conceived of as an assertion that such and such, or as an enquiry about so and so, and so on. "To me [Dummett] seems rather to be telling us to describe linguistic behaviour in a way that would obliterate, not deepen, the rational intelligibility that we know it has" (Heck 1997: 110). Apparently, Dummett points to our ordinary practice of making linguistic behaviour rationally intelligible but he insists on describing that behaviour in distinctly unordinary terms, terms which threaten to make inoperable our ordinary means of rendering an act rationally intelligible. Thus it seems that McDowell reads Dummett as suggesting that mind enters the picture because the basic behaviour in terms of which understanding is characterized can itself be rationally appraised. And it seems he is rightly sceptical about this. However, if we look at the long catalogues that Dummett provides of the sort of thing he is talking about (see Taylor 1987: 261; LBoM: 91) we see that he is considering the ordinary case: cases where we ask why someone asserted that . . . rather than that . . ., and so on. The examples he gives all presuppose content. Nowhere does he seem to envisage the process operating on the sort of behaviour basic to a full-blooded theory of meaning.

One therefore supposes that Dummett's point must have been rather different. I take it that what Dummett is driving at is closer to something like the following thought. He isn't concerned with, what might be seen as, the input side of the theory but with the output. His point is that the process of estimating a speaker's intentions requires that we see a speaker's capacity as not merely practical but as something of which she has some form of awareness. It makes no sense to ask why she enquired whether the train left on time unless we suppose that she has some awareness of the meaning of the relevant expressions. So to make room for rational appraisal of linguistic acts, the theory must characterize something that is a form of not purely practical knowledge and, in its ineradicable appeal to such a notion, the theory cannot but be anti-behaviouristic. So the theory avoids behaviourism not at its base but because what it delivers must be of an appropriate form for the process of rational appraisal.

Dummett's notion of implicit knowledge together with the insistence that such knowledge be manifestable is supposed to deliver the account that avoids both psychologism and behaviourism. However, the anti-behaviouristic component of his earlier characterization fails to distinguish cases where a level of reflective awareness of one's own practice has been arrived at (sufficient to enable recognition of a formulation of one's knowledge) from cases where it is simply the case that one's practice is guided by that knowledge. So the characterization is inadequate. It is this failure to explain how the knowledge involved in understanding is implicated in our use of language that exposes Dummett's position to accusations of collapsing into behaviourism. The appeal to rational intelligibility then is supposed to support the claim that such a notion of knowledge is required even if it cannot, as yet, be characterized. So behaviourism must be avoided, although quite how that is to be achieved remains unclear; it is just as unclear as is the character of the knowledge which constitutes understanding.

Let us move on to McDowell's other worry, which is based on Wittgenstein's considerations about the nature of following a rule. McDowell takes Wittgenstein to have shown that because there are indefinitely many alternative interpretations of one's necessarily finite use of language (described in content-free terms) there can be no full manifestation of one's understanding. So the basis of the publicity requirement necessitates a rejection of full-bloodedness. To take a well-worn example, no finite number of instances of my responding to the instruction "add two" can show that I grasp the instruction in the same way as you do. For it is always possible that I go on to respond to the instruction in ways that I take to be consonant with my previous uses but which deviate from your use. So, unless we can describe my behaviour as "applying the rule 'add two'", there is no way in which we shall be able to earn that licence on the basis of a description of my behaviour in non-normative terms, terms that don't themselves appeal to grasp of a rule. But (if we take grasp of a rule to be equivalent to grasp of a concept) this is to say that there is no full manifestation of grasp of a concept, if the behaviour that constitutes that understanding is to be characterized in terms that avoid ascribing any conceptual competence. So the rule-following considerations show that publicity requires renunciation of full-bloodedness.

It is important to get clear about exactly how the rule-following considerations are supposed to bite. On the one hand it seems that all we have is a finite number of instances of use that will be reconcilable with indefinitely many possible interpretations or attributions of grasp of a rule. So it may seem that the step from a sample of use to an attribution of following a rule just is problematic. What is, in fact, revealed is the problematic nature of this step *if* it is seen as inferential. For, given the defeasibility in the light of any further instances of use, the step cannot be one of deductive inference: no sample of use (even, *per impossibile*, were it to be infinite[9]) will guarantee an attribution of rule following. If, on the other hand, we see it as a step of inductive inference then the sample of use will form an evidential base for our attributions and the claim that we share meanings will be relegated to the status of a hypothesis. What we need to realize is that samples of use (if sufficiently large and varied) non-inferentially warrant attributions of following a rule. Dummett hints at this much when commenting on our ordinary practice of ascribing understanding (he also makes the useful observation that deviations from a given rule need not always be taken to defeat an attribution of following a rule: people forget what once they understood) (SoL: xiii). But this appearance is belied by his eventual insistence that we require full manifestation so as to have conclusive evidence for attributions of understanding. There cannot be conclusive evidence and the mistake is to think of use (described in Dummettian terms) as standing in an evidential relation to judgements about speakers' understanding.

Dummett's thought is that the Wittgensteinian considerations can be met by two concessions: first, an allowance that a speaker's understanding of an expression need only be *capable* of full manifestation in their use of it; secondly, a realization that meanings are scarcely, if ever, fully determinate: what we should go on to say in novel situations may not be determined by hitherto established meanings. Given these concessions, Dummett insists that "Wittgensteinian considerations do not have the power to demonstrate that it does not make sense [to speak of someone's having manifested every aspect of the meaning he attaches to an expression]" (SoL: xv).

However, Dummett surely has not taken the measure of the Wittgensteinian point here. He concedes that my use of the term "chair" may not determine how I shall apply the term when I encounter some new strange object that, perhaps, has some chair-like properties. But the Wittgensteinian point is that, though I have always applied "chair" to what I am currently sitting on, that is no sort of guarantee that if I am to go on in the same way as before (if I am to be faithful to my meanings) I shall continue to apply "chair" to what I am sitting on. For the question precisely concerns what it is to go on in the same way. Nothing that I can have done in the past ensures that, in order to continue in the same way, I *should* now call this a chair. So at no conceivable point has someone manifested every aspect of her meaning. For, to repeat, at no point is her future use bound by her past use under the constraint of continuing in the same way. Dummett's concession that future use is not completely bound by past use simply misses the depth of the Wittgensteinian point that future use is *in no sense* bound by past use.

We shouldn't, however, be rushed by this into thinking that the manifestation constraint is bogus. One manifests one's understanding in one's use, not in the sense of thereby conclusively justifying an ascription of understanding, but in the sense of defeasibly, but non-inferentially, warranting that ascription. There is no guarantee that a sufficient agreement in use will constitute an agreement in meanings since a judgement of the latter sort might always be defeated. But this does not entail that it is a hypothesis inductively supported by the evidence of agreement in use.

McDowell's way with the problem is rather different. He assimilates attributions of following a rule to cases of perceptual judgements: we see someone's meaning in their familiar use of familiar vocabulary. The point of this characterization is that it allows McDowell to see ascriptions of understanding as defeasible (in the same way that perceptual judgements are defeasible) and to see them as non-inferential. These features give him the tools to respond to the rule-following problem. My suggestion is aimed at retaining these two elements – thereby earning a similar solution to the rule-following problem – without appeal to the perceptual view. It allows the basis for ascriptions of understanding to be speakers' use described in Dummettian terms.

How does this discussion relate to the issue of full-bloodedness versus modesty in a theory of meaning? The theory of meaning attempts to give an account of the constitution of speakers' knowledge of language. A modest theory of meaning fails to give any substantive such account for a base class of vocabulary. We need to distinguish two questions. The first is this question about the constitution of speakers' knowledge and the second is that of the basis on which that knowledge is ascribed. I've recommended that the basis for ascribing understanding is use (described in terms which don't presuppose concept possession) but that such ascriptions are defeasible. Thus the use that forms the base for ascriptions of understanding fails to be constitutive of understanding. And now we need to reassess the first question in the light of the answer to the second: what sort of description of the constitution of understanding have we a right to expect? Should we satisfy ourselves only with an account of our manner of making attributions of understanding and let go of the constitutive account? And if we seek a constitutive account can this be full-blooded or must it be modest?

Let us pursue Dummett's discussion of Wittgenstein on following a rule a little further. He grants that Wittgenstein has established that in the case of certain basic rules "there is nothing *by which* we judge something to be a correct application of them" (SoL: 460). This, he points out, is an epistemological claim from which the further metaphysical claim "that, if we never do make such a judgement in some particular instance, there is no specific thing that would be a correct application" (*ibid.*) does not follow. He admits that it is hard to see how the metaphysical claim fails to be entailed. If nothing informs our judgements about correctness then it seems nothing can determine what would count as correct in new instances. For otherwise there seems to be something that establishes what correct use is but which fails to have anything to do with the judgements we actually make. Nonetheless Dummett finds the metaphysical conclusion impossible to accept and hopes that a line can, in fact, be drawn under the epistemological conclusion.

Now one way of adopting such a position might be precisely to embrace modesty. Provided we confine our discussion within the sphere of rules there need be nothing suspect in refusing to see the correctness of an application as constituted by our judgements. If, for instance, we define a bachelor as an unmarried man (presupposing, in the process, an understanding of "man" and "unmarried") then what makes it right to apply "bachelor" to x is that x is a man and x is unmarried. That is, we don't find ourselves pushed into the absurd position of claiming that what makes it correct is securable communal assent to the application. But this means that the account of language use must always be given in normative terms and, for basic rules, there is no non-trivial account of what makes an application correct. Thus for a modest theoretician we can accept the epistemological conclusion but duck the metaphysical one by refusing to take on the metaphysical question; that, to use a modish phrase, is a question too far or, to use another, is an attempt to dig below bedrock. What we are supposed to realize is that in fundamental cases our judgements of correctness are responsible to nothing, but we have to realize this without being tempted to say that therefore there is no fact of the matter about correctness in hitherto unencountered cases. We resist the latter by a further realization; namely, that we cannot say what correctness of an application consists in in norm-free terms. So in some cases we shall have to say, for example, that what makes it correct to apply "red" to x is that x is red. Nothing more need or can be said.

There are, however, two distinct questions here. One – that raised by the issue of following a rule – is whether an account of the practice of following a rule can be given in terms of something other. The other is whether any account of content must presuppose contentful states. This is the question of modesty. To bring out the contrast let us focus on what might be a primitive expression of a rule in a theory of meaning, say: "x is red" is true iff x is red. Someone who understands the predicate red knows this rule. So the theory will be committed to statements of the form

S knows that "x is red" is true iff x is red.[10]

And this, for McDowell (and anyone of modest inclinations), is all the theory of meaning can achieve. At base, a rule is specified and understanding consists in knowledge of the rule. Dummett however insists that we specify what this knowledge consists in. But what form might such a specification take? Dummett asks himself what it is to grasp a basic concept and answers along these lines:

> It is to be able to discriminate between things that are red and those that are not. Such an ability can be ascribed to one who will, on occasion, treat red things differently from things that are not red; one way, among many other possible ways, of doing this is to apply the word "red" to red things and not to others.
>
> (See SoL: 98, I've substituted "red" for "square")

So in grasping the concept one possesses a certain ability, an ability that can consist in knowing something about a word, knowing, one might say, its rule of application. But the description of what it is to grasp this rule is not itself given in terms of grasp of some concept. True, the account uses the concept *red*, but it doesn't use that concept within a specification of the speaker's knowledge. We don't say that the speaker knows that "red" applies to red things; rather we say that the speaker discriminates red things from others by applying the word "red" to red things. So we specify in non-trivial terms what rule a speaker follows but we do not non-trivially specify anything that guides her use. So the epistemic point of the rule-following considerations is met. Note also that the specification doesn't attempt to reduce rule following to non-normative terms since what it specifies is *correctness* conditions. So it is at least not obvious that we cannot have a position which: (i) rejects the metaphysical conclusion of the rule-following considerations; (ii) accepts the epistemic conclusion of them; and (iii) has full-blooded ambitions.

Systematicity and molecularity

A systematic theory of meaning need not be compositional. According to a systematic meaning-theory, the meaning of a sentence will be determined systematically by the meanings of its component words and an understanding of the sentence will be described in terms of knowledge of these meanings. However, it may be that this knowledge can only be characterized in terms of a general linguistic competence or, at least, in terms of a competence with sentences of an arbitrary degree of complexity. Such are holistic meaning-theories. On the other hand, this knowledge might be characterized by reference to a competence with sentences whose complexity can be definitely circumscribed. Such are molecular or compositional meaning-theories. These descriptions are vague since the notion of complexity has not been glossed at all (it need not coincide with syntactic complexity). We can, however, do well enough for the moment without any such gloss. On a compositional theory, understanding is characterized in such a way as to impose a partial ordering (or something close to a partial ordering) on sentences: the understanding of a sentence will presuppose an understanding of a fragment of language and sentences in that fragment will be understandable independently of and prior to an understanding of the given sentence. In contrast, understanding as described in a holistic meaning-theory will not impose a partial ordering on sentences: understanding a sentence will involve an understanding of other sentences whose understanding in turn presupposes that of the given sentence. Understanding a language will thus be seen as a process of gaining ingress into a holistically interdependent system of meanings.

Dummett gives the following neat characterization of holism and its denial. Any account of the understanding of a sentence will require a speaker to know the identity of the sentence, that is, to know the component words and their ordering. But, clearly, this won't suffice for understanding. The question then is whether the additional component of understanding is uniform for all sentences or whether it is sensitive to the identity of the sentence. A holistic theory adopts the former view (citing, for example, a knowledge of the entire language as a possible second component). A compositional theory adopts the latter. Though this formulation of the distinction is neat, it is surely not equivalent to the former characterization. A theory that is holistic on the former construal may be compositional on the latter since the additional component may vary from sentence to sentence without thereby imposing a partial order on sentences.

Why should we adhere to molecularity? One line of argument takes its cue from thoughts about the nature of acquiring linguistic competence. Crudely, the thought would be that learning a language is (or, perhaps, must be) a progressive process. What we learn at a given stage provides the basis for our passage to more sophisticated capacities. Moreover, and crucially, it is thought that, in functioning as a basis, these more primitive linguistic capacities must be unmodified by the acquisition of more sophisticated capacities.

How true are these thoughts? Well learning a language is a progressive business and learning some bits of language necessarily presupposes some linguistic competence. So linguistic competence consists of capacities which admit of articulation into an ordered sequence. But the final thought is, at least as a general observation about learning, false. Dummett himself supplies examples of learning that satisfy the holistic scheme and thus raise a question here.

The learning of games need not fit the compositional scheme. As Dummett points out, playing dominoes involves a capacity to identify each domino but this capacity is related only to a general competence with the rules of dominoes. This, however, doesn't supply a counter-example to the stability involved in the progressive view because learning dominoes is not a progressive process. Being able to play the game is a matter of having internalized all the rules and no rule forms the base for understanding further rules. Chess might provide a more troubling example. Understanding the power of each piece involves a grasp of the ways in which it can move and take other pieces. The pawn can and must be converted into any other piece (though not the King) when it reaches the eighth rank. So fully to grasp the powers of a pawn involves a grasp of the powers of the other pieces. Since only one sort of piece has such a power there is no problem thinking of this in progressive terms. But now imagine that a second sort of piece (let's say the Bishop) has similar powers of conversion when it reaches one of the central squares of the board. Now an understanding of the powers of the pawn involves an understanding of the powers of the Bishop and vice versa. And indeed we could extend the case giving conversion powers to every piece other than the King. Seemingly, such a game, though complex, would be both understandable and playable but thoroughly holistic; the power of one piece would, in part, be determined by that of another so one's grasp of the power of one piece would not be a stable base on which to build our grasp of those of another.

From a Dummettian perspective the arguments are, perhaps, more obviously troubling. Dummett's philosophy is revisionist. He thinks that an outcome of philosophical reflection may allow us to see that our first-order linguistic practice is not in order as it stands and thus requires a revision of some kind.[11] His justification for being revisionist is built on his insistence on molecularity: a region of language that is incapable of being described in molecular terms therefore stands in need of revision. But since the original language was learned and spoken it's hard to see how molecularity could, from this perspective, be a mere consequence of the nature of language acquisition. Dummett is aware of something like this worry and he brings it to life in the person of Brouwer. How, he asks, could Brouwer have accused classical mathematics of meaninglessness in the face of his supreme competence in classical (topological) techniques? How could it be that we could acquire competence in a (sophisticated) practice yet somehow see that practice as meaningless on grounds of the nature of language acquisition? Or, to put the question another way, where do we find more stringent demands on the meaningfulness of a practice than non-collusive agreement in use (which is all that mere acquisition would deliver)?

Dummett's answer is that the point about acquisition is not simply one about what it is to acquire competence in a practice but about what it is to acquire specifically linguistic competence. So the motivation for molecularity depends essentially on a conception of the nature of language itself. Language is not merely a practice in which we can engage but one whose functioning should be open to view, at least, upon reflection. It won't do merely to describe the practice of using the language if that description does not exhibit the way the language works: we have to make sense of the practice.[12] Quite what this consists in is a moot point but the mere sense that there is something here to be done and something that holists refuse to recognize leads Dummett to accuse holism of intellectual lethargy. At any rate, the demand of molecularity takes on the form of a methodological maxim. We ought to strive for a deeper understanding of our use of language unless we are faced with conclusive evidence against this possibility. Such evidence cannot come in the form of aspects of the practice that resist description in compositional terms since Dummett uses this constraint to justify his revisionism. To be sure revisionism is only plausible when it is moderate; faced with a choice between jettisoning molecularity and radical revisionism we should opt for the former.[13] But what should count as moderate and as radical revision is, of course, something of a vexed question.[14]

Let's set that question aside in the attempt now to clarify what, for Dummett, is involved in making sense of a linguistic practice. A good route into this issue is to focus on Dummett's criticism of one influential holist: Quine. One way of thinking about Quine's ideas is to see him as extending a Fregean view. Frege thinks that the meaning of a word *is* its contribution to the meaning of sentences in which it occurs; we can only account for the meaning of a word as it occurs in the context of a sentence. Quine thinks that this lesson applies to sentences: we cannot think of the meaning of a sentence in isolation from its occurrence in a theory. His reasons for this extension of Frege stem from his rejection of the accounts of meaning offered by logical positivists who, in their different ways, had attempted to give an account of the meaning of a sentence in terms of the sensory experience that would constitute a verification of it. Quine objects to this, noting that "statements about the external world face the tribunal of sense experience not individually but only as a corporate body" (1953: 41); no sentence is confirmed or infirmed directly by an episode of experience, rather, a theory[15] must be modified when we meet with an experience which is recalcitrant. However, this thought is not essentially holistic. One way of incorporating it is to note that the way we verify a sentence is not simply a matter of undergoing a certain sensory experience but by carrying out operations, performing (both deductive and inductive) inferences and bringing to bear background knowledge. So the mode of verifying a sentence will necessarily involve its relations to other sentences: no sentence is confirmed or infirmed in isolation. This doesn't entail, however, that the content of a sentence is inextricably bound up with the theory as a whole. For the structure of the theory might be such as to allow for a partial ordering of sentences.

Quine's holism becomes apparent when we amplify this view by means of two further theses. The first is that no particular revision in an assignment of truth-values to sentences is dictated by a given recalcitrant experience. Rather, in the face of recalcitrance, we shall revise our theory simply under the pragmatic constraint of attempting to minimize further disruption in the body of the theory. The second thesis is that, conversely, we can modify our theory so as to revise the truth-value assignment of any sentence in the theory, provided that we are prepared to make compensating modifications elsewhere in the theory. That is, no sentence has a guaranteed truth-value, come what may.

The effect of these two theses is that meaning becomes a notion which is primarily applicable to the theory as a whole. The theory consists of a set of sentences in relation to one another, together with a relation that determines whether or not an experience conforms with it. (Dummett calls this "the conformability relation".) The empirical significance of the theory (a significance which distinguishes it from other theories) is determined by the experiences with which it is conformable and by its permissible revisions in the face of recalcitrant experience. And now it seems that the meaning of individual sentences can only be given in relation to the theory as a whole (in the same way as the meaning of an expression is given by its role in sentences, the meaning of a sentence is given by its role in the theory and in possible modifications of the theory). The problem that Dummett perceives in this view emerges from Quine's second thesis. Since any sentence is apt to be revised, nothing fixes the relations between sentences of the theory, so no sentence has a definite role to be described in this way. Moreover, we cannot even characterize the empirical significance of the theory since, to do so, we should have to state its conformability relation. This statement then becomes a sentence of the theory, which, in view of the second thesis, is apt for revision in accordance with the conformability relation. So to grasp the significance of this sentence – its role in theory – we already have to have a grasp of the conformability relation. Thus that relation cannot be communicated.

A consequence is that holism of this variety leads to the denial of the possibility of a theory of meaning. Dummett thinks it is false because it cannot account for the communicative role of language. You and I may differ over our use of a certain term. That difference may be merely a terminological divergence (e.g. I use "red" to include things you would call "orange") or may be a substantive disagreement. We have a terminological divergence when we operate with theories whose empirical significance is the same but which differ syntactically). The question is: how do I tell whether the empirical significance of your theory is the same as or different from mine? No sample of your assignment of truth-values to sentences can determine the matter, for any divergence here is always explicable as *either* a terminological divergence or a substantive disagreement. Thus to know what you mean by endorsing or rejecting a sentence I need to know everything you believe. But then you cannot tell me anything: communication is entirely otiose. Another problem is that even if I knew your entire theory I still would not know what you mean unless I also knew the conformability relation. But if you were to tell me this then it would be a sentence of your theory, one whose meaning I need somehow to arrive at. So the meaning of your utterances cannot be conveyed to me unless I happen to light on the correct conformability relation. One might think that one builds up a knowledge of another's conformability relation by witnessing patterns of revision in the face of experience. Bear in mind, however, that the conformability relation is a relation between the theory and all possible experiences. We cannot make any headway in determining it for a given theory from a sample of revisions unless we can proceed in piecemeal fashion, taking a certain pattern of revision in the face of certain experiences to be relevant to the conformability relation of sentences within a certain region of language. But that, precisely, is to eschew the holistic picture in favour of a molecular view.

This gives us some reason for thinking that there are problems in the holistic view. But what we want to be clear about is the source of the holistic mistake. The holist refuses to acknowledge sentences that are analytically true (at most she supplies an ersatz notion of analyticity: stimulus analyticity). Now what distinguishes an analytic sentence is not that (considered syntactically) it is irrevisable but that when it is revised this must be either in response to discovery of a mistake in its proof (if it has one) or as a result of a change in meaning in one or more of its components. In the latter case the revision of the sentence must be accompanied by an elucidation of the new meanings of the relevant components. And here is the rub for the holist. For, in holistic terms, this is to say that revision of an analytic sentence must be accompanied by a change in the conformability relation. But, as we've seen, there's no way in which one speaker can express to another the nature of her conformability relation. There is no linguistic activity that can achieve this end. And the reason why there isn't, is that all linguistic activity is reduced to the assignment of truth-values to sentences; no role for the distinctive activities of elucidation and explanation of meaning is allowed for. If, in contrast, we take particular note of these aspects of language use then we shall be concerned with the justifications offered for asserting a sentence and explanations offered of when it is correct to assert a given sentence, and so on. That is, we shall be concerned with the way in which a determinate sense is conferred on a sentence, the analytic connections which hold between that sentence and others.

What Dummett is insisting on is that, as philosophers of language, we should allow room for the ordinary linguistic activity of policing and monitoring our own and others' use of language. This activity necessitates that speakers have something of a reflective understanding of the nature of their practice: as speakers, we don't simply enforce a set of rules but attempt to understand aspects of the practice both in an attempt to elucidate them but also in the process, where the need is felt, of deliberately modifying them. The consequences of recognizing elucidation as a linguistic activity at the level of the theorist (i.e. of the philosopher of language) are twofold. For it provides both a richness of linguistic structure, which it is the job of a theory to reflect, and also a context for the very activity of theorizing. Elucidation is essential to conferring sense on expressions, and the sense of an expression is, at least in part, determined by the way it is elucidated. So recognizing the activity of elucidation gives us something that might form the subject matter of a theory. However, the theory itself is the outgrowth of this very same activity of elucidation; it is the attempt to push elucidation further than ordinary speakers do. The impulse for this push stems from an urge to systematize. Systematization is an entrenched feature of the way in which we attempt to understand phenomena present in both science and mathematics.

Dummett's thought seems to run along these lines. As speakers, we engage in the process of elucidating meaning. In individual cases we either achieve complete clarity about a term's meaning or revise the meaning so as to achieve clarity. This activity is integral to our use of language as part of rational activity and of subsuming our linguistic activity under our own capacity for rational appraisal. Admitting this feature of our use of language is part of our conception of ourselves as rational agents. The theoretical turn is an attempt to do systematically what, as practitioners, we do in individual cases. It is justified because systematization is an important and, in many instances, an ineliminable ingredient in our attempt to understand a phenomenon. In the case of language we would thus need special arguments to show that this phenomenon is not susceptible to being understood in a systematic way. Though, at this stage, we cannot rule out the possibility of such an argument, such an argument would have to show a systematic theory of meaning either to have no explanatory value or to be impossible to construct. Moreover it would have to show either of these things while admitting speakers' ability to clarify meanings. And the question now is: why does the elevation of our explanatory interests to a theoretical level disfigure them? Only if we distort the distance between our selves as practitioners and our selves as theorists does this question appear to have a sensible answer.[16]

Summary

Dummett insists that whenever a theory of meaning attributes a certain piece of knowledge to speakers it must also say what possession of this knowledge consists in. A theory of meaning is a theory of understanding and, if the core of the theory is not articulated from the beginning in terms of speakers' capacities, then the conversion of this core into a theory of understanding is by no means a trivial process.

The business of saying in what possession of a piece of knowledge consists is tied up with the insistence on the publicity of meaning. Dummett argues that an essentially private ingredient of understanding is completely unjustified by the explanatory role of the concepts of meaning and understanding and is alien to, indeed subverts, the communicative role of language. When we explain in what possession of a piece of knowledge consists, we explain how possession of that knowledge is fully manifestable in a speaker's behaviour. Knowledge might be explicit or implicit. The problem of explaining what constitutes manifestation of a piece of linguistic knowledge infects implicit knowledge and that problem Dummett never completely resolves. The rational aspect of language use entails that it cannot be conceived of as a purely practical capacity but its implicit character entails that it cannot be conceived of as theoretical. Rather we need to move away from this dichotomy to make room for a notion of knowledge which has a practical aspect but which is also the object of our awareness.

Dummett goes on to claim that a theory of meaning should be full-blooded, not modest, and molecular, not holistic. A full-blooded theory of meaning aims to give a full account of the meanings of all expressions in the language in terms that don't presuppose grasp of any concepts. We considered McDowell's objection to such an animal, the crux of which is that, in attempting to avoid psychologism by insisting on publicity, Dummett's constraint of full-bloodedness forces him into a behaviourist position. The defence of Dummett was long and complex but it involved three ideas. First, Dummett thinks that the account we aim for is one which characterizes language use as an activity of rational agents. So the final account is one which cannot be behaviourist. Secondly, McDowell's use of Wittgenstein's discussion of rule following fails to be decisive. If McDowell's own position constitutes an adequate response then there is little reason to think that a modified Dummettian position couldn't retain full-bloodedness and also offer a response. Finally a suggestion was made which allowed characterization of a speaker's capacities in concept-free but not norm-free terms.

Molecularity is an important, though often misunderstood, strand in Dummett's thinking. It supplies a constraint on an acceptable theory of meaning and is motivated in part by considerations about the nature of language and language acquisition and in part by Dummett's conception of philosophy and philosophical method. At its most simple, Dummett's thought runs like this. He sees no reason why we should not be able to describe language in molecular fashion and also sees molecularity as allied to our proper philosophical ambition. So, to reject molecularity at this point would be an act of intellectual irresponsibility. However, he also argues that only a molecular account can give us a proper perspective on the functioning of our own language. The sort of explanation we want is not thoroughly alien but is an outgrowth of the reflective grasp we have of our own language, which we deploy in very ordinary uses of language: in selecting the most apt words or in offering explanations or elucidations. The philosophical enterprise simply harnesses this reflective capacity in a systematic enterprise.

The theory of meaning now retreats to the background – it doesn't leave the stage – as we move on to discuss Dummett's characterization of realism.

Chapter 3

The characterization of realism

What is realism?[1]

A realist believes that there is a mind- and language-independent world. More specifically, since a realist is usually a realist about something or other, a realist about this and that believes that this and that is independent of mind and language. What fills the place of "this and that" will normally be a certain subject matter, range of entities or realm; one is a realist about mathematics or about the past or about other minds, and so on. So if we're searching for a general understanding of realism we need two things. First we need a general characterization of the sorts of things one might be a realist about. And, second, we need an explanation of the notion of independence of mind and language since, as it stands, the notion has no very clear content.

Michael Dummett is justly famous in the contemporary philosophical world for having offered a characterization of realism which is both general and whose content is, or at least promises to be, clear. The general applicability of his account suggests a way of seeing diverse disputes as sharing elements of a certain form. It also helps us to pick out in diverse cases what is essential to the dispute about realism from incidental features of the particular dispute. As we shall see Dummett thinks that in many cases this suggests forms of anti-realism which are more plausible than their traditional forms.

The basic thought in Dummett's characterization of realism is that we should delineate the scope of a realism by viewing it as concerned with a range of *statements*. Of course, realism isn't then a view about the mind- and language-independence of those statements. Rather it is a view about how those statements relate to reality. So accompanying this shift in focus is a relocation of the dispute from one which is overtly and, apparently, purely metaphysical to one which is semantic: a realist about a certain range of statements holds that those statements have a certain semantics. A semantic theory when applied to a certain statement aims to describe the manner in which that statement is determined as true or false in accordance with its construction. Realists across a wide variety of disputes will thus, it is hoped, propound semantic theories which share a common form or forms. In explaining the shared features of realist semantic theories Dummett gives an explanation of the notion of mind- and language-independence which sponsors the intuitive notion of realism.

Realist semantic theories

A realist about a certain range of statements thinks of those statements as describing a reality whose existence and character in no way depends on the manner in which we portray it to ourselves or on our ability to disclose its nature. Statements within the range are thus rendered true or false merely by the nature of external reality and are so rendered irrespective of whether or not we can come to know their truth-values. So a realist semantic theory adopts a notion of truth which determinately either applies or fails to apply to any statement in the range: as we shall say, the notion of truth applies bivalently or we have a bivalent notion of truth. Such a semantic theory will, for obvious enough reasons, be called a two-valued semantic theory. An alternative way of making this claim – one which introduces a terminology that will often be employed – is to say that a realist semantic theory adopts a notion of truth which determinately either applies or fails to apply to all statements whether or not they are *decidable*. For present purposes a decidable statement is one for which we can guarantee a verdict on its truth-value by instituting a decision procedure.[2]

However, this characterization fails to capture realism in its entirety. The reason is that it focuses simply on the realist view that statements are rendered determinately either true or false but fails to shed any further light on the manner in which the truth-values of statements are determined. A semantic theory aims to elucidate this aspect of the way language (and/or thought) relates to the world and it is an aspect that is significant for the metaphysical dispute. An orthodox procedure is to base the two-valued semantics on a notion of reference, taking it that singular terms function to refer to objects and that predicate expressions have semantic values (depending on one's taste, these might be properties, functions or extensions). The truth-values of simple statements will then be determined by whether the object referred to has the property or lies within the extension which is the semantic value of the predicate expression. For example, the sentence "Socrates is mortal" will be true just in case the object referred to by "Socrates" has the property of being mortal or falls in the extension of the predicate "is mortal". So realism consists not merely in the adoption of a bivalent notion of truth but also in a "face value" construal of the relevant statements, for instance, in taking it that putatively referential terms are genuinely referential. So, as Dummett says, a realist semantic theory will adopt a two-valued semantics based on a notion of reference.

The effect of Dummett's semantic construal of debates about realism is twofold. First, as just mentioned, it enables us to see these diverse disputes as sharing a common form. If, instead, we thought of realism as a view about a certain range of entities then we would miss the potential similarities between realism about, say, other minds and realism about the past (where no range of entities seems to be under discussion). We might try to achieve a general overview while avoiding Dummett's semantic manoeuvre by considering states of affairs rather than entities. But this would only be successful had we a conception of states of affairs which was separable from that of truth makers. If not then the talk of states of affairs ushers in the semantic construal by the back door. It is also prima facie possible for a realist and an anti-realist to agree on questions of ontology but to diverge only over whether they think of a certain range of entities as being mind- and language-independent. For instance, one might be a Platonist about arithmetic in that one thinks that numbers are abstract objects (i.e. numerical terms purport to refer to certain objects) which exist (i.e. numerical terms succeed in referring to those objects) but reject arithmetic realism on the grounds that one thinks of the existence of numbers as mind-dependent, or on the grounds that arithmetic truth is not bivalent. In allowing for the possibility of such anti-realisms Dummett's construal of realism facilitates the development of rejections of realism which are more plausible than those which reject or demote the status of an ontology.[3] For instance, on the ontological approach it is tempting to see the anti-realist as espousing a view according to which a certain range of objects is constructed by us. The notion of construction is, however, metaphorical and it is hard to see how it is to be made more than that. We'll return to an aspect of these ontological questions when we examine the relation of anti-realism to reductionist views.

A second feature of Dummett's semantic characterization emerges only given his particular view of semantic theory.[4] Dummett thinks that a semantic theory must form the base of a theory of meaning. And, given this feature, a problem with traditional disputes about realism is (potentially) avoided. Traditionally realists and anti-realists have propounded their respective views about a given subject matter but, short of uncovering an incoherence in an opposing view, it is unclear what considerations would decide the matter. In locating a semantic theory within the theory of meaning, Dummett thinks that we thereby have a means of arbitrating the metaphysical dispute: the metaphysical dispute concerns a choice of semantic theory and that choice will be dictated by the appropriate theory of meaning. So *if* we accept Dummett's view of semantic theory and *if* there is a metaphysically neutral conception of the theory of meaning then we seem to have a systematic means of attempting to settle metaphysical disputes about realism. Dummett perhaps overstates the case when he says that the theory of meaning "lies at the foundation of the whole of philosophy" (T&OE: 309), but given this framework the philosophy of language is certainly the basis of metaphysical disputes.

We have arrived at Dummett's semantic conception of realism by an attempt to gain a general understanding of realism and to clarify the notion of mind- and language-independence in the intuitive conception. Another strand of thinking is that a realist attitude is warranted only where we consider that a certain range of things forms part of the ultimate furniture of the world. If realism is thought of in these terms then its opposition seems to be one or another form of reductionism. And, indeed, many traditional disputes about realism have taken just this form. So what is the relation between anti-realism and reductionism?

Anti-realism and reductionism

Let's follow Dummett in calling the class of statements about which there is a metaphysical dispute the disputed class. A reductive view claims that the truth of statements in the disputed class reduces, in some manner, to the truth of statements in another class, the reductive class. Now it might be that the reduction holds because we can translate any statement in the disputed class into a statement in the reductive class. Or it might be that, although no such translation is possible, the truth of any statement in the disputed class is completely determined by those in the reductive class. In the first case we have a full-fledged reductionist thesis, in the latter a weaker thesis, that of reductivism. Dummett gives two reasons for why the reductivist thesis might be preferred. First, the truth of a statement in the disputed class may not depend upon any finite set of statements in the reductive class. So no translation will be possible. For instance, it may be that the truth of an ascription of a mental state depends upon truths about behaviour without there being any finite set of statements about behaviour which guarantees the truth of an ascription of a mental state. Alternatively it may be that statements in the reductive class presuppose the vocabulary of statements in the disputed class, so there cannot be any reduction of the one vocabulary to the other by a process of translation. Examples of this are the reduction of mathematical truth to provability and perhaps the reduction of the truth of past tense statements to statements about currently available evidence and memory (it seems impossible to characterize documentary evidence and the content of memory reports without using the past tense itself).

Classic examples of reductive views are phenomenalism – the reduction of statements about material objects to statements about experience – and behaviourism – the reduction of statements about mental states to statements about behaviour. It is important to note that in both these cases the reductive view is being espoused as an analysis of statements in the disputed class. That is, the reduction is supposed to give the meanings of statements in the disputed class. A feature of these reductive views, which have been taken as paradigmatic forms of anti-realism, is that the notion of truth applicable to the disputed class remains bivalent. And this, understandably enough, has been taken to be a problem for Dummett's analysis of realism. For surely he cannot have provided a good analysis of realism if classical forms of anti-realism come out as realist according to the analysis.

But Dummett has a good response here. In the two examples cited a statement in the disputed class will be explained in terms of (a complex of) subjunctive conditionals drawn from the reductive class. Thus a statement about material objects will be equated with

statements about the experiences one would have in certain circumstances and a statement about another's mental state will be equated
with statements about how she would behave in certain circumstances. And now what Dummett says is that it was only blindness to
the essential nature of realism that led these would-be anti-realists
to cling to a realist notion of truth. If they had seen the connection
between realism and truth they would have regarded the bivalent
notion of truth as something to be challenged *and* would have seen
their reductive view as supplying the motive for such a challenge. For
instance, consider the ascription of bravery to Jones (to use one of
Dummett's well-worn examples). According to the behaviourist the
truth of "Jones is brave" will depend on the truth of a statement (or
statements) of the form "If Jones were to be placed in such and such
circumstances then he would behave thus and so". Similarly "Jones is
not brave" will be true just in case the opposite conditional, "If Jones
were to be placed in such and such circumstances then he would not
behave thus and so", is true. But why should we suppose that one or
other subjunctive conditional must be true? In general, we don't
suppose that just one of "If such and such were to happen then P" or
"If such and such were to happen then not-P" must be true, since it
may be that whether P or not-P holds in the hypothesized circumstances will depend on further factors. Thus, in the behaviourist case,
the reduction of mental ascriptions to subjunctive conditionals about
behaviour should provide the basis for questioning whether the
appropriate notion of truth for the former is indeed bivalent. So there
is a connection between reductionism and Dummettian anti-realism:
reductionism may provide the reason for a denial of (Dummettian)
realism.

But this match is only one possibility. It is possible for reductionism to run counter to anti-realism. For instance, a materialist might
think that the truth of the subjunctive conditional "If Jones were to
be placed in such and such circumstances then he would behave thus
and so" depends on the configuration of Jones's neuro-physiology. If
his neuro-physiological structure is thus and so then the conditional
statement is true; if not, then its opposite is true. So here a reductive
view – the reduction of statements about behaviour to statements
about neuro-physiology – provides a justification for maintaining
bivalence. So a reductive view can actively support realism. Indeed
Dummett dubs such positions "sophisticated realism".

I remarked above that realism is not merely a view about the truth
of statements in the disputed class, it is also a view about how truth-

values are determined. So the paradigmatic or, as Dummett says, naive realist bases her semantic theory on a face-value construal of those statements. So it is certainly true that a realism which incorporates a reductive thesis is a retreat from this paradigm of realism. The difference between these forms of realism is still semantic but now the focus of attention is the notion of reference rather than that of truth. And here Dummett thinks that there are cases and cases.

One sort of case is nicely illustrated by Frege's example of reducing statements about directions to statements about lines. Frege points out that we can introduce talk about directions on the back of talk about lines by fixing the meanings of statements of identity among directions in terms of relations between lines as follows:

The direction of a = the direction of b iff a is parallel to b.

Let us set aside questions about whether this provides an adequate explanation of direction talk: assume it does. Then what we have here is a reductive thesis and moreover one which has no obvious implications for the notion of truth. If we think truth applies bivalently to statements about parallelism among lines then we shall endorse a bivalent notion of truth for statements about directions. If we think not then we won't. However Dummett thinks this *is* a retreat from realism (even if we cling to a bivalent notion of truth) because the notion of reference for directions is otiose in the semantic theory. The semantic theory for statements about direction will proceed by translating such statements into statements about parallelism among lines and then will provide a semantic theory for such statements. Now in the translation process the singular terms for directions are eliminated in this sense: there is no singular term in the statement about parallelism among lines that corresponds to the term for a direction. So the semantic theory dissects the manner in which the truth-value of a statement about directions is determined without having to invoke, and without supplying, a notion of reference which applies to direction terms.

Contrast this case with the following, in which direction talk is reduced to talk about lines by an explicit definition of directions, namely,

The direction of a is the set of lines which are parallel to a.

Here, although directions are treated reductively (directions are reduced to sets of lines), the reduction supplies a singular term for the direction term. So it supplies a reference for the direction term and thus the notion of reference as applied to terms for directions plays a genuine role in the semantic theory.

Now Dummett does not want to deny that in the first case terms for directions succeed in referring. But he does want to say that the first view distances itself more from realism about direction statements than the second view does. One might wonder what the rationale for this position is. For, if the crucial consideration for realism concerns the notion of mind- and language-independence, then it is not clear why the nature of the semantic theory that underpins the realist notion of truth should be relevant. One might put this point (benignly) in terms of states of affairs. What the independence notion concerns is the independence of states of affairs from our knowledge of them and means of describing them. The structure of the semantic theory can be seen as depicting the structure of the state of affairs. And now it seems that realism (if restricted to the independence idea) need have nothing to say about the structure of states of affairs; it simply affirms their independence. On occasion, to be sure, these questions will be linked (as in the case of simple behaviourism) but it is not clear why the need to invoke a notion of reference in the semantic theory should, in itself, have any relevance to the independence idea. And indeed in the discussion of directions it had no relevance.

I do not think we can make proper sense of Dummett here unless we think of him as also attempting to shed light, in semantic terms, on the intuitive idea of the ultimate furniture of the world. So there is supposed to be a sense in which an object is thought to be properly part of reality when it participates in the proper semantic theory for the relevant region of language.

The label "realism" and the set of ideas that accompany it are, of course, important; they link styles of argument in different spheres and serve to group together and to differentiate various philosophers and philosophical systems. They are part of our philosophical heritage. Dummett's work has, to be sure, done much to focus thought on what realism might be. Despite this there is a sense in which Dummett might be seen as deflating controversy about realism *per se*. The metaphysical yearning which underpins discussion of realism is a craving to know how our language relates to the world, or, at least, when we have a proper semantic theory (a semantic theory which is the base of a theory of meaning) then our metaphysical quest will be over. Whether we call a certain semantic theory realist or anti-realist will be of comparatively minor importance.

Another point to bear in mind is that Dummett doesn't think that the label realist or anti-realist will apply merely on the basis of formal properties of the semantic theory. We can pick out which properties of a semantic theory are relevant to realism (e.g. use of a bivalent notion of truth, basing the notion of truth on a notion of reference) but whether a semantic theory counts as realist or not will depend upon the nature of its plausible competitors. Dummett gives the example of definite descriptions as treated by Russell and by Frege and Strawson. Russell maintains a bivalent notion of truth at the expense of not treating definite descriptions as referring terms. The Frege–Strawson position, in contrast, accepts truth-value gaps (allows that certain sentences may lack a truth-value) but retains (something of) a referential view of definite descriptions. It is hard to characterize one position as being more realist than the other but impossible to see the debate between these views as metaphysically neutral. On the other hand, *both* positions can be seen as different modes of retreating from a realism of the Meinongian kind which views all definite descriptions as having a reference, even if the referent, on occasion, fails to exist.

Thus it might be fair to interpret Dummett, first, as recommending that we tackle the metaphysical dispute by attempting to construct a semantic theory and, second, as pointing to metaphysically significant differences between semantic theories.

Let's pause to consider a difficulty for Dummett's semantic approach (and possibly too for his conception of semantic theory). Recall the two semantic theories mooted for statements about directions. The first eliminates terms for directions as referring terms while the second gives informative specifications of those references. For this reason Dummett wants to regard the second as constituting a more realistic view than the first. But, note, this is not because he thinks that the first account should lead us to deny that direction terms refer (SoL: 240). Instead he endorses a version of Frege's context principle according to which a term's functioning as a singular term combined with its occurrence in true statements suffices to guarantee it a reference. But can Dummett consistently allow this? He views semantic theory as part of the theory of meaning so if we are legitimately to suppose that a certain semantic relation obtains this must be because a proper account of meaning leads us to ascribe this relationship. But now the semantic theory which is the base for the theory of meaning for statements about directions makes no appeal to reference yet we are supposed to be entitled to use the context principle to justify an ascription of reference to direction terms. Thus a semantic relation is postulated which lies outside of the proper semantic theory.

In discussing this issue Dummett says, "nothing is gained by a philosophical protest to the effect that 'there are not really any such things as directions'" (SoL: 240). So it seems Dummett is, on the one hand, impressed by overt features of the first-order practice (namely, the singular-termhood of terms for directions and our commitment to truths about directions); however, on the other hand, he thinks that there is a philosophical or meaning-theoretic project required to reveal the way the practice actually functions. These two views come into tension because he allows the first to lead to thoughts about the semantics of the language but he also insists that the second approach is the only justification for semantic propositions.

We may, however, be able to dispel this tension. What we need is a principled method for allowing certain semantic propositions to stand even though they form no part of the proper semantic theory. One way to achieve this is to realize first that we can always give a semantics for a region of language homophonically. That is, we can exploit the language in specifying its own semantics in the manner of clauses such as,

(i) "dog" refers to dogs
(ii) "the direction of a" refers to the direction of a.

Clauses of this form are, all but, trivial; in essence, they are comments on the syntactical character of appropriate expressions. Now we might use such a semantics as a base for a theory of meaning by explaining what a knowledge of each of these clauses consists in. In the case of directions this knowledge will consist in a knowledge of how to determine the truth of statements involving directions and this, in turn, will involve a knowledge of how to transform such statements into statements about lines and parallelism. Thus, in explicating the nature of the relevant knowledge, we provide a more interesting semantics for the language, one which explains and doesn't merely presuppose the way the language functions. The proper semantics forms part of the theory of meaning which explicates the homophonic scheme, so it underpins rather than supplants it. Thus, provided we take (the right sort of) direction statements to be true, there is no reason why we shouldn't take this to commit ourselves, given the like of (ii), to the existence of directions themselves.

However, the semantic theory will, at the same time, illustrate the manner in which we have departed from realism.

Different sorts of reason for rejecting bivalence

According to the above, a necessary ingredient of a realist view is adoption of a bivalent notion of truth, a notion which determinately either applies or fails to apply to each statement in the disputed class irrespective of our ability to come to know whether it does or not. Realism thus seems to demand a conception of reality according to which the way things are may outrun our ability to know how they are. That is, realism seems committed not specifically to a bivalent notion of truth but to a notion of truth which goes beyond our possible knowledge. In the jargon, a realist notion of truth is one which is epistemically unconstrained. So ought we not to distinguish different sorts of reason for rejecting bivalence? Some will involve rejection of an epistemically unconstrained notion of truth, and thus will count as anti-realistic. Others won't and might be consistent with realism.

In his "Truth Conditions, Bivalence and Verificationism" McDowell takes the defining property of realism to be a commitment to an epistemically unconstrained notion of truth. He then goes on to argue that one might be convinced by what he calls the verificationist argument to reject (i.e. to refuse to assert) bivalence. However, he claims that there is no route from such a position to a rejection of realism since such a position need not result in novel (i.e. non-truth-conditional) specifications of sense. So it would be possible to refuse to endorse bivalence but to retain a truth-conditional account of meaning making use of an unreconstructed notion of truth, a notion of truth which is not epistemically constrained. In this way McDowell opens up conceptual space for a position which is, in his terms, realist but sceptical about bivalence.

In a similar vein, the following seems to be a possibility. A neutralist about the future thinks that the truth of future-tense statements is constituted by present tendencies: a future-tense statement is true if it is true in all continuations of the world which are consistent with present tendencies, false if it is false in all such continuations. She is likely to take certain future-tense statements to be indeterminate (true in some continuations and false in others) and so will reject bivalence. However, she need not think of truth as, in some sense, always lying within our compass: present tendencies may determine a future-tense statement as true but do so in a manner which we need not be able to discover.[5]

Dummett himself puts and answers an objection of this form (SoL: 263–6). Having characterized realism in terms of adherence to a classical two-valued semantics he wonders whether realism should instead be seen as a view about the objective determination of truth-value independent of our knowledge, rather than as a view about bivalence as such. If the truth-value of a statement is objectively determined then that should suffice for a realistic view; the manner in which it is so determined should be irrelevant to the metaphysical dispute.

We've already encountered Dummett's response to the second form of worry, which is to point out that the status of a position as realist will depend on the character of opposing semantic theories; realism is not purely a matter of the form of the semantic theory but a question of the forms of competing semantic theories. In this manner Dummett can hang on to the intuition that reductionist positions are anti-realist while still insisting that the most important anti-realist component of such positions is their capacity to motivate a rejection of bivalence. But can a similar response be effective against McDowell, whose contemplated position specifically eschews reductionism (the specification of sense is to be truth-conditional)?

We'll need to look in a little more detail at what McDowell envisages. He claims that Dummett's objections to a truth-conditional conception of sense presume that a truth-conditional conception of sense will make use of a bivalent notion of truth. We'll come to Dummett's objections in the next chapter. For now we need only note that they form the crux of Dummett's argument against realism. McDowell tries to distinguish adherence to the principle of bivalence from realism. He does so by sketching a position which refuses to endorse bivalence yet which adheres to a truth-conditional account of sense. If such a position is possible and if it warrants the title "realist" then McDowell will have shown that a realist might accept Dummett's arguments against bivalence but cling to the defining thesis of realism.

Tarski's work gives us the technical machinery for defining truth in a formalized language. Later philosophers, pre-eminently Davidson, have tried to build on Tarski's work in constructing a theory of truth for natural language. The upshot of such a theory will be the systematic generation of theorems that specify the truth-condition for each sentence in the language. So if we have a sentence, S, the theory will then provide a theorem of the form "*S* is true iff *P*". The generation of such theorems is made possible by the use of deductive machinery and a finite set of axioms which specify the denotations of singular terms and satisfaction conditions of predicates. Truth is thus reduced to more primitive semantic notions and what we have can justifiably be claimed to be a theory of truth. We then note that a global constraint on the theory is that it systematically generates acceptable theorems specifying the truth conditions of each sentence in the language. A theory which can achieve this will be a theory whose theorems can be taken to specify the meaning or sense of each sentence in the language. What we have is a truth-conditional account of sense. In traditional implementations of this programme the deductive machinery used to generate theorems is taken to be classical. That is, we use a logic which adheres to the law of excluded middle: "$P \vee -P$" is logically true, for any proposition, P. Such an account will deliver a commitment to bivalence: S is true iff P, S is not true iff $-P$, P or $-P$ so S is true or S is not true. But McDowell notes that we can avoid commitment to the principle of bivalence if instead of taking classical logic to be the logic of our theory we adopt intuitionistic logic, which refuses to accept the law of excluded middle.

One source of interest in intuitionistic logic arises out of a challenge to the orthodox truth-conditional construal of meaning for mathematical statements. Whereas in classical logic the meaning of a logically complex statement is explained in terms of the truth-conditions of its component statements such an intuitionistic account explains what counts as a proof of a complex statement in terms of what counts as a proof of its components.[6] So in the classical case the sense of the logical constants are given as truth functions while in the intuitionistic case they are given as proof functions. So here a novel conception of sense is in play. When we generalize beyond the mathematical case this novelty will be retained since the meaning of the logical constants won't be given simply in terms of truth-conditions but will be given in terms of conditions in which a sentence is known to be true. McDowell concedes this but still insists that in the case of basic sentences the specification of sense will be truth-conditional so, fundamentally, there need be no reconceptualization of the nature of reality. Fully to deal with McDowell's position would require an excursion into the issue of modesty versus full-bloodedness in a theory of meaning.[7] That was one of our ports of call in the last chapter. I don't intend to revisit it here. At this point I want only to make a few remarks about the relation of a non-epistemic conception of truth to the principle of bivalence. The relevance of the issue for the present has less to do with the coherence of realism than with its characterization.

Dummett taxes himself to find a conception of realism which has clear content. So it is a fair question to ask what shows that someone who adopts intuitionistic logic but offers a truth-conditional account of the sense of certain basic sentences has a non-epistemic conception of truth. Presumably McDowell's thought is that, since such a theorist will make no attempt to reduce truth to epistemic norms and since the meanings of undecidable sentences are given truth-conditionally, the notion of truth is one which is (potentially) verification transcendent. However nothing in the theorist's repertoire commits her to a notion of truth which applies in the absence of our capacity to determine that it does apply. The only thing which could do so, namely endorsement of bivalence (or equivalently adherence to classical logic in the presence of a truth-conditional account of sense), is something which she studiously avoids. So, while it is true to say that rejection of bivalence is not tantamount to adoption of an epistemic conception of truth, its rejection is equivalent to agnosticism about whether or not truth transcends verification; such an agnostic position should be distinguished from fully fledged realism. Since there would be no discriminating such a character from McDowell's theorist, there would be no content to the distinctively realist credentials of the latter.

Another way of making this point is to come at it from the rather strange dislocation in McDowell's theorist's account of logic. Recall that the meanings of basic sentences are to be given in terms of truth-conditions but logical connectives are to be explained in terms of what it is to know the logically complex sentence to be true. This gives rise to an intuitionistic logic. But why should we not introduce another set of logical connectives by recourse to a non-epistemic notion of truth and thus resuscitate classical logic? The reason presumably is that a notion of truth which transcends verification (as opposed to one which is not known not to transcend verification) is not known to be available. So describing the theorist as an agnostic[8] *anti*-realist is an apt portrayal of the theorist's position. Thus Dummett's point stands: a rejection of bivalence is a rejection of realism.

Semantic deflationism

The essence of Dummett's position is that the debate about realism should be pursued as a debate about semantics and, crucially, about the notion of truth. Answers to a set of philosophical problems are to be found by asking certain questions about the notion of truth. This presupposes that there is enough "depth" to our concept of truth for it to support such answers. One brand of thought about truth precisely denies that truth possesses the requisite depth. Minimalists or deflationists about truth argue that our concept of truth is all but captured via (some version of) the disquotational schema,

"P" is true iff P.

So the truth predicate functions simply as an instrument of endorsement. Its usefulness is to be found in the way in which it enables endorsement of a sentence by attaching the truth predicate to a name of that sentence. This allows one to generalize over a range of sentences[9] or to endorse a sentence without having to utter it. Now if deflationists are right in their major claim there would be no significant enquiry into the nature of truth and so no such enquiry directed towards metaphysical ends. Dummett's characterization of realism would thus be threatened.

One response to this worry might simply be to deny minimalism. And, indeed, on some understandings of that position this may be the correct response. But a more interesting way of exploiting the debate would be to use it to reflect on how, in just what sense, Dummett's position requires a departure from minimalism. I'll move on to consider that question shortly. But one might also see Dummett's position as challenging minimalism, for if the notion of truth can indeed be made the focus of metaphysical investigation then a minimalist construal of truth must be false. One minimalist, Paul Horwich (1990), has accepted this challenge. His attempt to rebut it poses a problem for Dummettians. I turn now to that.

Horwich denies that realism should be understood in terms of truth. Instead he offers an opposing conception. He begins from two supposed features of our ordinary conception of things. On the one hand we are inclined to think of the world (or regions of it) as being metaphysically autonomous, as being independent of us. On the other hand we think that we can make unproblematic knowledge claims about the world: the world is seen as being epistemically accessible. The anti-realist (and she might come in a number of guises) sees an irresolvable tension in these two lines of thought. Consequently she'll find some way of denying the independence of the world or of revising or rejecting our claims to know. Thus the anti-realist might, Horwich claims, implement the supposed lesson of this tension in three broad ways: by denying the existence or independence of the putative facts at issue, by denying our claims to know in the relevant area (namely scepticism), or by offering a reductive thesis. The realist, in contrast, thinks that both features can, on reflection, be harmoniously combined. Nothing in this depiction of matters implicates the notion of truth: we don't encounter a notion of truth either in the characterization of the underlying source of the dispute or in the particular claim made by the anti-realist in advancing her position.

One striking feature of Horwich's proposal is his nonchalance in helping himself to the notion of metaphysical independence. Dummett's programme gets going because he takes it that that notion requires clarification, that its content is unclear and needs to be made out. Horwich's pat formula of "metaphysical independence" can surely be accused of lacking any clear content. He might, however, claim that this is all to the good since the notion of independence is only clarified by reference to the manner in which it is denied by the anti-realist. Horwich's claim then is that the mooted forms of anti-realism don't make distinctive claims about truth. Perhaps not (though it is far from clear that a reductive anti-realism such as behaviourism shouldn't best be seen as advancing a claim about the truth of statements about mental states) but, if this is the right reading, then Horwich surely begs the question against a Dummettian characterization of the dispute simply by not considering a Dummettian anti-realist.[10] Here's one form of anti-realist who advances distinctive claims about truth; why doesn't Horwich see her claim as a way of denying the independence thesis?

Horwich is happy to talk of facts and their existence. So a realist about one or another subject matter might claim (along with her epistemological reassurance) that such facts exist independently of our thought and talk. Facts make statements true (Dummett would deny that we have any access to the notion of a fact other than as the truth makers of statements). So if the facts exist independently of our knowledge of them certain statements are true (or false) independently of our knowledge, or capacity to know. So truth is epistemically unconstrained and it seems that one version of the independence idea does at least have *consequences* for our conception of truth. We can now see Dummett as claiming that since the notion of truth has some theoretical weight to pull we can treat this link as being more than simply consequential but as illuminating the content of the realist's position. Further skirmishing would then have to concern the theoretical utility of a notion of truth. We'll look at that below. Now I want to pause to consider in just what sense Horwich can, and needs to, deny truth's role in the metaphysical dispute.

It is no part of the minimalist's thesis to deny the utility of a notion of truth in formulating certain claims. So it may be that one (or perhaps the) way of formulating a claim of the right level of generality to count as a realist or anti-realist view will involve recourse to a notion of truth. But this, according to the minimalist, should not lead us to misconceive the debate as one that is about *truth*. So, if truth is simply used as a device facilitating expression of a general point of view, there need be nothing minimalistically objectionable in characterizing realism with respect to a class of statements as a belief that the truth predicate there applies bivalently, or in characterizing anti-realism as a belief that the truth predicate applies bivalently only when a statement is decidable. But once this concession is made we'd then want the minimalist to provide some criterion for deciding exactly when a claim is one that is about truth. Otherwise it is not clear that any part of Dummett's prosecution of the debate is minimalistically objectionable. One possibility would be to gloss the use of the truth predicate as an expressive device when it is eliminable. Here elimination might be either by recourse to substitutional quantification (which would make endorsement of bivalence equivalent to adhering to the law of excluded middle) or by appeal to the notion of a fact. The first option raises issues to do with the semantic justification of logical laws and the relationship of the semantic to the syntactic principle. Horwich himself wants to make a distinction here. In his discussion of vagueness he admits the applicability of classical logic, and so, given the equivalence principle, of bivalence. But he distinguishes between truth and determinate truth. Arguably, the realism issue will similarly focus on a notion of determinate truth. So substitutional quantification wouldn't provide an acceptable eliminative mechanism. The question thus settles on that of the relative priority of the notions of truth and fact.

And here the minimalist faces a dilemma since either the notion of fact is explained via the (minimal) conception of truth or it can be given a more substantial characterization. The first alternative leaves it obscure as to how the realism debate is to be conceived

independently of the notion of truth. The second alternative threatens minimalism since, armed with an account of facts, one would be
in a position to characterize truth in terms of correspondence to facts.
Indeed in his discussion of the notions of fact and correspondence
Horwich is at pains to point out that the platitudes connecting these
notions don't support an account of facts which goes beyond the minimal theory of truth. In other words, he impales himself on the first
horn of the dilemma.

What the above argues for is that an expression of realism will
either make use of the notion of truth or will naturally devolve into
such a claim. But Dummett thinks that realism concerns adoption of
a certain notion of truth (or semantic theory). So what we need is reason to think that truth itself is or should be the focus of attention in
disputes about realism. Now if we think that we ought to provide a
semantic theory for language (as part of constructing a theory of
meaning, say) and, in particular, a semantic validation of logic then
we shall already need to question both the form of such a theory and
what notion of truth will be implicated in it. So the question about
realism, given its involvement with the notion of truth, will be settled
in the course of that enterprise, provided, of course, that we can
engage in that business without betraying a realist or anti-realist
outlook from its outset.[11] Now a minimalist will buttress her position
by denying any substance to these projects. So the focus of the debate
now shifts to the legitimacy and interest of semantic validations.
That issue will permeate through the last two chapters, and Chapter
6 in particular. Thus we leave the matter somewhat inconclusively
here. A characterization of realism in terms of a notion of truth can be
made relatively uncontroversial. But whether we *ought* to characterize realism in this way – whether we make progress in resolving
issues to do with realism by so doing – depends on our attitude
towards semantic theorizing.

I want now to draw this discussion of minimalism to a close by
considering some of Dummett's thoughts about truth itself. He
argues that the source of our concept of truth emerges from a need to
distinguish between, on the one hand, the truth of an assertion and
our grounds for making it and, on the other, the content of what is
asserted from a speaker's purpose in asserting it. We discussed the
second distinction in the first chapter (see, in particular, Appendix
1). The first distinction is relevant to the issue of minimalism. For
Dummett claims that when we consider the role of many sentences in
more complex sentences (particularly their role as antecedents in

conditionals) we are forced to distinguish the truth of an assertion from what warrants its assertion and in so doing we arrive at a conception of truth which cannot be explicated in minimalist terms. Consider the sentence "There will be a deluge tomorrow" and let us say that we know very well what would count as the best possible evidence for its assertion. This would suffice for an account of how the sentence should be used on its own to effect assertions. But we use the sentence to assert such things as "If there will be a deluge tomorrow then the bottom paddock will be inundated" and we cannot by any means explain the content of this conditional assertion by adverting only to the consequences of an availability of evidence for the antecedent since the evidence for the assertion of the sentence is consistent with its falsity – since such evidence is defeasible.[12] Rather we need to consider the situation given the *truth* of the antecedent. But if minimalism is right then truth is explicated via the equivalence principle. So, for our sentence, we shall have "There will be a deluge tomorrow" is true iff there will be a deluge tomorrow. The thought behind the account is that the truth of the sentence will be explicated simply via an understanding of the sentence as used on its own to make assertions. But then truth won't be available to perform the explanatory work we require of it: the minimalist account fails us.[13] So Dummett's thought is that, although we are not very aware of the origins of our notion of truth, our linguistic practice is informed by a conception of truth which contrasts with the mere availability of evidence. And this forces us to adopt a more substantial notion of truth than minimalism will allow. If Dummett is right then, of course, his view of the realism debate as a debate about truth is secured. But minimalism about truth (in the wake of Horwich's book (1990) and, to some extent, Wright's account of realism and truth (1992)) has emerged as a difficult and controversial issue. I won't now allow myself to be diverted by it further.

Summary

It is often assumed that, for Dummett, a realist is anyone who accepts a bivalent notion of truth. Although this is an important feature of Dummett's conception it is a vast oversimplification of his position. It is better to see Dummett as recommending that metaphysical debates about realism should be seen as disputes about the correct semantics for a region of language. The reasons for this recommendation emerge from a number of sources. First, Dummett's concern in considering metaphysical disputes about realism is to arrive at a view about the character of these disputes in general. Only by moving up to the semantic level can we gain a sufficiently general overview. Secondly, a frustration with many debates about realism is that the opposing positions lack clarity; the terms of the debate are contested and thus we have no way of resolving the dispute. The semantic approach promises to give clear content to the opposing positions and, since the acceptability of a semantic theory is arbitrated by the theory of meaning, we have a principled way of deciding between opposing semantic theories. So it is quite clear that one cannot appraise the merits of Dummett's characterization of realism in isolation from his views about the nature of the theory of meaning.

Dummett points, not to a single form that a realist semantic theory must take, but to aspects of a semantic theory which are (or may be) relevant to the realism issue (depending on the form of competing semantic theories). Those features can be seen as giving content, in semantic terms, to the intuitive ideas of mind- and language-independence and to that of being part of the ultimate furniture of the world.

Dummett's semantic construal of the realism debate has attracted many critics. Many of these do not consider the characterization in the context of his views about the theory of meaning. In this chapter we've looked at two problems: one raised by McDowell and the other by Horwich. McDowell raises no problem about the semantic construal itself, rather his claim in effect is that Dummett mislocates the crucial realism relevant issue: acceptance of bivalence is not crucial, acceptance of an epistemically unconstrained notion of truth is. I defended Dummett by noting that McDowell's contemplated realist is no such thing. Minimalism about truth provides a problem which is less easy to restrict. Although some problems in Horwich's attack on Dummett's semantic view were mooted I also noted that this issue would depend on one's attitude in general to semantic theorizing.

As we noted, given the semantic construal of the metaphysical dispute, resolution of the dispute will occur within the theory of meaning. Dummett argues that meaning-theoretic considerations undermine realist semantic theories. We now turn to that challenge to realism.

Chapter 4

The challenge for realism

Grant the following premises.

* Premise 1: We understand sentences for which we lack a decision procedure – that is, undecidable sentences.
* Premise 2: If an expression has a semantic value its possession of that value must be justified by the character of speakers' understanding of it. (Sense determines reference.)
* Premise 3: A speaker's understanding of an expression must be capable of being fully manifested in the use she is able to make of it.

Now, if realism holds, truth applies bivalently to all sentences (or, perhaps better, statements). In view of premise 2 this supposed fact must be justified by the character of speakers' understanding of those sentences. Moreover, premise 3 ensures that this understanding must be capable of full manifestation. So the question is: what manifestable feature of speakers' understanding shows that the sentences they grasp are subject to bivalence? Where the sentences concerned are those we can recognize (in suitable circumstances) as being either true or false, the question is easy to answer. The ability to recognize the sentence as true or as false is itself the manifestable feature of speakers' understanding of them which shows that truth applies bivalently. But premise 1 informs us that this fails to exhaust the range of sentences that speakers understand. So our question now becomes: what manifestable feature of speakers' understanding shows that truth applies bivalently to undecidable sentences? And this question is rather more difficult to answer.

A speaker's understanding of a sentence might consist in an ability to offer a verbal explanation of it. Where it does so, the account of her understanding is unproblematic but equally the question of whether truth applies bivalently becomes one of whether truth applies bivalently to the explanans. Clearly there cannot be any ingress into a region of language which is undecidable from one which consists of sentences which are purely decidable. For using the resources of the latter we can only frame explanations of sentences which are themselves decidable. Thus at a certain point there will be concepts or operations expressible in language (paradigm examples being the past tense; subjunctive and counterfactual conditionalization; and quantification over unsurveyable domains) that give rise to the phenomenon of undecidability. And the question must be focused on the introduction of these operations. A speaker's understanding of such an operation cannot transcend the use she is able to make of it. But how can she have attached a use to an operation which demonstrates that truth applies bivalently to undecidable sentences? By hypothesis she will be incapable of putting herself in a position to recognize the truth or falsity of the sentence. So it appears that there is nothing she can do which shows that the sentence is determinately either true or false. Realism is refuted, given our premises.

To put the point slightly differently, the realist must maintain that in understanding an undecidable sentence speakers grasp something (usually this is conceived of as a truth-condition) which determines that the sentence is determinately true or false. But what would distinguish such a character from one who grasps something slimmer, something which is constituted by (or delivers only) a sensitivity to whether or not appraisable conditions warrant the assertion of the sentence? It seems that all one is able to do with the sentence is exhausted in such a sensitivity and that this would fail to determine that the sentence is determinately true or false when we cannot discover which it is. So the extra ingredient of understanding that the realist is forced to ascribe becomes something that is not manifestable. Once again, realism is shown to be incompatible with our premises.

If realism is to be defended then one of the premises will have to be denied or shown not to support its application in the argument. Premises 1 and 3 are not to be questioned here – the former because it is evident and the latter because we have already discussed and examined it – although it's worth recording that a position which diluted the manifestation claim might not result in an argument against realism. Thus one might defend realism by opting for a requirement of less than full manifestation, perhaps insisting only that a difference in understanding between two speakers be capable of manifestation. The question is whether such a position delivers an account of understanding which construes meanings as publicly accessible. Dummett rejects such accounts because he still thinks that they demote the status of speakers' agreement in meanings to something that is, at best, a hypothesis.[1] So the only defences of realism we shall here consider are, first, attempts to find holes in the application of premise 3 and, secondly, a rejection of premise 2.

Realism and manifestation

The argument applies premise 3 by taking it that a speaker will have to manifest her understanding by an exercise of an appropriate recognitional capacity (a capacity to recognize the sentence as true or as assertible or, perhaps, a sensitivity to whether or not presented evidence justifies the assertion of the sentence) and it might be argued that this fails to take into account other aspects of a speaker's use of the sentence. This view of use might be seen to be impoverished either because one might have a richer conception of what a speaker is able to do with the sentence itself or because one might want to take into account the use of the sentence as a component of other sentences.

I shall begin by considering an example of the first sort of strategy. In embracing modesty, McDowell provides himself with a richer conception of what is available to view in a speaker's use of language. So, for him, one manifests one's grasp of the truth-conditions of, say, "Caesar crossed the Rubicon" because one is able to use that sentence to assert *that* Caesar crossed the Rubicon. Thus McDowell's realist can respond simply enough to the manifestation challenge.

Now part of the question about the legitimacy of this strategy will simply take us back to the issue of modesty versus full-bloodedness in the theory of meaning. I don't propose to tread that ground again now.[2] But there is one aspect of the question that I think is worth speculating upon here. Let us suppose that we accept Dummett's characterization of realism. Suppose also that we think of realism as making a claim that anti-realism simply refuses to make. Then we are likely to see the realist as incurring a burden of proof. Dummett's challenge might then take a looser form: with what right, he asks, do we credit ourselves with grasp of realist truth-conditions? If we do grasp such truth-conditions then McDowell has an answer to the question of how that understanding is manifested. But how do we justify the antecedent? That question has no obvious answer. Thus, as long as she sees no need to justify her position, the realist can fall back on aspects of her own view to rebut Dummett's challenge. But once she accepts the need to offer a justification then, even if we allow for modesty, an acceptable response will be far from trivial.

As an example of the second sort of strategy we might begin with Loar[3] who attempts to defend realism (about the natural world) by showing how a realist might meet the manifestation challenge. His thought is that the manifestation challenge will be met provided we are given an account of meaning that coheres with the slogan "meaning is use". A holistic conceptual role account of meaning[4] will, he argues, legitimate realism while portraying meaning as use. However, he opens his defence with an argument which, although inconclusive, is supposed to motivate realism as a natural part of our view of the world. The argument captures a tempting realistic line of thought and is worth pondering.

Loar's conception of realism differs significantly from Dummett's. He advocates a disquotational (or minimalist) view of truth. So, where Dummett takes the realism issue to be *about* truth, Loar cannot concur. However, this doesn't mean that truth is not essentially involved in *stating* the realist's position. Loar accepts this but now departs from Dummett once again in construing the issue in modal terms. Whereas Dummett is primarily concerned with whether the notion of truth adopted is one that applies bivalently, Loar is concerned with the modal question of whether *it is possible* for a sentence to be true though unverifiable. I won't here question the relevance of this shift of focus, so let us move on to consider the supposedly natural train of thought which indicates that this is indeed a possibility.

Take a sentence, say a sentence about the past, which we are sure is true – for example, "Beethoven died in 1827." How do we know this sentence to be true? Presumably on the basis of a number of records made at the time, which appear to be reliable and which have survived. Our knowledge thus rests on a set of contingencies. Although it might be unlikely, it might have been the case that these contingencies each failed to hold, in which case we wouldn't have known that Beethoven died in 1827. But it would still have been *true* that he died in that year. So it's possible for the relevant sentence to be true but unverifiable.

Another realist thought akin to this one runs as follows. Only an extreme constructivist will buttress her anti-realism by insisting that the relevant facts are brought into being by our investigations. So, in cases where those investigations yield knowledge, our epistemic powers are supposed (even by anti-realist lights) to be responsive to facts which don't owe their existence to an exercise of those powers. So the facts might have obtained in each of the following counterfactual circumstances: we had not exercised those powers; the powers were less than they actually are; the powers could not have been exercised because of various external factors. So the facts might have obtained even if we hadn't come to know them (in the first case) or even if we couldn't, in some sense, have come to know them (in the last two cases).

Note that, even were the argument successful at this stage, realism would not have been substantiated. What would have been shown is that realism – or a notion of truth which transcends verification – is part of our view of the world. To move from this to a justification of realism we would need, in addition, to show how we manifest an understanding of sentences whose truth transcends verification. I turn to Loar's attempt to discharge that obligation shortly. But first let us review the argument (which, even if it failed to justify realism, would be a potent criticism of anti-realism).

Dummett takes the argument simply to beg the question. He grants that we can describe cases where the possible course of events deprives us of the ability to know what, in fact, we do know. But this doesn't address the relevant question, which is whether we can conceive of states of affairs as determinately obtaining independently of our knowledge. So, in the example about Beethoven, it is true that Beethoven died in 1827 and true too that we might not have known this. But that reflection would have no bite were we in a position of ignorance: it wouldn't justify the assumption, in those circumstances, that "Beethoven died in 1827" is determinately either true or false. The example has us envisaging a certain possibility from a position of knowledge, it doesn't speak to the crux of the difficulty, which concerns what we are entitled to assume in a position of ignorance.

Loar's contention, however, was that such examples demonstrate a possibility of some generality. What we learn from the case of Beethoven's death is that, although we know when this happened, we might have been deprived of this knowledge. Analogously, we are ignorant of whether "Beethoven breakfasted on boiled eggs precisely two weeks before his death" is true or false. Might we not here be in precisely the sort of position we envisage with respect to "Beethoven died in 1827"? If not, wherein lies the disanalogy between the two cases?

Let's suppose that the analogical reasoning holds up. What would we have succeeded in showing? The possibility envisaged according to the analogy is that "Beethoven breakfasted on boiled eggs precisely two weeks before his death" might be either true or false despite our (current) inability to know which. This may not license the assumption that the sentence has a determinate truth-value irrespective of our ability to disclose it (for that we'd need some evidence that the envisaged possibility were realized) but we would be unable automatically to rule out the assumption. That is, the example suffices to show that the anti-realist cannot *deny* the assumption of determinate truth-value. But that was never, or need never have been, the anti-realist's contention. The anti-realist simply prescinds from making that assumption. Or, to put the matter slightly differently, we can conceive of two sorts of anti-realist, each marked by her respective attitude to this assumption: the agnostic anti-realist simply prescinds from making the assumption; the forthright anti-realist denies it.[5] The argument is problematic only for a forthright anti-realist. Her agnostic cousin is unaffected by it. Thus part of the lesson of this discussion is that Loar's modal conception of realism is insufficiently weighty: it is compatible with a moderate (i.e. agnostic) anti-realism.

The possibility Loar aims at establishing is that of a sentence which is true though unverifiable. The notion of verifiability and its relation to that of decidability are often a source of confusion. What Loar is concerned with is the possibility of a sentence's being true yet there being some bar to us discovering its truth. Now if that bar makes it impossible to discover the sentence to be true, if, that is, there is some absurdity in supposing that we know the sentence to be true, then under most likely readings of anti-realist negation[6] we should be entitled to *deny* the sentence. Thus, if the anti-realist has a credible notion of negation[7] then this cannot be the sort of situation Loar is contemplating (it's hard anyway to see how *all* modes of discovering a given truth could have been ruled out *ab initio*). Rather we are asked to think of a sentence for which we lack a decision procedure and for which we also lack decisive evidence. He then claims that such a sentence might nonetheless be true. And so it might. (The sentence about Beethoven's breakfast might well be true. This is presumably part of what I commit myself to in reserving my judgement, given my present state of ignorance.) But that quite simply fails to establish that truth transcends verification.

Let us now move on to consider how Loar thinks the manifestation challenge should be met. (If Loar has an answer here then the previous argument will still have been useful to him. For then it will seem that the agnostic anti-realist's reservations about the realist assumption are unmotivated.) Loar advocates a "holistic conceptual role theory" of understanding according to which the understanding of a sentence consists in (and so its meaning is given by) certain dispositions to use the sentence: dispositions to use the sentence in reasoning (including inference and the construction and acceptance of theory), in relation to perception and in relation to action. So given a sentence, S, there will be a complex story to tell about how qualified speakers are disposed to use it. Since the account is embedded solely in facts about use (or, more strictly, dispositions to use) the account, plausibly, will satisfy the requirements of manifestation. What needs to be explained on such an account is how it is that in understanding S a speaker understands a sentence whose truth transcends verification. For Loar this amounts to providing an explanation of how one can coherently think that S is true though unverifiable. And now the previous argument is recycled since, according to Loar, it is part of our theory of nature that our ability to determine whether or not S is true depends upon contingent relations between us and the relevant states of affairs. So, despite the fact that the meaning of S is given (in part) by reference to an ability to recognize whether or not it obtains, we can still conceive of S being true independently of our ability to recognize it as true because we have a theory of nature which presents a picture of how that recognitional ability operates. According to that picture a successful exercise of that recognitional ability is only ever contingently related to the relevant state of affairs.

So Loar thinks we need two steps to get to realism. First we have a holistic conceptual role account of understanding. We then need to explain why sentences understood according to this model are subject to a verification transcendent notion of truth. That question might seem – especially if one has Dummettian inclinations – to be a question about what semantic account is legitimated by this theory of understanding. But that isn't Loar's approach. Rather he answers that question by explaining how it is that speakers come to form a conception of verification transcendent states of affairs. This they do, according to him, by mastering a certain theory of nature. So the answer to the question is that our theory treats our sentences as subject to a verification transcendent notion of truth. That is, the question is not answered by looking "externally" at which semantic theory is justified but by looking "internally" at the way our theory portrays our practice.

Now this is surely a very odd idea. *If* I have mastered a certain theory of nature then, according to Loar, a verification transcendent notion of truth is warranted. Why? Well, because that theory of nature treats sentences as subject to a verification transcendent notion of truth. However, the manner in which the theory treats those sentences is surely irrelevant unless we take it that the theory is true. And now it seems that the "internal" aspect of the approach withers. For what counts now is simply the truth of a certain theory about how our recognitional capacities relate to truth-making states of affairs. *Speakers'* mastery of that theory need not be taken into account. This does not mean that the argument is nugatory; it might still challenge the anti-realist position by making that view collide with an entrenched part of our worldview. However, it does mean that this second argument simply collapses into the first (motivational) argument, the argument, that is, which we've already discussed and dismissed.

An alternative form of holism might, however, seem more conducive to the realist's needs here. The flaw in the conceptual role approach emerges as a result of the breadth of use it is prepared to encompass. It thus takes into account use within certain theories whose interpretation is taken as unproblematic (itself a questionable position for a theory of understanding) and so brings into question not merely the character of the theory but its truth. One might still be a holist, and thus enrich the resources for describing how understanding is manifested, but attempt to narrow the focus of what is taken to be meaning-determining use. An example of such a strategy would be to confine one's attention to inferential role, that is, the role of a sentence within deductive inference.

The holistic element in this thought consists in the idea that the meaning of a sentence will not be determined in isolation from its role in inferential practice in general. However, the meaning of any particular sentence won't merely consist in this role, rather the role will determine a definite content for each sentence. The thought then is that mastery of the canons of classical logic shows that one grasps, not simply the role a sentence plays within a system of classical logic, but realist truth-conditions for sentences with which one is adept in reasoning. In other words, grasp of a realist notion of truth is manifested precisely in one's ability to reason classically.

Is there any plausibility in the idea that proficiency in classical logic could constitute grasp of a realist notion of truth? Dummett (EoI: 376–7) thinks not. He grants that training in the principles of classical logic might well lead us to presume that we had such a notion of truth but that presumption doesn't in any way show that we indeed grasp a notion of truth that fits this conception.

Revisionism about inferential practice holds that our actual practices of reasoning stand in need of justification and can be found to be in error if no acceptable justification is forthcoming. If revisionism is a defensible stance then one will need to provide some justification of classical inferential practice. If that justification appeals to a realist notion of truth then the justification will have to explain what constitutes grasp of this notion of truth. If the reply is that this is constituted by grasp of the principles of classical logic then the justification becomes circular.

If the justification is given in some other terms then it's not evident why a realist notion of truth is implicated at all.[8] To be sure, once the law of excluded middle is conjoined with the equivalence principle we could infer that every sentence is either true or not true (false).[9] But since truth doesn't play a role in justifying the law of excluded middle it's not clear that the corresponding semantic principle is not simply an informal means of endorsing that law.[10] That is, *if* classical logic is taken to be acceptable then an endorsement of bivalence cannot be distinguished from an acceptance of the law of excluded middle unless the former is being put forward as a way of *justifying* the latter. Since, in the present case, one eschews such a justification it is at least arguable whether or not a realist notion of truth is indeed implicated.

To put the point slightly differently, the account claims that use of classical reasoning manifests grasp of a realist notion of truth. However, if a realist notion of truth is not involved in the account of one's grasp of classical principles of reasoning then it seems clear that there is a way of understanding those principles *without* grasping realist truth-conditions. And this undermines the original claim. If, on the other hand, a realist notion of truth is involved in explaining grasp of classical principles of reasoning then our judgement about the acceptability of those principles of reasoning will await a justification of ascribing grasp of realist truth-conditions to speakers; we won't be able to move in the reverse direction as the proposal intends.

Another move is, however, available to the non-revisionist. In the absence of a justification for her practice the non-revisionist might still think that she ought to be able reflectively to make sense of it. This doesn't quite push us back to revisionism since the notion of making sense of a practice might be loose enough to nullify any threat of having to revise our practice. There might be better and worse ways of making sense of a practice and one way might always be to describe the principles or rules governing the practice. So this non-revisionist might go on to claim that the best way of making sense of classical reasoning appeals to a realist notion of truth. However, note that now the position has changed quite radically. The thought now is not that mastery of classical logic manifests a grasp of realist truth, but that the best way for a *theorist* to comprehend the practice appeals to a realist notion of truth. The question of what manifests grasp of a realist notion of truth thus remains hanging. So, on this view, the defence of realism would be that we might be led to ascribe semantic properties to our sentences which aren't justified merely by the character of speakers' understanding. But that is to challenge the second premise of the argument. We focus now on that.

Realism and the notion of sense

The effect of adhering to premise 2 is that any assumption made in the theory of reference must be justified by appeal to facts about the character of speakers' understanding. Since sense is that ingredient of understanding that is relevant to the determination of reference, the theory of reference must be validated by a theory of sense. Dummett's argument is then to the effect that a realist theory of reference cannot be validated by a plausible theory of sense (and, for Dummett, a plausible such theory must be one which guarantees the publicity of meaning). So one way of resisting Dummett's argument would be to find an alternative way of justifying a theory of reference. However, one might wonder where, other than in the core of a theory of meaning, we should "place" a theory of reference.

Hilary Putnam (1979a) exemplifies precisely the sort of character we've just been envisaging in rather abstract terms. Putnam attempts to defend realism by rejecting what is essentially a Fregean assumption of premise 2. He insists that the only credible way to think about understanding is to think of it as an ability to use the language. He then (in effect) concedes Dummett's point that such an account of understanding won't validate a realist notion of truth. In fact, such an account won't make use of a notion of truth at all but will instead focus on speakers' use of sentences in response to appropriate evidential situations. So what, asks Putnam, is the point of a theory of truth and reference? His answer is that we encounter the need for such a theory only when we turn to a different explanatory task, namely, that of explaining the contribution that linguistic behaviour makes to the success of overall behaviour. The notion of truth enters the picture because, if our beliefs are true, then we tend to get what we want. When we engage in the enterprise of explaining success we'll need to explain the reliability of our learning strategies. Since one of the ways of learning about the world is to employ deductive inference we shall need to see those practices as truth preserving. And since the logic underlying our inferential practice is classical (and so obeys the law of excluded middle) and since the simplest explanation of classical logic's preservation of truth appeals to a realist notion of truth, that notion of truth will be validated via an inference to the best explanation.

So the broad form of Putnam's strategy here is to admit a theory of understanding which fails to determine the semantics for the language. We arrive at the semantic theory only by grafting a substantial theory – an explanation of the contribution that linguistic behaviour makes to successful behaviour – onto the theory of understanding. So we move from a theory of understanding to a semantic theory by means of some substantial theory. In Putnam's case this substantial theory is an explanation of success but that is only one of a number of possible options. Others (e.g. Papineau (1987) and Millikan (1984)) have recommended that the right sort of account is one which focuses on teleology, that is, on the biological proper function of expressions. And still others claim that causal or contextual relations between speakers' use of language and worldly items are responsible for those items assuming the status of referents: we adopt a causal theory of reference.

How should we proceed? Some of the arguments for these non-Fregean conceptions directly challenge Dummett's Fregean assumption. These arguments call for a rebuttal. That is, if Dummett's position is to survive, we need to see what is wrong with these arguments. But a second obligation remains since, unless something is shown to be wrong with the alternative conceptions, premise 2 will seem unmotivated and the argument against realism correspondingly lacking in compulsion. I'll turn to these in turn: first the challenge to Fregeanism, then the fault in non-Fregean pictures.

Michael Dummett

Challenges to Fregeanism

In this section I shall look at a challenge to Fregeanism which derives from the work of Putnam and of Kripke on reference and which is often taken to support the need for a causal ingredient in the reference relation.

Kripke attacks descriptive accounts of names and, since he assumes that a Fregean account of the sense of a name is to be given descriptively, he takes himself to be attacking Frege. So one way of defending a Fregean view of names would be to reject assimilating his view to a descriptive account. But let us concede the point to Kripke and consider his argument. I'll focus first on Kripke's use of modal considerations. If the meaning (sense) of a name is to be given by a definite description then that conferral of meaning on the name should support certain necessities. So, for instance, if the sense of "St Anne" is given by means of the definite description "the mother of Mary" then it seems that "St Anne is the mother of Mary" must be necessarily true. But that cannot be right since it makes perfect sense (and, in fact, is true) to say that "St Anne might not have been the mother of Mary."

That cannot quite settle the matter for it is surely necessarily true to say that "The mother of Mary is the mother of Mary" yet we can still say (meaningfully and truly) "The mother of Mary might not have been the mother of Mary", meaning that the person who gave birth to Mary might not have done so. We need to be a little more careful about what is happening in the case of descriptions and why names are disanalogous. In the description case we have the following two sentences:

(i) Necessarily, the mother of Mary is the mother of Mary.
(ii) The mother of Mary is necessarily the mother of Mary.

In the first sentence the necessity operator has wide scope and the description has narrow scope. The resulting sentence is true. In the second sentence the description has wide scope and the necessity operator has narrow scope. The resulting sentence is false since it is contingent that the person who gave birth to Mary actually did so (she might not have for any number of reasons).

Now let's consider the following two sentences.

(i)′ Necessarily, St Anne is the mother of Mary.
(ii)′ St Anne is necessarily the mother of Mary.

Here the sentences don't seem to express different propositions. In each case they seem to be false since St Anne might not have given birth to Mary. So where there is a scope distinction in the case of descriptions there is none in the case of names; "St Anne" is not synonymous with "the mother of Mary".

Kripke goes on to explain the situation by saying that although the reference of "St Anne" might be fixed by means of the definite description "the mother of Mary" the latter does not give its meaning. Because of this "St Anne is the mother of Mary" is knowable a priori but since (i)′ is false it is contingent: we must distinguish metaphysical from epistemic necessity. Finally the point of difference between a name and a definite description is that, although each functions as a designator (serves to pick out a particular individual), a name is a rigid designator (it designates the same individual in each possible world) while a definite description can be used either as a rigid designator (if it has wide scope) or as a flexible designator (if it has narrow scope).[11]

Although the phenomenon Kripke has lighted on is undeniable his interpretation of it is not. Dummett is suspicious of the distinctions (between fixing the reference and giving the meaning and between epistemic and metaphysical necessity) to which Kripke helps himself in describing the phenomenon. In support of his suspicion Dummett deflates the importance of the phenomenon.

Dummett wants to retain the idea that the meaning (sense) of a name might be given descriptively. Nevertheless it is clear that names and descriptions function differently in modal contexts: different conventions govern relative assignments of scope. So could we not simply allow that the meaning of a given name might be given by means of a description but accept that different general conventions govern our use of names and descriptions? We have a general convention that names, in modal contexts, always have wide scope.

There is one worry about the proposal and one sense in which Frege was clearly wrong to conflate names and definite descriptions, distinguishing only the category of singular terms. The proposal takes it for granted that the categories of names and definite descriptions can be distinguished by some feature other than their behaviour in modal contexts. For, if not, then the convention cannot engage with linguistic practice. However it is surely clear that names and definite descriptions are different: the latter have semantically relevant structure and the former do not. From "The black dog is lazy" we can infer "Something black is lazy". In treating "the black dog" as a singular term with no semantically relevant structure Frege was clearly wrong. But recognizing that structure enables us to distinguish the two categories independently of any discussion of modality. So the convention can have a meaningful application which explains the behaviour of the respective categories of expression in modal contexts.

One might think that Dummett's account poses a potential problem for his molecularist inclinations since there seems to be a difference in meaning between names and descriptions which only emerges when we consider their use in sentences that are more complex than the simple ones by means of which we plausibly form our understanding. So it seems that our original understanding is incomplete and can't be seen as a stable basis on which our understanding of the complex sentences is built.

There is something right about this worry. Our understanding of a given name or definite description is only complete when its use in any context flows from that understanding together with a grasp of the relevant context. But this seems to mean that in grasping the meaning of a name we need to form a conception of the convention governing names in general. The appearance might, however, be denied. We might think of the convention not as being integral to an understanding of names and descriptions but as being integral to an understanding of modal notions *given* an understanding of names and descriptions. What we want anyway to focus on is how we form our understanding of the relevant modal sentences. If molecularity is not to be compromised we want to see this understanding as accruing by bringing together linguistic expertise which is independently acquirable. And now it's hard to see what genuine worry one might have. Given an understanding of names and descriptions we form a conception of the convention. To understand the modal sentences we then bring these two pieces of understanding together (with whatever else needs to be understood, e.g. an understanding of a given predicate). Nothing here hints at a harmful ramification in which the partial order of understandings is threatened.[12]

Dummett's deflation thus appears to be a plausible strategy. However, it would be hard to see the deflationary account as apt if Kripke had brought to light two genuinely distinct notions of necessity: how could these conceptions and the states of affairs they portray be a mere product of adopting a linguistic convention? The account must be supplemented by motivating a scepticism about Kripke's distinction between epistemic and metaphysical necessity. The seeds of scepticism aren't hard to find. For it seems odd that in fixing the reference of the name "St Anne" we should thereby come to know a priori the contingent fact that St Anne is the mother of Mary. Moreover our knowledge of this fact is entirely analogous to our knowledge that the mother of Mary is the mother of Mary.

Recall that the reason we were given for separating names and descriptions was that the latter exhibited an ambiguity in modal contexts which the former lack. So, if we take the sentence "Necessarily, the mother of Mary is the mother of Mary" we can read this in a manner in which the definite description has narrow scope (in which case the sentence is true) or in a manner in which the definite description has wide scope (in which case the sentence is false). In contrast, "Necessarily, St Anne is the mother of Mary" is supposed to be unambiguously false. But that isn't quite the full story. For Kripke grants that "St Anne is the mother of Mary" is a priori knowable, it is epistemically necessary. So, in fact, the sentence comes out true when the necessity operator is read as epistemic necessity, but false if read as metaphysical necessity. One might therefore suspect, as Dummett does, that we have the *same* phenomenon at work in either case. In the one case it is explained by means of the notion of scope, in the other by means of a distinction between two sorts of necessity. But it's the different modes of explanation which distinguish names from definite descriptions, not something intrinsic to their respective behaviours.

Kripke's form of explanation thus appears to be spurious. It arises primarily from focusing on the modal status of *sentences* rather than on the nature of the property, which the sentence involves. If we distinguish between accidental and essential properties and note that being the mother of Mary is an accidental property of a person then the same form of explanation is apt in both the case of names and that of definite descriptions. So it is true of any person (no matter how picked out) that she might not have been the mother of Mary. So both "St Anne might not have been the mother of Mary" and "The mother of Mary might not have been the mother of Mary" can be interpreted as being true and the explanation in either case is the same, namely, that being the mother of Mary is an accidental property of a person. And note also that in each of these sentences the name and definite description respectively has wide scope. It is this which licenses our attempt to determine the truth-value of either sentence by considering the status of the relevant property (as being essential or accidental). Similarly the necessity, that is, a priori knowability, of each of "St Anne is the mother of Mary" and "The mother of Mary is the mother of Mary" is explained by appealing to the meanings of its components.

The crucial point is that we often fix the reference (that is, *pace* Kripke, give the meaning) of a name of a sort of object by appealing to what is, for that sort of thing, an accidental property. The consequence of this is that the referent's possession of that property is knowable a priori but that this doesn't, of course, alter the fact that the property is accidental for that sort of thing. Why should this phenomenon pose a problem for the notion of sense? Why, that is, should a proponent of the notion of sense be committed to the ludicrously strong view that the sense of a name should be given by means only of uniquely individuating *essential* properties?

Kripke's modal argument does not comprise the whole of his attack on the notion of sense. Here I won't aim for exhaustiveness but will restrict myself to what I take to be his strongest non-modal argument. If a name has a certain sense, that is, determines its referent by means of certain properties how could it be that we come to discover that the referent doesn't have some (or all) of those properties? For instance, let us suppose that it's part of the sense with which most people use the name "Gödel" that Gödel discovered the incompleteness of arithmetic. How could it then be discovered that Gödel stole his findings from some now long forgotten and ill-used student? How, indeed, can we make sense of such a discovery? To make the example even more forceful we might suppose that the single piece of knowledge possessed by most competent speakers about Gödel is that he was the discoverer of the incompleteness of arithmetic. So this exhausts the putative sense of the name.

Dummett's answer to this problem is essentially that there are cases and cases. Sometimes when we use a name we aim to be referring to whomever in life bore that name. So, though we might only know of Gödel that he was the discoverer of the incompleteness of arithmetic, we aim to be referring to that person who, in life, was called "Gödel". We might then discover that the person who discovered the incompleteness of arithmetic did not go by the name of Gödel. In other cases we are less concerned by what name the relevant person went under. So, Dummett suggests, it might matter little to us to discover that the giant whom David slew did not go by the name of "Goliath". It matters little since *we* use the name "Goliath" to refer to that giant. So Dummett's suggestion is that this feature is not a pervasive one infecting all names and that where it does occur the piece of individuating knowledge is either not the only such knowledge (at least, if we focus on the community as a whole) or it is supplemented by other criteria for determining the reference of the name (such as that the putative referent was called by that name in life). In the latter sort of case Dummett says that "here it is the *tradition* which connects our use of the name with the man; where the actual *name* came from has little to do with it" (T&OE: 143). According to Kripke's alternative causal account there is no more to our use of a name other than a causal chain leading back to the bearer, each link of which involves an intention to preserve reference. In contrast, Dummett thinks that this account is too weak. In some cases the descriptive explanations offered of a name are paramount (e.g. "Goliath"). In others we need to look not simply to the causal origin of any utterance of the name but to the causal origin of an utterance which is in accord with standard use, that is, an utterance which is informed by the normal explanation of the name. Even in the latter case the description used in the explanation may fail to be true of the bearer of the name because the reference relation is fixed by the causal origin of the belief expressed in the explanation. So the reference of "Gödel" would be determined by the causal origin of the belief that Gödel discovered the incompleteness of arithmetic. Note that no circularity is involved in using a belief about Gödel in specifying the reference of "Gödel" since we don't presuppose that speakers grasp this fact about the belief in grasping the name. Rather the point might be that we accept that the explanation now offered of the name "Gödel" originates in an attribution made by speakers who were capable of identifying Gödel by other means (perhaps ostensively) and that that attribution might have been mistaken. So the thought seems to be that something like the linguistic division of labour[13] functions diachronically. Or, it seems that our practice is informed by a knowledge that we hold our use responsible to features, of which we may not be apprised, of the original introduction of the name. Although, to be sure, we may not be aware of what precisely we hold our use responsible to, we are aware that we hold our use responsible to factors of a particular sort. Thus qualified speakers would know what would settle the question of the reference of a name such as "Gödel" and therefore no very substantial deviation from a theory of sense is called for.

Putnam makes natural kind terms the focus of his attention. Here again the point is that what speakers understand fails to determine the reference of their terms. So, once again, the second premise in

Dummett's argument against realism will be threatened. Putnam's first example indicates a phenomenon which is analogous to those Kripke highlights. Very often a speaker will succeed in effecting a reference by use of a term although the knowledge which she has about the term's bearer(s) will be inadequate to distinguish that (or those) thing(s) from others. So, for instance, Putnam unashamedly admits that his botanical knowledge is so meagre he is unable to distinguish an elm from a beech. Nonetheless he is able to refer to elms by the use of the word "elm" and to pass on useful information about, say, a copse of beech trees to botanically more informed acquaintances. The reason why his use of "elm" succeeds in referring cannot be found in anything that informs Putnam's use of the term but rather rests on the fact that his community contains experts who are able to distinguish the one sort of tree from the other and that Putnam defers to these experts in his use of the term. So Putnam argues that we must acknowledge a division in linguistic labour. Dummett endorses this point, using it to argue against the idea that a public language should be seen as an overlapping of idiolects. However he insists that a theory of sense can easily encompass the phenomenon. Putnam fails to grasp the sense of "elm" completely but his reference succeeds because his community includes members who do grasp this sense completely (and Putnam defers to them). So the example fails to trouble the general thought that reference is mediated by sense, although the community will be the primary locus of attention rather than the individual.

Putnam, however, pushes the point further. He asks us to consider a Twin Earth which is atom for atom identical with this, other than the fact that on Twin Earth the chemical composition of the stuff that has all the phenomenal characteristics of common table salt (it tastes like salt, can be used for pickling, dissolves easily in water, etc.) has some other chemical composition. Now since Twin Earth replicates Earth it possesses a *doppelgänger* for Putnam. Both Putnam and his twin would seemingly attach the same sense to the term "salt" since (apart from the fact that they are physically qualitatively identical) they use precisely the same features to apply the term "salt" to stuff in their respective environments. However, Putnam contends that his term refers to sodium chloride whereas his twin's term refers to some other stuff. So sense does not determine reference.

Now Putnam thinks that this example will work no matter how sophisticated or primitive his and his twin's community are in matters chemical. So even if the two communities lack any notion of chemical composition it is still the case that his and his twin's terms differ in extension. Dummett is sceptical. Were someone from such a community to encounter the stuff which goes by the name "salt" on Twin Earth[14] she would call it "salt" and, given that there is no chemical knowledge which she holds her use responsible to, there is no sense in insisting that she would be wrong to do so. Alternatively if the knowledge that this stuff differed in chemical composition from what she normally calls "salt" came to light, it is simply underdetermined whether we would say that salt has more than one chemical composition or that the other stuff was not salt. A decision on the meaning of the term "salt" would be called for. So Putnam's point doesn't seem to have quite the generality he claims for it.

If, however, we consider twins whose communities have a fairly extensive battery of chemical tests for determining the composition of a substance then we approach something akin to the elm–beech case and the phenomenon of the linguistic division of labour. The only difference would be that in this case the experts might not have exploited the tests in distinguishing the two sorts of stuff. But the community would possess a clear notion of the manner in which the reference of their respective terms would be determined.

Yet another scenario is, however, conceivable. For although there may be no precisely circumscribed set of tests for determining the nature of a sort of stuff we may, nevertheless, have enough chemical sophistication to have a notion of sameness of stuff, a notion of sameness which depends upon similarity of underlying chemical composition. In such a case we might introduce a term by means of a sample, determining its extension by insisting that it is to apply to the same stuff as the sample. In so doing, we would be holding our use of the term responsible, not to a particular way of determining the reference (unanticipated advances in chemistry may render it quite obscure precisely how the reference of the term will, in fact, be determined), but to the nature of the stuff itself. And, in this case, it would seem that Putnam and his twin might be relevantly similar – might agree with respect to any conceivable ingredient of sense – yet their respective terms differ in reference simply because of the nature of the stuff in their environment.

The case now resembles that of the name "Gödel" as described above. In both cases it is a feature of our use of a term that we hold our use responsible to something other than expertise possessed within the community. In the present case this is because we allow our use to be responsible to, at most, the findings of future scientific investigation whose form cannot now be anticipated. In the "Gödel" case this is because we hold our use responsible to features about how past speakers introduced a term. So, though in both cases we have some conception of what would determine the reference of a term, what actually fixes that reference is some fact or facts of which we, qua speakers, may not be apprised.

Dummett claims that "In using words of a language a speaker is responsible to the way that the language is used now, to the presently agreed practices of the community; he cannot be held responsible to the way people spoke many centuries ago" (T&OE: 430) or, he might also have said, to the way we might come to use language. So Dummett thinks that the Fregean doctrine needs to be modified only to take account of the social aspect of language use. However, Putnam's point seems to be that the way we currently use language incorporates responsibilities to aspects of the way the world is, aspects whose mode of discovery need not be (explicitly or implicitly) factored into the conferral of meaning.

One might want to counter that a notion such as that of sameness of stuff must be given content by reference to criteria for determining sameness of stuff. But that's an anti-realist thought and so is one which shouldn't play any part in formulating a challenge to realism.[15]

Dummett wants to assimilate Putnam's cases to that of indexicality.[16] Here we have a feature of present linguistic practice which involves the world yet is not regarded as a problem fundamentally affecting Frege's notion of sense. Certainly the manner in which we envisage a term being introduced, namely, "Salt is the same stuff as *this*", suggests that something very akin to indexicality is in play. Consider an ordinary case of introducing a name by saying, for example, "Fido is that dog" (using the demonstrative to pick out the appropriate dog). In so doing we set up a way of identifying the dog (presumably by his gross appearance) which correlates with the sense of the name as thus established. Similarly when we say "Salt is the same stuff as this" we set up a way of identifying salt (presumably by its distinctive phenomenal qualities). We have a criterion of identity for dogs, or, less controversially, we have a notion of sameness of dog. Now no matter what method of identification we use in conjunction with "Fido" it may be that it fails: Fido's appearance may change drastically, or the place may suddenly become awash with Fido look-alikes. Were we to find ourselves in such a position we would attempt to determine the reference of Fido by applying our notion of sameness of dog and attempting to discover whether a given dog is the same dog as that originally demonstrated. What considerations may count in this investigation and whether, in any given case, it will be successful cannot be prejudged. So in this sense we hold our use responsible to facts about the world.

Does this case challenge Frege's notion of sense? One would think not. For one way of seeing that doctrine is as encapsulating the idea that, if one understands a term, one knows how to determine its reference. There's no sense in which I fail to know how to determine the reference of "Fido" even if I can't be guaranteed to determine that reference (infallibly and in all circumstances) and even if what collateral information may aid that determination cannot be circumscribed. Insofar as it impinges on the notion of sense Putnam's case appears to be entirely analogous to the present one.

It remains true that two introductions of the name "Fido" might be relevantly similar, yet the term might be introduced with a different reference on each occasion (there might be two dogs bearing the name "Fido" who are uncannily similar to one another in appearance and, perhaps, character). So two speakers who acquire an understanding of "Fido" in these circumstances might be psychologically identical (in relevant respects). What this shows is that knowledge of sense cannot be characterized in narrow psychological terms. What a speaker needs to be able to do is to set about determining whether a certain presentation of an object is a presentation of the same object made on another *particular* occasion: the determination of reference is made relative to that particular occasion, which therefore must figure in the account of a speaker's knowledge of sense.[17] The general point would be that knowledge of sense is comprised of a certain set of capacities with respect to objects or sorts of objects in one's environment.

The fault in non-Fregeanism

If the previous section is substantially correct there may be no (extant) good reason for renouncing Fregeanism. But what is wrong with its opposition?

Recall Putnam's defence of realism by renouncing Fregeanism. In his reply to Putnam, Dummett is clearly intrigued by a view which is so alien to his own. However, he cannot bring himself to accept a position which distances the semantics of language from conscious aspects of speakers' use. He finds it incomprehensible that there might be any explanatory value in a semantic concept which isn't tied to the way speakers consciously use language. But what exactly is the worry here?

Dummett assumes that, in order for us to make explanatory use of a notion of truth, that notion must be one which we can comprehend. And now it might appear that the original problem resurfaces: we need to explain how a theorist grasps realist truth-conditions. That, however, would be over-hasty. Tarski has shown us how to define truth in a language given that we understand the language (or that we can assume a translation scheme). The problems infecting a truth-conditional account of meaning involved an inversion of this dependency, that is, the attempt to explain meaning in terms of an assumed notion of truth. But since Putnam thinks that we can give a use-based account of understanding those problems don't emerge and the Tarskian procedure should be available. So given that we understand the language what prevents us forming a conception of the requisite notion of truth for an explanation of success?

We might put the point as follows. Dummett seems, in his objection to Putnam, to be claiming that we cannot form a conception of the realist's notion of truth. But that surely means that we cannot form a conception of realism since realism is, according to Dummett, to be identified[18] with adoption of such a notion of truth. So Putnam's defence of realism now seems to fall together with Dummett's characterization of realism. But let me expand the point a little more carefully. What Dummett claims is that we cannot grasp realist truth-conditions; we do, however, understand what it is to attribute realist truth-conditions to sentences and in this sense we comprehend realism. But now surely Putnam can say that it is only in this latter sense that he needs a notion of truth in an explanation of success: when we come to explain how language makes its contribution to achieving success we find that we need to assume that we grasp sentences which have realist truth-conditions (and not that we grasp those truth-conditions themselves). So Putnam's defence and Dummett's characterization of realism seem both to stand. In either case they stand or fall together.

Dummett, however, has a further worry. It is this: given the overt features of language use, there may be a number of semantic theories with which it can be reconciled. So the option of one or another semantic theory over the others will be underdetermined, unless we attempt to ascribe an implicit grasp of the relevant semantic concepts to speakers. Thus he points out that other semantic theories than the two-valued one yield classical logic and, conversely, that the use of classical logic in reasoning with vague predicates will yield a two-valued semantics which many would find deeply counter-intuitive. Since the choice of semantic theory is not being dictated by the nature of speakers' understanding of language there is no way to arrive at what should properly be seen as the genuine semantic theory. The theory may spell out a relation in which our terms stand to worldly items but why, he asks, should we see that relation as reference?[19] If that relation doesn't figure significantly in the account of speakers' understanding of the language, Dummett contends that there are no grounds for identifying it with reference, even if our terms seem thus to be related to what we should ordinarily see as their referents.

Two points might be made in response to Dummett here. First, it isn't clear quite why understanding-theoretic constraints need to be appealed to in motivating a choice of semantic theory. Success-theoretic constraints might provide a similar motivation. Presumably, after all, the account of success won't simply be parasitic on formal features of the semantic theory but will take into account the nature of our perceptual apparatus, our causal embedding in the world and the way the world is (or the way our best theories represent it as being). And, when Dummett asks for an explanation of why the relation fixed on is reference, he can be given an answer. The relation is reference because, by means of it, we give an account of how the truth-conditions of sentences depend systematically on how their components are thus related to worldly items. That we're characterizing *truth*-conditions is shown by the role truth plays in explaining success.

Secondly and relatedly, Putnam makes the point that Dummett focuses too narrowly on the role of truth in justifying inferential practice. According to him "[it] is not that the laws of logic determine our concept of truth, but that our *entire* theory, including our theory of the relation of language to the speaker's environment, determines our concept of truth" (1979b: 228). So Putnam's account is holistic. Dummett's image of his opposition seems to be that we have first to consider our first-order use of sentences and then impose an assign-ment of truth-conditions from the theorist's point of view. In such a case the most important, if not the only, element in determining the properties of those truth-conditions will be inferential practice. Putnam, in contrast, thinks that our theory (or theories) will itself (themselves) treat our sentences as having truth-conditions with certain properties. A semantic theory can and must cohere with these aspects of our worldview; there is no external semantician's standpoint. Our semantic theory is part of our theorizing about the world and our place in it. (Compare with the discussion of Loar above.)

Thus it might seem that Dummett's adherence to Fregeanism depends entirely on the rejection of the holistic element in the non-Fregean's account of understanding. However, perhaps a little more might be said in defence of Fregeanism. I suggest that Dummett is right in thinking that allowing a gap between semantic theory and the theory of understanding has the consequence that the choice of semantic theory is unmotivated. But I think he is wrong in thinking that the problem is in the notion of truth adopted by the semantic theory. Rather the problem, as he suggests, infects the notion of reference. To anticipate, the point will be that once we adopt the non-Fregean conception of the relation of reference to understanding we cannot properly motivate a choice of a referential scheme. The result of this is that Dummett is right: a credible notion of reference is not available to the non-Fregean. However, it seems to me that the basis for this suggestion only emerges from Putnam's writings of a few years later (see Putnam 1983).

Putnam is well known to have offered his own challenge to (metaphysical) realism by utilizing results from model theory.[20] That challenge poses a problem for the metaphysical realist by asking how, given these results from model theory, she is able to specify the intended interpretation of language. The problem she seems faced with is that of referential indeterminacy. Putnam's challenge is problematic both because the details of the argument are contended and because it is not completely evident why technical results in model theory pose a problem for metaphysical realism in particular.

I cannot pursue the first issue here. But, if the argument can be acceptably rehabilitated (and I think it can[21]) then I suggest its more natural target is not metaphysical realism but non-Fregeanism. If this is right then the two attacks on realism (those of Putnam and of Dummett) are not separate, rather each is incomplete without complementation by the other.

Both metaphysical realism and non-Fregeanism think of the world as being independent of our thought and talk about it. But the relevant notion of independence differs. In the last chapter we looked at Dummett's attempt to cash the appropriate metaphors of independence as they apply to realism. The conclusion was that realism conceives of the world as being independent of our epistemic capacities: the world may transcend our ability to have knowledge of it. In contrast the non-Fregean thinks that there is a semantic independence of language from the world in this sense: according to the non-Fregean a description of language which issues from an account of speakers' understanding of language will not determine semantic relations such as reference relations. This view of things comports nicely with the model-theorist's project, namely, to take a formal characterization of language and then to investigate possible interpretations of that language by means of set-theoretical structures, which represent the world. So the challenging thought for the non-Fregean now is this. If Putnam's argument is right and if model-theoretic results represent the way it is with natural language, then natural language suffers from indeterminacy of reference. Thus, if we want to reject that uncongenial conclusion, we shall have to find some way of resisting the putative lessons from model theory. The Fregean seems to have an easy way of doing so: the model-theorist's picture is precisely at odds with her insistence that sense determines reference. In marked contrast, the non-Fregean seems to embrace the model-theoretic picture. Of course this doesn't show that the non-Fregean cannot find some other means of resisting this application of model theory. But until she does so her position is questionable.

Summary

Dummett's argument against realism depends crucially on both his Fregean conception of the place of semantic theory and his requirement of manifestability. Given these planks Dummett's challenge is, in essence, that we cannot manifest grasp of realist truth-conditions. Thus our sentences or statements do not have realist truth-conditions.

Two attempts to rebut this challenge were considered. Both were attempts to enrich the terms in which one might describe what constitutes manifestation of understanding. The first attempt involved an acceptance of modesty, the second an acceptance of holism. The first was found wanting because, once the realist accepts a burden of proof, it is simply not evident that the truth-conditions which modesty credits speakers with grasping are indeed realist truth-conditions. The holistic arguments we considered seemed to fail because they take speakers' grasp of realist truth-conditions to be constituted by a certain linguistic competence, either grasp of a certain sort of theory or grasp of inferential practice. The first approach was criticized because it not only implicates the internal properties of the theory but relies on the theory being true. The latter approach was criticized essentially because truth, on this scheme, was usurped from its justificatory role. Once truth is usurped it is obscure whether we have any grounds for crediting speakers with grasp of realist truth-conditions. We then considered whether we might fill this gap by reinstating truth, not in its justificatory role, but in an explanatory role. However, we noted that this was now to attack, not the narrowness of Dummett's conception of what counts as manifestation of understanding, but his Fregean conception of semantic theory.

Dummett sees semantic theory as lying at the core of a theory of understanding and this allows him to develop constraints on an acceptable semantic theory. We've seen some reason both for rejecting challenges, derived from semantic externalism (Kripke's and Putnam's arguments), to this position and for rejecting the opposing (non-Fregean) standpoint. The problem we hinted at was that a non-Fregean position will have an impossible task in accounting for the reference relation.

So if these considerations are persuasive we need a non-realist conception of sense. What form will such an account take? Chapter 5 takes up this question.

Chapter 5

What is anti-realism?

There are many ways of rejecting realism and thus many sorts of anti-realist. In this chapter we shall confine our attention to anti-realist positions spawned by the supposed success of the challenge to realism which we looked at in Chapter 4.

If the challenge to realism is successful we cannot give an account of meaning that makes use of a semantic notion that is verification transcendent. In particular, in the presence of undecidable sentences, we cannot appeal to a bivalent notion of truth. Now it might seem (and Dummett often gives this impression) that a consequence of this is a rejection of truth-conditional accounts of meaning. That is, we would give an account of meaning in terms other than truth-conditions and then allow an account of truth to issue perhaps in Tarskian fashion.[1] But this isn't obvious. It may be that we can give an account of an anti-realistically acceptable notion of truth and then use this notion in a truth-conditional account of meaning.[2]

What notions might an anti-realist appeal to in providing such accounts? An anti-realist will only make use of a notion which, when applied to a sentence, yields something that can be ascribed as implicit knowledge to speakers and which thus can be manifested by an appropriate exercise of recognitional capacities. So the notions that might be put to work by an anti-realist will be epistemic: for instance, notions of justification, warranted assertion, verification, falsification and so on. Can truth be explained in these terms? Can meaning? In this chapter we will consider these questions, first with reference to mathematics – which provides the only extant example of an anti-realist meaning-theory whose detail has been, to some extent, filled out – and then with reference to empirical discourse –

here the issues won't concern the details of such a theory, since none exists, but will concern the principles underlying construction of such a theory.

If you understand a (declamatory) sentence then it seems you are able to make a whole series of judgements about the use of that sentence in various situations. You will know what circumstances confer truth on the statement and what circumstances confer falsity on it. You may also have a conception of some of the circumstances which count as evidence for the sentence or which count as evidence against it. Or, perhaps more accurately, your knowledge of the meaning of the sentence, combined with collateral information, will involve your being able to classify at least certain evidential situations appropriately. You may also have a conception of some of the circumstances in which the sentence is correctly assertible and/or is correctly deniable. Conversely, in giving an account of meaning, it seems we must utilize one (and Dummett assumes only one (see below)) of these listed features. Now there is room for debate about exactly how meaning is implicated in each of these features. But what is clear is that there is no complete explanation of any one of them which eschews all appeal to meaning: what counts as evidence for a sentence must depend, at least partly, on the sentence's meaning. And now the thought is that one of these features will determine the meaning of the sentence and that for each of the other features of that sentence there will be a uniformly applicable means of deriving the meaning-involving element in it from that one. For example, one might start from a position that characterizes the sentence's meaning in terms of (some of) the conditions in which it is correctly assertible. One would then test the adequacy of this account by its ability to furnish accounts of the meaning-involving elements in fixing what counts as evidence for or against the sentence.

One of the problems with a truth-conditional account of meaning is that it is difficult to see how one explains a speaker's sensitivity to evidential situations on the basis of her grasp of a verification transcendent truth-condition. Witness, for instance, the classic problem of other minds, in which a link between grasp of the truth-condition and behavioural evidence is supposed to be forged in accord with the (spurious) argument from analogy. On the other hand, if meaning is explained in terms of one of these epistemic notions it need not be difficult to explain the relevant notion of truth, though the expense of that will be to give up the assumption that truth is epistemically transcendent.

Use-based theories of meaning: mathematics and proof

Mathematics provides the most promising ground for an epistemic account of truth. The reason for this is that proof provides a secure enduring warrant for assertion: proof guarantees truth.[3] In contrast, in empirical discourse a sentence might be evidentially well supported or correctly assertible yet fail to be true. So it is harder to see how, in such cases, truth might be defined in terms of an epistemic notion. We'll return to the empirical case shortly but for now let us concentrate on the notion of provability in mathematics.

As we've just remarked, a sentence is true if provable. Conversely, in rejecting the assumption that truth might outrun our epistemic span, one accepts that if a sentence is true it is provable, since proof (*pace* Brouwer and Gödelian platonists) is our only access to mathematical truth. So, for an anti-realist, truth and provability would seem to coincide extensionally. Thus we might identify truth with provability and then offer a truth-conditional account of meaning. That is, we would aim to characterize a sentence's meaning in terms of its truth-, here interpreted as proof-, conditions. So, having made this identification, the theory of meaning would aim to characterize in some systematic manner the proof-conditions of each sentence.

Instead of having clauses of the form

S is true iff P

we would have the following

S is provable iff P.

A sentence is provable just in case there is (in some sense) a proof of it. So a natural move would be to cash the previous clause as

S is provable iff there is a proof of S, i.e. there exists a construction, C, such that C is a proof of S.[4]

One problem with this account is that it explains the meaning of, what might be, a logically simple sentence in terms of a logically complex one, an existential generalization.[5] Let's set that problem aside for the moment, for it's clear that the proposal suffers from a more fundamental difficulty. We need to be able to ascribe knowledge of such clauses to speakers and that raises the usual Dummettian question of what constitutes manifestation of such knowledge. Clearly a speaker would have to know what it is for a construction to be a proof of S and what it would be for there to be such a construction. However, whether or not there is a proof of a given sentence is not something we can be guaranteed to determine. So the question is: what would comprise knowledge of what it would be for there to be a proof of, say, Goldbach's Conjecture? One thought might be that a speaker would have this knowledge were she able to determine whether or not Goldbach's Conjecture has a proof. Quite obviously that would be an absurd demand: we understand sentences in advance and independently of our ability to furnish proofs or refutations of them, and acceptance of the demand would entail that we only understand decidable sentences. Another thought is that the speaker has a conception of the existence of a proof which is quite unconnected with our ability to obtain a proof. But then there is nothing a speaker could do to manifest her grasp of this conception; if the proof might exist undetectably then a speaker cannot manifest her conception of its existence by an exercise of her recognitional capacities. It only remains that a speaker's conception of the existence of a proof must be linked to her possession of a proof, in which case, to know what it would be for there to be a proof would be to know what it would be to possess an appropriate construction, to know what it would be to be presented with a proof. So the existential element in a speaker's knowledge appears to vanish, for it amounts only to a sensitivity displayed towards constructions with which she is presented. A speaker understands a sentence when she knows what it would be for a given construction to be a proof of that sentence. So we characterize proof-conditions of a given sentence by characterizing the condition a construction must meet in order to be a proof of the sentence. And this relation between a construction and a sentence – the proof *relation* – is decidable: we are supposed to be able to tell, when presented with a construction, whether or not it is a proof of a given sentence. So the proof-conditional account of meaning characterizes understanding a sentence as knowledge of what would be a proof of that sentence. Possession of this knowledge is constituted by an ability to discriminate between constructions which are and those which are not proofs of the sentence. This ability is fully manifestable in an exercise of recognitional capacities.

The theory of meaning will attempt systematically to characterize what counts as a proof of each mathematical sentence. It thus departs from a truth-conditional account (even where truth is identified with provability); we don't characterize the truth- (or pro*vability*-) condition of each sentence but the condition a construction must satisfy in order to be a proof, i.e. the sentence's proof-conditions. The theory will achieve its aim by characterizing what counts as a proof of a complex sentence in terms of what counts as a proof of its constituents. In other words, we presuppose that we know the proof-conditions of a sentence's constituents and explain the sentence's proof-conditions on this basis. The characterization is recursive. The meaning of each logical constant is captured by explaining the proof-conditions of those complex sentences in which it is the dominant operator, again, in terms of the proof-conditions of their components. The scheme has been well studied, since it forms the basis of an account of intuitionistic logic derived from Heyting. In outline, Heyting (1971) offers the following stipulations of the meanings of the logical constants:

&, ∨, ∃:

&: A proof of A & B is any construction of which it can be recognized that it is a proof of A and a proof of B.

∨: A proof of $A \vee B$ is any construction of which it can be recognized that it is a proof of A or a proof of B.

∃: A proof of $\exists x F x$ is any construction of which it can be recognized that it is a proof of Ft for some t in the domain.

→, ∀:

→: A proof of $A \rightarrow B$ is any construction of which it can be recognized that applied to any proof of A it yields a proof of B.

∀: A proof of $\forall x F x$ is any construction of which it can be recognized that applied to any t in the domain it yields a proof of Ft.

We'll move on to discuss the adequacy of these specifications shortly but it is well to note an immediate disanalogy with the classical case. Analogous clauses for the classical constants framed in terms of truth have an appearance of circularity. Consider, for instance,

"$A \vee B$" is true iff "A" is true or "B" is true.

Here the right-hand side uses the meta-linguistic equivalent of the very constant we are attempting to define. This needn't, in itself, render the scheme circular or vacuous since the sentences flanking the constant are of a particular sort: they all involve use of the truth predicate. But given the equivalence principle this restriction on the form of the relevant sentences amounts to no restriction on the contents involved. Contrast this with the intuitionistic case where again each constant is defined by use of its meta-linguistic equivalent. But here the sentences flanking the constant each relate a construction to a sentence by means of the proof relation, i.e. they are of the form "*C* is a proof of *A*". As we noted, such sentences are decidable. Thus, unlike the classical alternatives, the intuitionistic clauses offer a genuinely reductive explanation of the meanings of the logical constants; the full use of the constant is reduced to its use in the context of certain decidable sentences.

We now have, in outline, a model for an anti-realist theory of meaning. The task in the second half of this chapter will be to consider how the model might be generalized to empirical discourse. In Chapters 6 and 7 we shall consider whether a credible account of this form can be reconciled with the arguments for anti-realism. Now I want to turn to a more detailed examination of the form the theory will have to take. This discussion involves some technicality and some readers (those less interested in the proof-theoretical account of the meanings of the logical constants) may want to skip it or to return to it later.

Proof and canonical proof

Dummett criticizes Heyting's account of the meanings of the logical constants. He accepts that the stipulations succeed in establishing a framework within which the meanings for the logical constants must be established (any acceptable account must confer meanings on the logical constants which satisfy Heyting's stipulations) but he thinks the stipulations, as they stand, fail to determine definite meanings for them. Let's first have Dummett's worries before us. He (EoI: 389–403) gives three reasons for thinking that, as they stand, the stipulations contravene the molecularity requirement. These difficulties infect the second set of stipulations for "→" and "∀" in which a proof is a construction which is applied to other constructions or to objects in the domain, respectively. The first problem is specific to the stipulation governing the conditional in which we are required to quantify over proofs of the antecedent. Since we impose no restriction on proofs of the antecedent we must include proofs which proceed via sentences of arbitrary degree of complexity or, indeed, which proceed via the conditional itself. So we are attempting to characterize the meaning of "→" by quantifying over a totality in which it is included. Russell called such definitions impredicative. So the claim is that the impredicativity of the meaning stipulation entails that we cannot give an account of the meaning of a conditional which presupposes only an acceptable fragment of the language (*ibid*.: 390). I'll call this the circularity problem.

Here's an example of how it might arise. Consider the following (awful) proof of the antecedent in $((P \ \& -Q) \to -Q) \to P$:

1	(1)	$P \ \& -Q$	A
2	(2)	$(P \ \& -Q) \to -Q$	A
1	(3)	P	1&E
1,2	(4)	$P \ \& ((P \ \& -Q) \to -Q)$	2,3&I
1,2	(5)	P	4&E
1	(6)	$((P \ \& -Q) \to -Q) \to P$	2,5CP
1	(7)	$-Q$	1&E
	(8)	$(P \ \& -Q) \to -Q$	1,7CP

Here "A" is assumption, "E" signals the elimination rule for the relevant constant, "I" signals the introduction rule for the relevant constant, and "CP" is conditional proof. The proof is truly horrible but it is a valid proof of the antecedent. So when we quantify over proofs of "$(P \ \& -Q) \to -Q$" in the meaning stipulation for "$((P \ \& -Q) \to -Q) \to P$" we must be quantifying over a range of proofs that includes the above. But that proof includes "$((P \ \& -Q) \to -Q) \to P$" at line 6. So the meaning stipulation for that sentence quantifies over a range of proofs that includes proofs involving that very sentence. The meaning of the sentence thus presupposes the meaning of proofs in that range and the meaning of some of those proofs presupposes the meaning of our original sentence (since it is included in those proofs). The stipulation is thus circular.

The other difficulties concern the manner in which the putative proof is to be applied. First, if, in applying the construction, we are entitled to use rules of inference which allow elimination of the dominant logical operator then the stipulations impose no constraints whatever on what is to count as a proof either of a universally quantified or of a conditional sentence. If, say, we choose to regard P as a proof of $A \to B$ then, provided we are entitled to use *modus ponens* in applying it, the meaning stipulations will ratify it as a proof. Since then, when presented with a proof of A, we simply use P as a proof of $A \to B$ followed by a step of *modus ponens* to arrive at a proof of B (*ibid*.: 393). P will then satisfy the meaning stipulation. I'll call this the vacuity problem.

Lastly, when presented with a construction which putatively has the properties required of a proof, i.e. when appropriately applied it ostensibly yields an appropriate construction, we may need a supplementary argument in order to convince ourselves that the proof does indeed satisfy these requirements. The informal proof is thus constituted by the construction together with the supplementary argument. That is, the capacity to recognize a proof of the sentence is constituted both by a grasp of the construction and an ability to follow the supplementary argument. This means that if we have imposed a restriction on the notion of proof as used in the stipulations we shall be in danger of contravening that restriction through our use of supporting argument: once again we are faced with the threat of holism (*ibid.*: 399). I'll call this the supplementary argument problem.

Dummett argues that in order to circumvent these problems we need to distinguish proofs as more generally conceived from meaning-determining or canonical proofs. The thought would be that meaning is established in terms of a restricted class of proofs which don't always coincide with our epistemic routes. For we may know a sentence to be true, not on the basis of possession of a canonical proof, but because we are in a position to see that we could construct a canonical proof: the possibility of obtaining a canonical proof suffices to give us knowledge of the truth of a sentence. Now, only if we can characterize a notion of canonical proof and frame the stipulations in terms of canonical proofs can we be satisfied that we have conferred coherent meanings on the logical constants. But this means that Dummett needs to provide an account of the notion of canonical proof.

Dummett accepts the obligation and attempts to discharge it by finding an apt model for canonical proofs: he exploits the notion of normalized proofs in a natural deduction system. We need now to digress briefly to explain that notion. A natural deduction system is a formal system in which the use of each logical constant is captured by specifying rules governing its introduction and elimination. In a normalized proof we proceed from the premises of the proof by use of elimination rules (if necessary) and then by introduction rules (if necessary). So such a proof does not have a "local maximum", that is, it includes no sentence which results from the use of an introduction rule and is the object of an elimination rule (that is, no sentence such as line 4 in the little proof above). A normalization result will demonstrate that each proof in a formal system containing a certain set of introduction and elimination rules can be transformed into a normalized proof. The important thing (for our purposes) about a normalized proof is that each sentence of the "elimination branch" of the proof is syntactically less complex than a premise of the proof and each sentence in the "introduction branch" of the proof will be less complex than the conclusion of the proof. So the (syntactic) complexity of sentences in the proof will be restricted by that of the premises and conclusion of the proof. And the important thing about a normalization result is that it entitles us to restrict the meaning stipulations for the logical constants in a formal system to normalized proofs.

Normalized natural deduction proofs thus would seem to provide an ideal model for canonical proofs; they appear to establish the truth of a sentence in accord with its meaning by decomposing premises and then constructing the conclusion. The proof has no redundant steps and is, in a sense, completely direct. We can also see that, were canonical proofs akin to natural deduction proofs, the circularity and vacuity problems would vanish. Circularity would not arise since if, say, we are quantifying over normalized proofs of the antecedent of a conditional then such proofs cannot include sentences more complex that the antecedent itself so, in particular, cannot include the conditional. Thus we do not presuppose a grasp of the conditional in explicating its meaning. Similarly the vacuity problem is solved since it only arose because we failed to exclude use of elimination rules in arriving at a conclusion. But in a normalized proof the conclusion must be arrived at by means of an introduction rule.[6]

However, solving the supplementary argument problem involves a more recondite exploitation of the notion of normalized proofs. Dummett now appeals to the notion of a fully analysed proof, that is, a proof in which each of the steps of the proof is not reducible to a sequence of shorter steps (EoI: 400). Take C to be the formal analogue of a given sentence. Then rather than simply considering normalization for the set of derivations of C we instead consider the normalization of the set of derivations of C^*, where C^* is the conditional whose consequent is C and whose antecedent is the conjunction of axioms of the form "$A_i \rightarrow$ there is a proof of A_i of such and such a kind", where each A_i is a constituent of C. So we assume that, if we have a precise characterization of the manner in which a given sentence may be proved (if it can be proved at all), we then need simply to consider those constructions which, applied to such proofs, would produce the desired conclusion.

I take it that Dummett's point here is this. The supplementary argument is provided to show that the construction with which we are presented does indeed transform *any* proof of the antecedent into a proof of the consequent. It is, therefore, essential to the full meaning of the intuitionistic conditional, since the proof of B from A is not simply a proof of B from A as hypothesis but is a proof of B from possible proofs of A. Now, where C is $A_1 \to A_2$, we can systematically limit the set of proofs we need to consider if, for each constituent, A_i, of C we have, as an axiom, "$A_i \to$ there is a proof of A_i of such and such a kind". Thus we need to consider proofs of C^*, which, once formalized in an adequate system, will be, one hopes, the subject of a normalization result.[7]

There are a number of problems with Dummett's use of the notion of normalized natural deduction proofs. I'll confine myself here to, what seems to me, the most basic problem.[8] As I remarked, normalization applies to particular *formal* systems. In contrast, the notion of canonical proof is a notion that applies to the informal development of intuitionistic mathematics. So canonical proofs cannot be identified with normalized proofs, rather they are modelled on them. Application of this model will thus depend on formalizing a given intuitionistic theory of mathematics and this raises the question of what constitutes an adequate formalization. Without returning a full answer to that question, we can, I think, insist on at least the following: a formal proof of a given sentence must be a formalization of an informal proof of its analogue.[9] This guarantees, what we might call, structural adequacy in the formalization and it appears to be a necessary condition, if informal proofs are to be modelled on formal proofs. The question is: how do we assure ourselves that we have achieved structural adequacy? Obviously we cannot run through the proofs in each theory for comparison, we can only compare the sets of proofs by means of our grasp of what, in general, characterizes a proof in either theory. In the formal theory this is given by the introduction and elimination rules, while in the informal theory it must be given by informally accredited rules of inference. Were we to have these before us, we could construct an inductive proof of structural adequacy. The problem, though, is that this all presupposes that we have achieved a reflective grasp of the informal practice itself. In particular, it presupposes that we have a representation of the meanings of the logical constants from which the inferential rules flow. This, however, is precisely the role for which Heyting introduced the meaning stipulations. And now it's clear that Dummett's recommended process of justifying those stipulations will be circular: in order to embark on it we need to assume not only that we have a grasp of the stipulations but also that we have a coherent representation of what it is that we grasp.

It might easily seem anyway that Dummett has overstated the difficulty here. Let us focus first on the circularity problem. The problem arises because in the stipulation for the conditional we quantify over proofs of the antecedent, among which will be proofs which proceed via the conditional itself. But what is required to grasp quantification over the antecedent? Presumably what's needed is a general grasp of the significance of universal quantification and a grasp of the domain of proofs of the antecedent. The first piece of knowledge is not regarded as problematic. So where does the problem arise with regard to the second piece of knowledge? Surely one grasps the relevant domain just when one has a conception of what qualifies a construction as a proof of the antecedent. But that is just to know the proof-conditions of the antecedent, which is just what the recursive account in general takes for granted: the proof-conditions of each sentence are characterized in terms of those of its components. This doesn't quite get us off the hook since it may simply appear that, given the indefinite potential complexity of proofs, we have generalized and not solved the problem. But we can extricate ourselves from that bind if we simply insist that the meaning stipulations give a recursive characterization of *canonical* proofs. Having accepted the need for a distinction here between proofs and canonical proofs we can also see that the supplementary argument problem can be dispensed with. For the supplementary argument is presented to show that a certain construction is a canonical proof. It cannot therefore itself be part of the canonical proof, although it may form part of a proof. The vacuity problem remains. Recall that that problem arises from being too lenient in the ways in which a construction might be applied. To make any progress here we need to think about the relation of canonical proofs to proofs.

A proof is a construction which recognizably yields a canonical proof. However, a proof of, for instance, a conditional must also be something which can be applied to a proof of the antecedent to yield a proof of the consequent. We need to demonstrate that the latter holds given the account of proofs as yielding canonical proofs. This can easily be done, given an elasticity in the notions of applying and yielding, notions which are central to the intuitionistic account. However, once that is done the distinction between proofs and canonical proofs threatens to collapse. For then it will be the case that the proof of the conditional can be applied to a canonical proof of the antecedent to yield a canonical proof of the consequent. That is, a proof will be a canonical proof. To solve this problem, we need to specify (canonical) modes of application and of yielding in the recursive account of canonical proof. So a canonical proof of a conditional will be *canonically* applicable to canonical proofs of the antecedent to yield *canonically* a canonical proof of the consequent. Once we do this successfully the vacuity problem will be solved, provided applications involving use of elimination rules are not counted as canonical. We can allow an elasticity in the notions as used to define proofs, and perhaps exploit that elasticity in explaining the indefinite extensibility in our notion of proof (arguably the lesson of Gödel's theorems[10]). We may also be able to put this idea to work in developing an account of a species of a priori knowledge. The account would explain a priori truths as consequences, in a broad sense captured by the relation of proof to canonical proof, of meaning stipulations. But with those sketchy hints at what might be another story we should return to our narrative.

We've learned that the anti-realist account of meaning will depart from a truth-conditional account in two respects. First it will characterize a sentence's meaning not directly in terms of its provability-conditions but in terms of what constitutes a proof of the sentence, its proof-conditions. That is, we might say that grasp of what it is for a sentence to be provable accrues from or is constituted by a knowledge of when a construction with which one is presented is a proof. So, although the end result is a theory according to which understanding might be seen as grasp of anti-realist truth-conditions, an anti-realist notion of truth does not play a fundamental role in the theory. Secondly, the theory will not characterize what is particular to the meaning of an individual sentence as its proof-conditions but as its canonical proof-conditions, the former being given a general explanation in terms of the latter.

Use-based theories of meaning: the general case

In this section we shall consider the broad form of a theory of meaning which takes a subset of a sentence's conditions of use to determine its meaning. However, our interest in such a creature takes a distinct Dummettian slant, for two reasons. First, we are assuming that, in the presence of undecidable sentences, a truth-conditional theory of meaning won't make the right connections with speakers' abilities to use sentences. Secondly, our preferred use-based account of meaning will have to be molecular. In Chapter 2 we left the matter of molecularity in somewhat vague terms. We noted that the requirement emerges from Dummett's insistence that we be able to make sense of a linguistic practice. Though there's no conclusive argument in favour of such an approach to language, Dummett thinks that it is well motivated by the character of language – by what it is to learn and understand language – and that it would be a kind of abnegation of intellectual responsibility to renounce this ambition. To be sure, this hardly makes things crystal clear. So the task ahead is not easy. We shall be trying to fill in the pieces of Dummett's conception of a use-based theory of meaning but will also be trying to elucidate a little further the character of his requirement of molecularity. One might well prefer to tackle these issues separately and to take the latter first, but I don't think we can; Dummett's thinking about molecularity is, at least partially, appreciated by considering how he applies the requirement. We begin with three ideas at the heart of his discussion of molecularity and then move on to consider motivations, criticisms and an opposing view.

The nature of a linguistic practice is determined by conventions governing correct use and there are, as we noted at the start of the chapter, a number of aspects to the use of any given sentence: for instance, a sentence is correctly asserted when a warrant for its assertion is available; it is asserted on the basis of inductive evidence; it is used as a basis in an inference; it is correctly denied in certain circumstances; one should withhold judgement about its truth or falsity in certain circumstances. Not just any combination of these aspects of use is possible: some combinations are plainly incoherent, others are simply incomprehensible. Few will object to a condemnation of practices which incorporate incoherent combinations of uses, but Dummett, as a molecularist, wants to be far more strenuous about the sorts of combination he is prepared to accept. Three important notions feature in the substance of Dummett's strenuousness: notions of harmony (and of stability), of conservative extension and of single component meaning-theories. We will look at each of these in turn.

One applies the notion of harmony to assertions, noting that these have two fundamental aspects of use: first, a sentence is correctly asserted only if certain grounds are available and, secondly, making the assertion incurs certain commitments, certain consequences are inferable from legitimate assertion (one is committed to the legitimacy of one's assertion and, thereby, to the holding of these consequences). These two aspects of the use of an assertion need to be in harmony; the one sort of use must be seen as "flowing from" the other. One wants to see what we take as the consequences of an assertion to be justified, given what are taken to be grounds for the assertion. Or, in other words, the consequences of the assertion must be in harmony with the grounds for the assertion. Similarly, one wants to see what we take as grounds for an assertion as being required, given what are taken to be consequences of the assertion. Or, in other words, the grounds of the assertion must be in harmony relative to the consequences. Failure of harmony of the consequences relative to the grounds leads to the pernicious result that we may infer conclusions as consequences of an assertion which we are not entitled to draw, given the grounds justifying the assertion of the sentence. Failure of harmony of the grounds relative to the consequences leads to the serious, but less grave, error that we fail to infer all the consequences which the grounds for the assertion entitle us to infer. The first sort of failure means that, merely on the basis of having made an assertion, a conclusion becomes available, which wouldn't necessarily have been available otherwise. The second sort of failure saps the assertion of its point: we cannot learn as much from the assertion as the epistemic position which warrants making the assertion entitles us to. Dummett thinks we must police our linguistic practice so as to ensure that we avoid both sorts of failure: the grounds of an assertion must be shown to be required, given its consequences, and its consequences must be justified, given its grounds. Harmony in both directions is desirable (and of consequences relative to grounds is mandatory).[11]

A second notion employed by Dummett is a generalization of the mathematical notion of a conservative extension. In mathematics (one notion of) a conservative extension is that one theory, T_1, extends another, T, if the language of T is included in that of T_1 and any sentence in the language of T which is derivable from T_1 is derivable from T. So the thought, roughly, is that if T_1 is a conservative extension of T then when T is enlarged to form T_1 no sentence expressible in the language of T becomes derivable if it wasn't so before. Dummett generalizes this notion to language by thinking of one region of language as conservatively extending another when the one region is an enlargement of the original region and when no sentence of the original language is assertible after enlargement if it hadn't been assertible before. So the thought, roughly, is that a conservative extension of a region of language preserves the assertibility-conditions of sentences in that region. Let us consider an example. Suppose we have a language which enables formulation of present-tense statements and now suppose this is extended so as to enable formulation of past-tense statements also. Then, if we have a case of a conservative extension, no present-tense statement is assertible purely on the basis of having made a past-tense assertion. Now it is certainly true that we may well assert "The city is destroyed" on the basis of the past-tense assertion, "The volcano erupted." But here we don't have a definite case of a non-conservative extension, for either of two reasons. First one might hold that the present-tense assertion is only assertible given the assertibility of the past-tense sentence and our acquisition, by means of induction, of a piece of knowledge linking truths about the past to truths about the present, e.g. the truth of "If a volcano has erupted then a nearby city is destroyed"; the assertibility of the present-tense sentence is not a consequence purely of the meaning of the past-tense assertion but of that and a substantial claim. The notion of a conservative extension clearly need not rule out changes in our use of a sentence in response to a new piece of inductively acquired knowledge, which may only be expressible in the extended language. Secondly, although we may not have direct grounds for asserting "The city is destroyed" we might, plausibly, insist that such grounds are obtain*able* and the reason we might insist on this is that we claim that the conditional statement is only assertible if it provides a way of moving from a recognition that the grounds for the antecedent obtain to a recognition that grounds for the consequent obtain. Clearly the applicability of either of these strategies will depend on the case at hand. Here the first strategy seems more plausible.

What is the connection between the notions of harmony and of conservative extension? Suppose we have a sentence whose grounds and consequences are expressible in a certain vocabulary. Then, if the grounds and consequences are in harmony, any consequence of asserting our sentence is, in an appropriate sense, a consequence of the grounds, which must themselves hold if the assertion is legitimate. So any sentence expressing a consequence is, if assertible on the basis of the assertibility of our sentence, assertible on the basis of grounds expressible independently of the introduction of our sentence. Our sentence thus extends the original language conservatively. Conversely, if the grounds and consequences of our sentence are again expressible in a certain vocabulary, and if our sentence extends the language conservatively then a sentence in the original vocabulary is assertible on the basis of the assertibility of our sentence only if it was assertible within the unextended language. So, in particular, the (meaning-)consequences of our sentence must be assertible on the basis of sentences expressible in the original vocabulary (call them S). If we knew that those sentences, S, express the grounds for the assertion of our sentence then we'd know that harmony (at least in one direction) held. Now although we don't have the first piece of knowledge we have something close: whenever the grounds hold, the sentences S must be true (otherwise the consequence would become assertible on the basis of the assertibility of our sentence, contradicting the assumption that we have a conservative extension). That is, the sentences S are consequences of the grounds. So the meaning-consequences of our sentence are themselves consequences of that sentence's grounds: harmony holds. So, as long as we consider harmony and conservative extension in relation to grounds and consequences of assertion, they are equivalent.

Dummett often illustrates his discussion of harmony and conservative extension by reference to logic and its justification.[12] Perhaps for this reason many (e.g. Tennant 1987) have understandably, though I think mistakenly, taken these requirements to be a particular constraint on logic. The view is understandable because it seems plausible enough to think of the meanings of logically complex sentences in terms of their involvement in deductive inference. One then wants to say that deductive methods are valid just in case any warrant provided by deduction is not essentially new, that such a warrant coincides with the existence (or perhaps the availability, in some sense) of a non-inferential warrant (at least, where the sentence concerned is logically simple).[13] In other words, a deductive system is precisely constrained by having to be a conservative extension of the base class of logically simple sentences: no sentence in that class becomes assertible purely as a result of the introduction of deductive methods. It is less obvious that this is a general constraint on the introduction of new ways of talking, and, to some extent, less clear what it amounts to in other cases. Conversely, if it is a general constraint on the development of language then one might well wonder what is distinctive about logic.

The third, and final, notion we need to consider is Dummett's predilection for single component meaning-theories (see LBoM: 160). A single component meaning-theory will take one aspect of the use of sentences to be meaning determining and then will explain other aspects of the use of a sentence on the basis of this determination of meaning. So, for instance, one might explain the meaning of a given sentence in terms of the grounds that warrant its assertion and then go on to explain its overall use on the basis of this explanation of its meaning. In other words, the meaning-theory will incorporate a perfectly general component which will explain, given the grounds

for assertion of a sentence, what constitutes its (meaning-)conse-
quences. So the only bit of the theory which is particular to a given
sentence will be the account of its meaning in terms of its grounds for
assertion. In contrast, a dual component meaning theory will take
two elements of a sentence's use as particular to its meaning. So such
a theory might focus on both grounds and consequences. Again it
seems fairly straightforwardly to be the case that harmony is equivalent to insistence on a single component meaning-theory (at least, if
we restrict our attention to grounds and consequences of an assertion). For if harmony holds (in at least one direction) then we should
be able to derive the consequences of an assertion from the grounds or
vice versa. In which case only one aspect of use need be construed as
meaning determining. Conversely if only one aspect is meaning
determining then there must be a uniformly applicable procedure for
deriving the other aspect from that. That is, harmony (in at least one
direction) must hold.

Dummett thinks that our uses of a sentence should be constrained
to be in harmony with one another, that one region of language
should be seen to extend others conservatively and that meaning
should be explained by focusing on a single aspect of use. I've tried to
elucidate these ideas and have offered some reasons for thinking that
(if we consider only grounds and consequences of assertion then) they
are equivalent. What we need to do now is to go on to consider
Dummett's motivations for his stance.

Molecularity revisited

There's a clear sense in which the requirements of harmony and of
conservative extension mesh with thoughts about the progressive
nature of language acquisition. If harmony between the grounds and
consequences of a sentence, S, fails then the assertibility of S will
provide a warrant for asserting another sentence, C, which otherwise
would not have been assertible. So, if harmony fails, then a speaker's
understanding of C won't be complete at a stage prior to the introduction of S. S will thus have to figure in an account of the meaning of C.
But C was supposed to be a part of the meaning-determining consequences of S. Thus the meaning of each sentence presupposes that of
the other and we shall be unable to view understanding as a stage-by-
stage process, each stage of which is complete in itself. Conversely, if
understanding is such a stage-by-stage process then it is clear that

one stage must extend, without disrupting the meanings of sentences in the previous stage. So, in some sense, the one must conservatively extend the other.

Note an important assumption in this argument. We assume that learning a language is a progressive skill in that it accrues in stages, each of which is *complete* and thus survives intact the passage to increased linguistic competence. This, as remarked in Chapter 2, is not a general feature of learning nor a feature of learning a linguistic practice. For Dummett it is part of learning a *legitimate* linguistic practice.

Can we argue in a similar fashion from this conception of acquiring a legitimate linguistic practice to an insistence on single component meaning-theories? It isn't clear that there is an argument to be had for this conclusion. We might give the meaning of a sentence by reference to both of its grounds and consequences without disrupting the progressive view. The reason for this dislocation between the notions of harmony and of a single component meaning-theory arises because the argument in the case of harmony began from assuming that harmony failed in quite a radical way, namely, that we had a counter-example to harmony (we assumed that C would not have been assertible but for the assertibility of S). It just is not clear that a dual component meaning-theory needs to land up in a commitment to a counter-example to harmony. How might this situation arise? Well, recall that harmony was a view that one aspect of use be *derivable* from the other aspect. Given this relation of derivability, we seem driven toward a single component meaning-theory; one component is seen as meaning determining and the other as derived therefrom. But we might relinquish the stringency of requiring derivability here – and so contemplate a much weaker failure of harmony – without committing ourselves to the kind of counter-example used in the argument. In that event we might well adopt a dual component meaning-theory but see no reason in this to compromise the stage-by-stage view of acquisition. We'll see below how we might come to this position.

The nature of assertion

Let's return to the question of why a legitimate linguistic practice should admit of being seen in stages, as molecularism insists. Harmony is one way of insisting on this sort of molecular view. So if we had an argument for harmony we'd have an argument for molecularism. One line of thought begins with a consideration of the nature of assertion. If we focus on the grounds and consequences of an assertion it is easy to see the assertion as encapsulating an inferential passage from grounds to consequences. Dummett's insistence on harmony is an insistence that the inferential passage that a legitimate assertion encapsulates must be *logically* valid. Clearly the inferential passage must be valid; otherwise the meaning of the assertion will enable us to infer falsities from truths. But why should the inferential passage be logically, as opposed to materially, valid? Now one answer to this question is to note that the inferential passage is one that is forged by the meaning of the assertion. So it is given a priori. This, in itself, might incline one to think that the inferential passage should be logically valid. But, more to the point, it appears to militate against seeing it as materially valid. If the passage is materially valid then it seems that its ratification depends on an empirical investigation and anyone who grasps the import of the inference will understand how the inference should be empirically confirmed. And now we surely have an absurdity since we are attributing to speakers an a priori acceptance of the inference *and* a grasp of how it should be empirically ratified. Certainly any speaker aware of both of these aspects of her attitude toward the inference should, rationally, reappraise her attitude and this, apparently, is what the revisionary Dummett is asking us to do. The only way out of this position is to find a way for an inference to be material, yet not susceptible to empirical ratification, and thus capable of a priori acceptance. So far it is unclear how this might come to be.

Dummett also focuses on the nature of assertion in offering an argument in favour of single component meaning-theories (see SoL: 78). In essence Dummett's point here is that if we have two components in play then we shall be characterizing the assertion's correctness and incorrectness conditions independently of one another. Or, to be more accurate, subject to a constraint of consistency – so subject to the condition that we preclude cases where the assertion is both correct and incorrect – these conditions will be independent of one another. Now certainly the outcome of an act of assertion cannot be indeterminate: if an assertion is not (objectively) correct then it is incorrect; it cannot be neither correct nor incorrect. And, to be sure, there's no reason to think that such an outcome need be possible on this scheme, since knowing an assertion not to be correct may be to know that it is incorrect. However a weaker sort of indeterminacy is possible: we may know an assertion not to be incorrect without knowing it to be correct. And Dummett claims that even this would be in tension with the nature of assertion. We can bring the point out by means of the notion of commitment. When one is prepared to assert something one takes on a definite commitment; this is part of what it is to make an assertion. But if it is known that the assertion is not incorrect then, in making the assertion, one is protected from having to withdraw it. To be sure, one is also committed to the possibility of satisfying the correctness condition but, since this possibility cannot be closed off, it is always open. So provided the assertion is known not to be incorrect it can be made with equanimity; the correctness condition adds nothing to the content of one's commitment.[14] So our notion of assertion won't bear dual specification of an assertion's correctness and incorrectness conditions.

The surveyability of sense

For Dummett, language is not merely a practice, or set of practices. Rather it is a set of practices by means of which we convey meanings to one another and through which we communicate. As speakers, the meanings of individual expressions are in some sense present to us since, as we've already noted, it is a recurrent theme in his writings that we cannot think of the state of understanding as simply a capacity to engage in a pattern of use but that understanding also involves an awareness of meaning. Dummett's point is that speaking a language is a rational activity – the rational activity *par excellence* – and this entails that knowledge of meaning, in some way, guides use: meanings are consciously available to us in determining our linguistic actions. However, unless this thought is taken in the right way, it doesn't quite get us to molecularism since a holist may admit that the rules of use must, in some sense, be available to practitioners. What the holist will insist on though is that these rules simply issue in a pattern of acceptable use for expressions, in much the same way as the rules of chess confer powers on the individual pieces. But characteristically language enables speakers to do certain things (e.g. to assert that such and such or to ask whether this and that) and Dummett's point is that there would be no doing these things unless speakers were aware of doing so. So it would be wrong to describe speakers as internalizing a set of rules that issues in these capacities since this would allow that speakers have certain capacities but are unaware of what these capacities enabled them to do. Rather what we have to do is to construct a theory of meaning which articulates speakers' capacities but which makes it clear that these are capacities of which speakers are aware. So we cannot describe a system of rules (of which speakers may be aware) that holistically combine to determine the meanings of expressions. For then the meaning of an expression need not be something of which the speaker is aware. Rather we have to give an account of the meaning of an expression in such a way as to make it clear that the meaning itself is something the speaker can be aware of. For this to be possible, meaning has to be determined by a restricted set of uses.

Another point about our use of language is that we ascribe understanding to others on the basis of their use of language and hold speakers to certain commitments incurred as a result of their linguistic activity. It is hard to see how either of these could be achieved unless the meaning of an expression is something which, in some sense, is available to us.

As theorists, we seek for an explicit representation of the speakers' presentations of the meanings of expressions. The notions of harmony and of conservative extension are introduced into the theory of meaning as ways of ensuring that sense is surveyable, that is, that the meaning of any expression can be finally and definitively given by reference to a certain set of conditions. And, if we cannot circumscribe the conditions that determine the meaning of an expression, then it is utterly obscure how we could make meanings available to ourselves. So these notions are theoretical requirements that give content to the idea that meanings can be made available. Thus the pernicious consequence of a failure of these requirements is not an inability to acquire a practice (and thus its impossibility); rather it is that, as speakers, we fail to enforce and thus to incur determinate commitments, that there is nothing on which to base our rational use of language and that, as theoreticians, we shall be unable to gain a reflective understanding of the nature of our own practice. Holism – the rejection of these requirements – thus becomes a rejection of an attempt to gain this understanding and is an acceptance of the obscurity of our use of language. On such a view, sense becomes essentially unsurveyable and this threatens the possibility of conceiving of speaking a language as a rational activity. In fact, it seems that for Dummett holism is a kind of nihilism since it threatens our conceptions both of ourselves as rational agents whose rationality is essentially bound up with language use and of language as essentially involved in rational activity. In the absence of conclusive arguments for holism, we should strive, through the attempt to construct a systematic theory of meaning, for a reflective understanding of linguistic activity: insistence on molecularism becomes a methodological maxim – a symptom, to be sure, of our explanatory ambition but of an ambition that is well motivated by the nature of our subject.

These thoughts are core elements in Dummett's philosophy and are not to be questioned here. The question that faces us is whether the notions of harmony and of conservative extension are the right ways of unpacking their implications. Before turning to that question, though, I want to raise some prima facie problems for the insistence on harmony.

Defeasibility

An important feature of empirical discourse is that in most, if not all, cases we cannot lay claim to have achieved a warrant that *conclusively* justifies the assertion of a statement. That is, the best possible evidence that we can have for a claim will be defeasible: it is compatible with the obtaining of this evidence for the claim to be false. Moreover, the anti-realist theory of meaning will, if based on a notion of warranted assertibility, take certain warrants to be both meaning determining and defeasible (indefeasible warrants being unobtainable and indistinguishable from truth-conditions). So associated with a given assertion we shall have its grounds,[15] defeating conditions for those grounds and its consequences. It is tempting to identify defeating conditions with failure of a consequence, since, on the one hand, failure of a consequence certainly provides reason to withdraw a statement (and so, in some sense, is a defeating condition) while, on the other hand, a consequence of the assertion is that the defeating conditions don't obtain (otherwise the assertion must be withdrawn). But, if we do so, then we shall have to admit that harmony fails.

The important thing about a defeating condition is that it may hold together with the holding of a ground; this is precisely why the latter fails to guarantee the truth of the assertion. But, if we identify defeating conditions with the failure of a consequence, then this means that the holding of a ground is compatible with failure of a consequence. That is, the consequence cannot be derivable from the grounds, as harmony would insist. One might want to evade this position by distinguishing defeating conditions from consequences. But this ploy won't alter the substance of the point. For it will still be the case that there will be certain consequences of an assertion, namely, that defeating conditions don't obtain, which are not derivable from the grounds for assertion. So it seems that it is incoherent both to insist on harmony and to acknowledge, as an anti-realist seemingly must, the defeasibility of grounds for assertion.

Assertoric content and ingredient sense

Allied to this point is another. Many sentences share assertion conditions but do not have the same meaning: for example, "It will rain tomorrow" and "It looks as if it will rain tomorrow"; "Dummett is lighting another cigarette" and "It is assertible that Dummett is lighting another cigarette." So meaning cannot be determined by assertion-conditions.[16] Recall[17] that Dummett uses the difference between such sentences to explain the origin of our concept of truth. For him the phenomenon emerges from a consideration of the respective behaviour of each sentence in more complex sentences, in particular, the difference that results when each is subject to negation or used as the antecedent in a conditional statement. Incorporation of the phenomenon within the theory of meaning requires us to make a distinction between assertoric content and ingredient sense. Assertoric content pertains to the use of a sentence on its own. Ingredient sense is the contribution that any sentence makes to the sense of a sentence of which it is a (not necessarily proper) part. A semantic theory aims to characterize ingredient sense. And our phenomenon demonstrates that two sentences might have the same assertoric content but differ in ingredient sense. However, since ingredient sense is what semantic theory focuses on there is no need to depart from a single component account.

To be sure there can be no complaint about this as a mere description but, if Dummett's position is that the use of two sentences on their own need not differ at all yet their ingredient senses diverge, then his molecularism is jeopardized. For then there is no stable understanding of the sentence upon which our grasp of its role in more complex sentences is built. The partial order of sentence meanings is threatened.[18] Actually this is a little too strong since it may be that two sentences share their assertoric content but differ in ingredient sense because of the manner in which the assertoric content is determined in each case. So there would be some difference in the understanding of each sentence as used on its own, which might be exploited in accounting for the difference in ingredient sense. However, it's not clear quite how this difference would be exploited unless it figured as part of one's understanding of the relevant locution of the more complex sentence. And in that case ingredient sense would be derived from more basic differences in meaning. But, in utilizing the distinction against Kripke's attack on Frege, Dummett notes that "the difference between [the sentences] lies *solely* in their different contributions to the sentences formed from them by modalisation and negation; in a language without modal operators or auxiliaries, no difference could be perceived" (LBoM: 48). If we construe ingredient sense in this strong way then it poses a problem for the molecularity requirement.

There seem to be different cases here. What one says in relation to pairs of sentences relating to Kripke's discussion of names need not be similar to what one says about, say, our pair about its raining tomorrow. In neither case, but for different reasons, does a notion of ingredient sense seem to figure as fundamentally explanatory. In the former case this is for reasons suggested in Chapter 4. In the latter case this is because there is a difference in the use of the sentences as wholes since the overturn or defeating conditions (at least, of statements effected by utterances of each sentence on an occasion) differ. So it may be that one way of replacing the dubious notion of ingredient sense – dubious from the point of view of molecularism – is precisely to deny, rather than to insist on, a single component theory of meaning. So the issue which will bring this chapter to a close is this: is there a way of reconciling a dual component meaning-theory with, first, what we've uncovered of the motivation for molecularism, secondly, the argument we gave in favour of harmony and, thirdly, the argument that the nature of assertion requires a single component meaning-theory?

An alternative proposal

Let us begin by disposing of one feature of harmony. Harmony requires that the one set of use conditions be *derivable* from the other, and vice versa. In so doing, it supposedly ensures that the meaning of the sentence can be seen as determined by the one set of conditions, the other conditions "flowing from" these. This, we noted, guarantees that the sentence introduced will conservatively extend a fragment of language. But why should it be in place to demand such a guarantee? Two points need to be made here. First, the process of inter-derivability involved in harmony establishes our guarantee. However, since it would be thoroughly implausible to think of the process of derivation as part of a speaker's understanding, harmony doesn't show that speakers grasp the meaning of a sentence by grasping just the one set of conditions. In other words, unless we think of speakers as deriving the one set of conditions from the other in accord with harmony, the existence of harmony won't by itself justify any judgement about the character of speakers' understanding. Secondly, it is hard to see what would be wrong with an extension of language that happened to be conservative. If one region of language happens to extend another conservatively, even if it is not guaranteed to do so, then it seems we shall be able to see speakers' understanding of the original fragment as stable. The meanings of sentences in the original fragment will be given with respect to a restricted set of use-conditions in accord with what we've uncovered of the motivations for molecularism.

The problem with this position is that it suggests that it may be legitimate to introduce meanings which, as a matter of contingent fact, result in a conservative extension of a region of language. And this is tantamount to saying that we relinquish harmony and so relinquish the idea that the inferential passage encapsulated in an inference is logically valid, insisting only that it is materially valid.[19] As we noted, this appears to be an odd combination of ideas. For, if the inference is material, it stands in need of empirical ratification, but since it is established by conferring certain meanings on our terms, it is given a priori. Can we make these ideas cohere?

It is far from clear that we can, but one way out of the impasse *might* be as follows. It is apt to seem as if our linguistic practice is either guaranteed, by means of a proof, to be legitimate or it is empirically ratified. Neither can be reconciled with the nature of understanding; the former because the process of derivation is not incorporated in understanding, and the latter because the notion of empirical ratification is in tension with an establishment of meaning. But perhaps we are facing a false dichotomy here, which only emerges once we suppose that the practice stands in need of some sort of justification. It may be that we eschew both the need for a demonstration that we have a conservative extension and empirical ratification of this fact: that we have a conservative extension is a presupposition of the practice.

Consider an example. Let's assume we have a language for talking about present states of affairs. To this, we add a form of past tense for talking about the very recent past whose use is guided by sensitivity to current evidence. Now it may be that, if it were the case that things change only very slowly, past-tense statements come to be taken as grounds for asserting their corresponding present-tense versions, *and* that this connection is taken to be part of the meanings of past-tense sentences. So, for instance, knowing the meaning of a past-tense sentence will involve knowing that if the present-tense sentence for which it provides grounds is false then the assertion of the past-tense sentence is defeated. Now in such a case there will be occasions in which a present-tense sentence is assertible when it would not have been so prior to the introduction of the past tense. On a strong reading of assertibility (e.g. the actual availability of a warrant) then even Dummett admits that even for the case of logic we have to admit the possibility of such occasions. (Otherwise he thinks there will be no way to explain the usefulness of logic; see "The Justification of Deduction" in T&OE, and Chapter 6.) However, Dummett does insist that on a suitably weak reading of "assertible" we must be able to *prove* that occasions such as those described must be impossible (else our understanding of the present tense in the example is at stake). But why should we accept this obligation? Why shouldn't we take it that, on a suitably loose reading of assertible, such occasions don't crop up (i.e. that a present-tense sentence asserted on the basis of the truth of some past-tense sentence would have been assertible anyway)? For example, I can now assert "The cat is in the parlour" on the basis of the truth of "The cat was in the parlour", while still meaning by "The cat is in the parlour" just what I have always meant by it (that is, that it is assertible according to the original conditions of assertion). There won't be any way of offering the proof Dummett requires because the whole practice depends upon being in a world in which (observable) changes occur only slowly. But, given such a world, why should not such a practice develop, be learnable *and* be one of which we can make sense? We simply need to see the nature of the practice as being, in part, a product of the way the world is, as thereby incorporating presuppositions about the way the world is. The nature of those presuppositions is revealed by the combination of taking the truth of "new" sentences to warrant the assertion of "old" ones *and* taking it that there has thereby been no change of meaning in the "old" sentences.[20]

It might seem that this account militates against the slogan that meaning is use. If meaning is use, and use, undoubtedly, changes (and changes in a manner that cannot be shown – non-trivially, perhaps – to be trivial), then surely meaning changes too. In its crude form the objection cuts no ice since, as Dummett points out, the slogan is just a slogan whose content is to constrain admissible accounts of meaning. But the real question is: how are we to give substance to this idea that we assume that original meanings are preserved? What is the content of this, clearly tacit, assumption? An adequate explanation will, of necessity, appeal only to features of the practice itself. However, the features we need to take account of are not, as it were, first-order features about the use made of the relevant sorts of sentences but second-order features about the ascription of understanding.[21] If understanding is ascribed on the basis of speakers' use of the present-tensed language in response to present states of affairs (even when the language as a whole includes past-tense statements) then we have grounds for thinking that this use is canonical and that the use sponsored by the past tense is made under an assumed preservation of meaning. Thus the relevance of acquisition has far more to do with constitutive matters than with the epistemology of understanding. That is, the worry isn't that we need to describe language so as to make clear the mode of its progressive acquisition. Rather we need to be able to describe what is understood (the content of understanding) in order to be clear about how the language functions. The route to the former must be via an account of use and an account of the basis on which attributions of having acquired an understanding are made. Ascriptions of understanding are thus crucial in determining within the community what content is to be attached to various expressions and therefore in facilitating communication: we cannot think properly about language if we think of it merely as a set of patterns of use and neglect the role of practitioners in policing that use.[22]

Let us return to Dummett's argument which claimed that a dual component meaning-theory will, absurdly, allow a kind of indeterminate outcome to an act of assertion. If the argument is sound then it is a refutation of *one* conception of dual component meaning-theories. The argument works by using one of the components to show that the other component adds nothing to the commitments incurred by making an assertion. Could we implement anything like the same strategy to an account whose components are the grounds for an assertion and their defeating conditions? The commitments incurred in making an assertion are themselves dual: one is committed both to the availability of grounds and to the absence of defeaters of these grounds. The correctness of an assertion is linked to the fulfilment of both of these commitments, while the incorrectness is linked to the failure of either. Neither set of commitments can be shown to be vacuous given the background of the opposing component of meaning. And no indeterminate outcome is possible. So it seems credible that the content of an *assertion* can be characterized with reference to both of these components.

Summary

The chapter began with an acceptance of the argument of the previous chapter. Since we must eschew a realist notion of truth, the anti-realist will need to give an account of meaning in terms of an epistemic concept (prime candidates being verification, falsification, warranted assertion, warranted denial, justification). However, that account might either be direct or offer an account of truth in epistemic terms and then offer a truth-conditional account of meaning.

The first area to be investigated was mathematics and here we noted that the anti-realist will most likely give an account of meaning in terms of proof-conditions rather than in terms of her notion of truth (which is likely to equate with provability). When we examined the details of the anti-realist's theory of meaning for mathematics we found that it is necessary, if we are to be molecularists, to mark a distinction between canonical or meaning-determining proofs and proofs generally. We then considered how canonical proofs might best be characterized.

Our final investigation again raised the issue of molecularity, here in relation to empirical discourse. We focused only on theories of meaning which proceed directly rather than via an epistemic account of truth.[23] Dummett employs three ideas in giving content to the requirement of molecularity: harmony, conservative extension and single component theories of meaning. We discussed the relations between these notions and the rationale for each of them. The upshot of the latter discussion may have shed a little more light on the basis of the molecularity requirement: we need to circumscribe the meaning-determining uses of an expression to make it plausible that speakers have an awareness of the meanings of individual expressions. Moreover this awareness shouldn't be conceived of simply as an awareness of permissible uses but must also involve an awareness of the character of these uses, that is, an awareness of the sort of act accomplished in these uses.

I was critical of the way Dummett applies the molecularity constraint because he takes it to warrant the requirement of harmony. The problem with harmony is that it insists that one aspect of the use of an assertion be *derivable* from the other. I argued that Dummett fails to motivate the stringency of his insistence on derivability. True, we cannot accept the linking of the aspects of use of an assertion as a result of empirical ratification but this doesn't entail that they should be inter-derivable; rather they may be linked as part of the presuppositions of the discourse.

Our whole discussion was concerned only with the basic form which an anti-realist meaning-theory should take and with what concepts it will be based on. We have, at this stage, very little idea of the detailed anatomy of such an animal. As Dummett remarks, the difficulties attending a realist truth-conditional account are primarily matters of principle, the mechanics of such theories being comparatively well understood. The difficulties with anti-realist theory of meaning, conversely, appear to be difficulties of constructing its detailed workings.

Chapter 6 may thus appear to be premature at this stage of enquiry: we look at some of the possible consequences of an anti-realist theory of meaning. Specifically, we shall be considering the nature of the revision that such theories might demand in first-order practice. The potentially revisionary character of such theories, however, raises an issue of principle, and the investigation does help to clarify the nature of our mysterious, anti-realist, meaning-theoretic beast.

Chapter 6

The revisionary implications of anti-realism

That Dummett's anti-realist position has attracted a good deal of attention is partly due to its revisionary character. We appear to be provided with a purely philosophical argument which shows that ordinary practice is based on a deep misconception about the way we succeed in talking about the world. Perhaps the majority of contemporary philosophers (in the wake of Wittgenstein, Quine and the pragmatists) find revisionism of this sort hard to swallow: it smacks of a foundationalist appeal to a first philosophy. In this chapter we examine both the possibility of the revisionary position itself and the nature and extent of revision contemplated.

One note of warning: Dummett should not be identified with verificationists or positivists, despite his interest in verificationist accounts of meaning. Those views, in decreeing that certain sentences are vacuous or meaningless (typically those for which we lack a means of verification), are revisionary about content. In contrast, Dummett thinks that it would be quite wrong to question first-order practice in this way. His position *begins* from an acceptance that we understand a certain range of sentences (those which, by ordinary standards, we are competent to use) but then goes on to ask what that understanding consists in. So he couldn't espouse a revisionism in verificationist style. To put the point in terms of the notion of content, Dummett is not revisionary about which contents we grasp, he only suggests that, given our natural inclinations towards realism, we are apt to misconstrue the nature of that understanding. His revisionism then emerges when we enquire more deeply into the nature of understanding and realize that the manner in which we have conferred (and can confer) meaning on the sentences of our language won't support a range of inferences that, prior to reflection, we had taken to be uncontroversial.

Dummett's anti-realist position appears to have revisionary implications but, just as importantly, his philosophical outlook is inalienably *potentially* revisionary. First, he sets out conditions on the acceptability of a linguistic practice which there is no a priori reason to assume actual linguistic practice fulfils. So, given an unexamined practice, it just is an open possibility that philosophical investigation will reveal it to stand in need of revision. Secondly, one of the distinctive features of his philosophy is that he is thoroughly committed to the business of metaphysics but is also aware of the difficulties in attempting to advance metaphysical theses. In particular, he is alert to the threat of advancing metaphysical views whose content is purely metaphorical.[1] His solution is to explain the content of metaphysical positions in meaning-theoretic terms. Transposing the discussion to that key is important because it demonstrates a link between metaphysical views and our ordinary practice; we see how the former engages with the latter. Part of the content of a view will then be determined by its revisionary implications:[2] we might say that this is the operational content of the view. Thus, for Dummett, the significance of a philosophical position cannot be divorced from its revisionary implications; the potential for revision in philosophy should be embraced, not treated with suspicion.

The particular route by which Dummett's anti-realist arrives at a revisionary position proceeds via an insistence that we provide our inferential practice with a semantic validation. We'll need finally to think about whether an anti-realistically acceptable semantic validation of classical logic is achievable. But first we need to face two questions: (i) Is the business of providing a semantic validation of logic – a justification of deduction – legitimate? and (ii) Is the business a legitimate anti-realist concern? Dummett addresses the first question in what is an important paper in the philosophy of logic ("The Justification of Deduction", T&OE: essay 17). And Wright (1981) attempts to raise difficulties for specifically anti-realist endeavours to justify logic. Finally, Wright (1981) and Edgington (1981) – in very different ways – try to cast doubt on the supposed anti-realist rejection of classical logic.

The justification of deduction

How can it be in place to demand a justification of our deductive practice given that any justification we offer will itself involve deduction? Either the justification offered will make use of the very principles we are trying to justify, in which case the justification will be circular, or it will make use of different principles which themselves stand in need of justification, in which case we launch a regress. So a justification of deduction is simply not a possible project.

Dummett's answer to this challenge introduces a distinction in types of justification and notices a feature of the accusation of circularity. Looking first at the sort of circularity involved, Dummett notes that a principle of inference will not feature as a premise in its own justification, rather it will be *used* in the justification – let us call such justifications "pragmatically circular" and those in which the conclusion appears as a premise "blatantly circular". So, for instance, we might have the following justification of *modus ponens*:

> Assume that [P] is true and that [If P then Q] is true. Given that the conditional is true we know, by the meaning stipulation for the conditional, that if [P] is true then [Q] is true. So, by *modus ponens*, [Q] is true.[3]

Note that in drawing the conclusion which justifies *modus ponens* we infer by means of *modus ponens*. So, certainly, if *modus ponens* is not a sound principle of inference the justification is worthless. But the question is: is the justification itself worthless? Why should it have any more value than the following worthless justification?

> *Modus ponens* is a sound principle of inference.
> So *modus ponens* is a sound principle of inference.

Before we tackle those questions let's have Dummett's distinction among justifications before us. A justification may be either suasive or explanatory. If it is suasive it aims at convincing one to adopt what it justifies. So one might, for instance, have a suasive justification of the law of excluded middle (LEM), from an acceptance of double negation elimination (DNE), reduction ad absurdum (RAA) and laws governing "&" and "∨":

1	(1)	$-(A \vee -A)$	Ass
2	(2)	A	Ass
2	(3)	$A \vee -A$	2 ∨ I

1,2	(4)	$(A \vee -A) \& -(A \vee -A)$	1,3 & I
1	(5)	$-A$	2,4 RAA
1	(6)	$A \vee -A$	5 $\vee$ I
1	(7)	$(A \vee -A) \& -(A \vee -A)$	1,6 & I
	(8)	$--(A \vee -A)$	1,7 RAA
	(9)	$A \vee -A$	9 DNE

Thus anyone who accepts these other principles can be brought, in this manner, to accept the law of excluded middle.

In contrast, an explanatory justification doesn't aim at bringing one to accept something one didn't accept prior to the justification, rather it attempts to "make sense" of an aspect of our practice. As Dummett says, an explanatory justification of deduction attempts "to find a satisfactory explanation of the role of such arguments in our use of language" (T&OE: 296). So, very roughly, an explanatory justification of deduction will try to make sense of the practice of deductive inference. Quite what counts as "making sense" of a phenomenon and which questions such an explanation aims at answering can be allowed to remain vague (at least for the moment). The question that faces us now concerns the relevance of this distinction to the point about circularity.

Clearly any circularity, whether blatant or pragmatic, is an absolute bar to the use of a justification in its suasive role. There can be no convincing someone to accept something if the justification offered assumes what is to be justified either explicitly as a premise or in its mode of inferring. Clearly too, a blatantly circular argument can have no explanatory power since it always has precisely the same form. But why should a pragmatically circular argument have any more explanatory value?

Dummett's thought is that, where our interests are explanatory, we do not need to surrender our epistemic position in constructing a substantive justification. So, where our concern is in explanatorily justifying principles of deductive inference, we may legitimately use those principles in constructing the justification. In very broad terms there must be something right in this proposal. This something accounts for the fact that, whatever else one thinks of the business of naturalized epistemology, it is not a vacuous enterprise. But, in the present context one might well question the value of pragmatically circular justifications, even where these are only explanatory.

Susan Haack (1982) thinks that, since we shall be able to furnish such justifications for patently absurd rules of inference, such justifications are valueless. For consider her rule of *modus morons* according to which we may infer that [P] is true from the truth of [If P then Q] and of [Q]. The justification proceeds as follows:

> Assume that [Q] is true and that [If P then Q] is true. Given that the conditional is true we know, by the meaning stipulation for the conditional, that if [P] is true then [Q] is true. So, by modus morons, [P] is true.

The last step proceeds by means of *modus morons* but, since it is supposed to be legitimate to use *modus ponens* in its justification, no complaint can, apparently, be raised about this. The justification is, however, clearly valueless. Analogously the justification of *modus ponens* is entirely valueless.

We might attempt to break the analogy by pointing out that the justification of *modus ponens* uses a sound principle of inference whereas that of *modus morons* does not. True, but the justification was also supposed to provide some reassurance that the given principle of inference is indeed sound. We cannot therefore appeal to the soundness of a principle of inference in order to distinguish worthy from worthless justifications. Moreover, if we could provide such a justification no matter what rules of inference we happen to adopt, how can we set any store by the particular justifications we are offered?

That all seems right enough. But it ignores a feature of the justifications; it ignores their involvement with the notion of truth.[4] In order to show that the justifications are (potentially) valuable we need to show that we may not be able to furnish a justification of just any rule of inference we are inclined to accept. Take the following as an example. Let us suppose we accept classical logic. Suppose too that we become convinced that truth coincides with possession (in an appropriate sense) of a proof.[5] Can we justify the rule of double negation elimination (DNE)? What we need to show is that the truth of [not-not-P] guarantees that of [P]. So assume [not-not-P] is true. We can then reason as follows:

> [not-not-P] is true
> not-not-P, by the equivalence principle
> P, by DNE
> [P] is true, by the equivalence principle.

Clearly we shall be able to adapt this reasoning to justify any rule of inference which we accept. Equally obviously we shall be able to provide a proof of [*P*] if we have a proof of [not-not-*P*] (by using DNE), so our identification of truth with possession of a proof is safe.

But now consider the following. We know (see above) that LEM follows from DNE. So the following should be acceptable:

> [*P* or not-*P*] is true just in case either [*P*] is true or [not-*P*] is true, that is, just in case we possess a proof of [*P*] or a proof of [not-*P*].

This assumes that truth distributes over the disjunction and then applies our equation of truth with possession of a proof. However, we need not possess a proof of [*P*] or of its negation, even in a classical framework, since this would entail that every sentence is (classically) decidable. And now we seem to have a tension in our position.

There may be a number of ways of negotiating one's way through this situation. We might, for instance, rescind our commitment to truth distributing over the disjunction. But we might also take the above line of reasoning to cast doubt on LEM and thus to place us in a position of requiring, not merely an explanatory justification, but a suasive justification. In which case our previous justification will now appear thoroughly question begging.

Another way to appreciate just how an explanatory and pragmatically circular justification has bite is to exploit the device of an object language–meta-language distinction. Then, even if we suppose that classical logic is valid in the meta-language, we won't be able to justify DNE in the object language, given the identification of truth with provability. Since to suppose that [– –*P*] is true is to suppose that we have a proof of [– –*P*], that is, that we have a refutation of any refutation of [*P*]. But that is not to have a proof of [*P*]. So we cannot show that [*P*] is true.[6]

What is the moral of this little parable? Explanatory justifications are easy to furnish but, given a substantive conception of truth, we may find ourselves requiring a suasive justification. In setting out to construct an explanatory justification we bring our inferential practice together with a conception of truth.[7] There is no guarantee that in so doing we emerge with a consistent view. So the business of providing an explanatory justification can lead us to question the legitimacy of aspects of our practice. Conversely, a successful explanatory project does confer a legitimacy on an inferential practice which transcends our mere inclination to accept it.[8]

The motivation for a justification of deduction

If the last section convinces then there's no obvious reason for deny-ing the possibility of a justification of deduction. But that doesn't establish a good motive for requiring one. Dummett's insistence on a justification is supposed to flow from his rejection of holism. That is, molecularism supplies our motivation here.

Now it's certainly true that a holist might well eschew any interest in a justification of deduction. She might claim that the meanings of the logical constants are implicitly defined by our rules of inference and thus that our practice of deductive inference is self-standing. In con-trast, Dummett's molecularist will want to say that introduction of inferential practice must not interfere with the established meanings of sentences. Thus, if a sentence is assertible as a result of a process of inference, it must be the case that the sentence would have been assert-ible anyway. So, unless deductive inference is to disrupt our under-standing of a base class of sentences, it must constitute a conservative extension of that class: that is, inferential warrants must be shown to coincide (in some sense) with non-inferential warrants. And, in this way, we supply a justification of deduction. So the thought is that according to molecularism the transition from deductive innocence to deductive competence must be negotiated on the basis of a stable understanding of (a class of) logically simple sentences.

Wright (1993: essay 15) attempts to put some stress on this thought. There is, he thinks, no direct route from molecularism to a requirement that we offer a semantic validation of logic. The essence of molecular-ism is an insistence that one's understanding of a sentence (or sentences) be explicable by reference only to a proper fragment of language, the relevant fragments being such as to issue in a partial ordering of sentences. Why though should we partition language into a logic-free base onto which we graft logical machinery? Could it not be that each stage of language involves a complete logical competence? The meanings of the logical constants would be implicitly defined by the rules governing their use and one would understand them when one successfully masters their use. The implicit definitional view of logic could then be reconciled with molecularism by thinking of the stages of linguistic competence as demarcated by something other than logic. To summarize, Dummett assumes that logical complexity must reflect a notion of complexity given by the order of understanding. This assumption allows him to argue from molecularism to the need to justify deduction. But what is the argument for the assumption?

According to the implicit definitional view we acquire logical competence through immersion in a practice; we learn a system of rules by means of which we achieve warrants for assertion. No question about the relation of inferential to non-inferential warrants need arise in acquiring competence with these rules. So to be sure there is no argument from progressive acquisition to the need to justify deduction. But we long ago noted that Dummett's molecularism could not be justified simply by appeal to considerations about acquisition.[9] Rather Dummett insists on molecularism because he thinks that we need to be able to make a certain sort of sense of a practice. His thought here is that we can make no sense of the practice of inference unless we tackle the question of the relation between inferential and non-inferential warrants. If there is no sense in which the inferential warrant coincides with a non-inferential warrant then it is just not clear what the argument informs us of: the epistemic role of argument is rendered mysterious. Of course it may prove impossible to construct an acceptable explanation of this role but we shouldn't prejudge that issue by factoring deduction into the basic practice. So the methodological aspect of molecularism suffices to motivate a justification of deduction unless we have reason for thinking that this aim is misguided. We'll turn to that question presently.

Can an anti-realist require a justification of deduction?

Wright turns from wondering whether there is a good motive for investigating the semantic validity of logic to wondering whether the anti-realist can justify such a concern. He voices two major reservations, one of which is based on an interpretation of Wittgenstein's rule-following considerations which conflicts with the account offered in Chapter 2. I'll therefore ignore that reservation here and move on to the other.

The crux of this reservation is that a concern with semantic validations of logic will involve the anti-realist in talk about recognition transcendent states of affairs. By her own lights, the anti-realist should deny substance to such talk so her requirement of a justification of deduction becomes vacuous. Dummett's anti-realist wants to show her inferential practice to be a conservative extension of her non-inferential practice. But, for the anti-realist, this requirement will be vacuous unless we can recognize the unsoundness of our inferential practice. Granted that an inconsistent practice is non-conservative,

Wright's question is then: is there any recognizing, short of inconsistency, that one's inferential practice is non-conservative? Why, one might well wonder, should this be a problem?

The problem emerges when we notice that inferential practice occupies a normative position relative to non-inferential practice. That is, we use the results of inference to determine when we have made a mistake in our non-inferential practice. To focus on the example of arithmetic, a natural enough thought is that we have operational procedures of counting which establish a sense for numerical terms. We then feel that arithmetic truths must be faithful to the meanings of terms so established. So if, for instance, we determined by counting that there are 7 poodles and 12 terriers[10] then, were we to count the number of dogs, we would find, since $7 + 12 = 19$, that there were 19 of them. Of course this isn't quite right, if we were to count *correctly* then we should be guaranteed to find 19 dogs. So any counting procedure which comes to a different result would be mistaken (we'd have counted one or more dogs more than once, or we'd have included a dog not in the original set, or we'd have repeated or skipped a numeral in the process of counting). Thus a crucial role of the arithmetic result is to determine when we have made a mistake in implementing operational procedures. More generally, inferential criteria are normative with respect to operational criteria.

Now to recognize the non-conservativeness of inference we should have to be able to recognize that an inferential warrant obtains where no non-inferential warrant is available. To translate this general possibility to our example we should have to recognize that the arithmetic result provides a warrant for assertion where no warrant is obtainable by means of counting. But surely it is not too difficult to imagine such a situation arising. Say we believed not that $7 + 12 = 19$ but that $7 + 12 = 18$. Then, in the above case, were we to count the number of dogs (being very careful and not noticing any mistake), we would find that there were 19 of them. Thus the inferential warrant would collide with that provided by operational criteria. But that's just too quick. If we were convinced that $7 + 12 = 18$ then we wouldn't accept this clash, rather what we'd say is that we must have made some mistake in counting. Nothing can guarantee that no such mistake occurred because the sources of a mistake cannot be completely circumscribed. So it is always possible that some source of error has crept unnoticed into our counting procedure. Since such a saving hypothesis is always available there is no recognizing the non-conservativeness of an inferential practice.

But what does this argument show? It doesn't show that the non-conservativeness of an inferential practice cannot be recognized, only that it cannot be recognized in a single instance of applying both sets of procedures. If the inferential practice is indeed non-conservative then there will be a systematic divergence between inferentially and non-inferentially based judgements. When we attempt to explain this systematic divergence we shall need to globalize the hypothesis of a mistake and the consequences of doing so may lead us to a recognition of non-conservativeness. Wright's thought is that where we have a divergence we explain away the appearance of a clash between arithmetic and counting by saying that we must have made a mistake in implementing counting procedures. Further, since such a hypothesis is an open existential (it hypothesizes the existence of a mistake without giving any definite characterization of its nature) it is strictly indefeasible and so is always available. Granted, but what is the cost of a global appeal to such a hypothesis? If we suppose that we globally misapply counting procedures then we systematically misuse part of our own language. But that's just to say that we fail to understand correctly the meanings of numerical terms as established by our counting procedures and that, surely, is absurd. The only other hypothesis is that our inferential practice is non-conservative.[11]

Now we must accept that there is no point at which we are rationally constrained to explain the systematic divergence by globalizing the hypothesis of a mistake. So we are not forced to recognize non-conservativeness. Or, perhaps a better way of putting this point is that we cannot force an adherent of a deviant arithmetic to recognize its non-conservativeness. But what we can do is to point to a phenomenon whose explanation will require that recognition. Although it is always possible simply to refuse to offer an explanation of a phenomenon that shouldn't cast doubt on what we might come to recognize in seeking to give an explanation. An awkward customer may fail to recognize all kinds of thing but her awkwardness shouldn't impugn our capacities to do so.

Can an anti-realist accept classical logic?

This question is not quite as simple as it sounds. If we take a realist to be someone who accepts bivalence for non-effectively decidable sentences then realism seems to follow once we combine an acceptance of LEM with an acceptance of the equivalence principles ([P] is true iff P; $[P]$ is false iff not-P). So, since an acceptance of classical logic leads to realism, a denial of realism must involve a rejection of classical logic. Let us bracket that thought for a moment and ask instead the following question. Can an assertibility-conditions theorist accept classical logic? So the supposition is that Dummett's challenge to use of realist truth in an account of meaning and understanding is accepted and, consequently, we see the need to move to an assertibility-conditions account. The question then is: should this bar us from accepting classical logic?

In her "Meaning, Bivalence and Realism" (1981) Edgington tackles just this question. Her treatment is sensitive both to Dummett's challenge to realism and to his requirement of molecularity; it amply warrants pondering over. Her account applies to non-mathematical regions of discourse – discourse in which warrants for assertion are non-conclusive or defeasible – and begins with some worries about attempts to generalize the intuitionistic accounts of the logical constants. We return to some of these worries in the next chapter. We can here move directly to her positive account. Her thought is that we accept that the meanings of sentences (at least those which are not logically complex) are given by their assertibility-conditions (or perhaps a combination of these with defeating conditions). However the meanings of the logical constants are characterized differently; they are characterized in terms of a notion of degree of justification.

Edgington notes first that disjunction can be seen as a way of weakening an assertion. So an assertion of a disjunction, $P \vee Q$, is always at least as well justified as an assertion of P (or of Q) and, if there is no entailment between P and Q and no conclusive justification of either or of their negations, then an assertion of $P \vee Q$ has a strictly better justification than that of P (or Q). If, in addition, P and Q are incompatible then the degree of justification of $P \vee Q$ decreases (increases) according as the degree of justification of either disjunct decreases (increases). So if we modelled degrees of justification by a function, J, from propositions onto the real numbers (between, say, 0 and 1) then we'd have $J(P \vee Q) = J(P) + J(Q)$. Now it's important to note that these features about degrees of justification and, indeed, the degree of justification of either disjunct, are not products of the meanings of P or of Q. Rather these features are products of the meaning of disjunction, given the degrees of justification of either disjunct. The implication is that the ordinary practice of inference involves reasoning with propositions which we regard as justified to a certain extent; the meanings of logical particles are given by reference to a metric of justification. However, the meanings of individual propositions are not so characterized for it is a common occurrence for speakers to agree about the meaning of a proposition but to disagree about how well justified it is.

The negation of a proposition is then characterized as that proposition whose degree of justification varies inversely with the degree of justification of the proposition. Moreover when P is conclusively verified, $-P$ is conclusively refuted. So when $J(P) = 1$, $J(-P) = 0$. Similarly, when P is conclusively refuted, $-P$ is conclusively verified. So when $J(P) = 0$, $J(-P) = 1$. Also if the degree of justification of P decreases by some amount then that of $-P$ will increase by the same amount. So at all stages $J(P) + J(-P) = 1$. But since P and $-P$ are incompatible $J(P \vee -P) = J(P) + J(-P)$. Thus $J(P \vee -P) = 1$. So the disjunction of a proposition with its negation is always conclusively verified: LEM holds.

What we've been offered is a story – a plausible story to be sure – of how LEM and so, for our purposes, classical logic might be justified. It doesn't demonstrate the validity of classical logic since the only justification we've been given for taking $J(P) + J(-P)$ to be 1 is the situation when P is conclusively verified or falsified. But conclusive verification was not supposed to be applicable in these cases. However, this does not detract, so Edgington supposes, from her point.[12] Dummett had issued a challenge to classical logic via a set of constraints on ascriptions of understanding, Edgington rebuts the challenge by showing how classical logic might be reconciled with the relevant constraints.

Now we combine the truth of $[P \vee -P]$ (where P is not effectively decidable) with that of:

$[P]$ is true iff P
$[P]$ is false iff $-P$

to infer that $[P]$ is true $\vee$ $[P]$ is false. That is, bivalence holds for non-effectively decidable propositions.

Have we given an anti-realist justification of classical logic or have we succeeded in justifying realism? There are a number of points to make here. First, one might think of realism as adherence to a verification transcendent notion of truth and note that this claim is distinct from that of whether or not bivalence applies to non-effectively decidable propositions.[13] So, though Edgington would have justified the latter, realism would not be a consequence.

We've already looked at McDowell's argument, which shows that one might consistently eschew bivalence while adhering to a verification transcendent notion of truth. So the two claims arguably are distinct. But McDowell's point shows that there is no implication from an acceptance of a verification transcendent notion of truth to bivalence. But, if the distinction is to do any work for us here, we want to know whether the reverse implication holds, that is, whether adherence to bivalence entails adoption of a verification transcendent notion of truth. For, if that implication holds, Edgington will have a justification of realism even on this revised conception of it.

Wright argues that the implication fails since acceptance of bivalence for non-effectively decidable propositions entails only that we cannot guarantee that all truths are knowable. But that claim does not entitle us to assert that it is possible for there to be unknowable truths. To make this inference we would naturally appeal to the principle: "it is not necessary that *P*" entails "it is possible that not *P*". However that principle, though classically acceptable, is not intuitionistically acceptable. So for an intuitionist there is no obvious route from the one claim to the other. Could this possibly help in present circumstances? Clearly not, for we are now in a position of having accepted a justification of classical logic and are enquiring whether this delivers a justification of realism.

To digress slightly, it is worth noting that, for an intuitionistic anti-realist, making a claim that truth transcends knowability will be difficult anyway. For, on an intuitionistic reading of negation, to show (in an appropriate sense) the impossibility of knowing a proposition is to demonstrate its negation. So if there is to be a statement of realism that can be uncontentiously understood it won't take this form; focusing on a commitment to bivalence and our reasons for being so committed is far more promising.

Let us return to our question about whether Edgington's justification of classical logic delivers a justification of realism, and thus isn't an *anti-realist* justification of classical logic. Recall that Dummett's paradigm realist position doesn't involve mere acceptance of bivalence but involves adoption of a specific sort of semantic theory in which the notion of truth plays a certain role. Since truth here plays no substantive role in the semantic theory, only featuring in its disquotational aspect, the realism that would emerge from Edgington's argument is, at most, a sophisticated realism. So there are good grounds for seeing such a position as less than fully robustly realist.[14] Indeed we might question Edgington's use of the disquotational schema. Plausibly we might justify the use of classical logic in connection with vague predicates in just the way that Edgington proposes. We wouldn't, however, want to be committed thereby to claiming that any statement involving a vague predicate is determinately true or false. One way to resist that commitment is to resist application of the disquotational schema here and our reason for so doing would be a rejection, in the context of the current account of disjunction, of the claim that truth distributes over the disjunction.[15] So Edgington owes us a justification of her use of the disquotational schema: she fails to discharge this debt. So, *if* we have a justification of classical logic here, it may well be one that is consistent with anti-realism.

The main feature of Edgington's account is that our acceptance of bivalence is driven by a commitment to LEM and not vice versa. Let us now consider the latter commitment. According to Edgington we justify LEM by realizing that, whatever our epistemic position, the sum of the degree of justifiability of any proposition with that of its negation will be 1. Now Edgington models the notion of degree of justification of a proposition as a function from the proposition to the reals (between 0 and 1). She also thinks that the degree of justification will vary: for instance, the degree of justification of $-P$ varies inversely with that of P. What is the additional feature which determines how the justification for a proposition varies? A natural thought would be to take this to be the agent's epistemic position (or "state of information"). Another possibility would be to take the justifiability of a proposition to be determined by the way the world is, the justifiability of a proposition varying from one possible world to another. This latter interpretation would be to be realist about degrees of justification and this is not what Edgington has in mind. For, if it were, degrees of justification would be thoroughly objective, but Edgington allows that we may vary in our assessment of the salience of information and therefore differ in our apportionments of degrees of justification. Also Edgington is offering a justification of classical logic which ostensibly meets Dummett's contraints on an account of meaning. But it's no more obvious that an account of the logical constants based on a realist notion of degree of justification is any advance on one based on a realist notion of truth; how does the character of our understanding of a proposition determine that it has a definite degree of justification and that the sum of its degree of justification with that of its negation sums to 1?

Conversely if degrees of justification are subjective assignments made from a given epistemic position there will, presumably, be an epistemological cum psychological story to tell about the assignment but, given that, there won't be any problem in explaining the meanings of the logical constants. (Be careful to note that, although the assignment of degrees of justification may be in part subjective, the *notion* of degree of justification and thus the definition of the logical constants in terms of degrees of justification won't be in the least subjective.[16])

Let's follow Edgington and model the justifiability of a proposition as a function from epistemic states to real numbers between 0 and 1. Edgington assumes that the range of this function will be 0 to 1 inclusive. But with what right does she help herself to this assumption? Of course, if a proposition is verified its degree of justification will be 1 and if falsified 0. But to take it that the function has this range is to assume that the relevant epistemic states (those in which the proposition is verified and those in which it is falsified) exist. And now either we become realists about epistemic states (and, as we've just noted, the notion of degree of justification won't find a place in an account of understanding as manifestable) or we've assumed that the proposition is decidable, in which case, the justification provided of classical canons of inference will be unsurprising and irrelevant to the realism issue. Conversely, if the proposition is genuinely undecidable, then it is simply not clear what range of values the justifiability function will take.

How does this affect Edgington's justification of LEM? Recall that for her the negation of a proposition, P, is that proposition whose degree of justification varies inversely with that of P and such that $J(P) = 1$ iff $J(-P) = 0$ and $J(P) = 0$ iff $J(-P) = 1$. Now Edgington assumes that the range of the J-function realizes the conditions captured in the biconditionals; this allows us to infer that the sum $J(P) + J(-P)$ and thus that $J(P \vee -P)$, at these extremes, is 1. Since any decrease (increase) in $J(P)$ is precisely compensated for by an increase (decrease) in $J(-P)$, $J(P \vee -P)$ remains constant. But this reasoning only applies if we can assume that the extremes obtain. If not, we have no guarantee that $J(P) + J(-P) = 1$. To assume that the extremes obtain is to assume that P is decidable. And if we cannot be sure that the extremes obtain we cannot be certain of the value of $J(P) + J(-P)$. So LEM remains unjustified.[17]

Edgington might accept this, claiming only that Dummett's strictures on accounts of meaning don't preclude adoption of a certain policy of assigning degrees of justification. And, to be sure, this idea of adopting a policy fits well with the idea that assignments of degrees of justification will be, in some measure, subjective: since individuals might differ over how they weigh evidence, a policy decision is called for. Now, given that some such policies will deliver a justification of LEM, Dummett doesn't provide an argument against classical logic. The crux, however, concerns what we are committed to in adopting such a policy. And, though it seems right to talk of policies here, a policy must be acceptable. For instance, one couldn't adopt a policy under which the degree of justification of a proposition was other than 1 when it was verified. Thus adopting a policy might well incur epistemological and/or metaphysical commitments. And what I've just tried to show is that Edgington's preferred policy would commit us to claiming that all propositions are decidable (that there is an epistemic state in which each is either verified or refuted). We might just as well explicitly make this assumption and offer a much more direct but thoroughly dubious justification of classical logic.

Summary

In this chapter we've seen reason for accepting the potentially revisionary character of Dummett's philosophy. Contrary to much contemporary thought Dummett has no qualms about this; it is closely linked with what he sees as the content of a given philosophical position. A theory of meaning, however, should aim to give a representation of linguistic practice as we find it. We are forced to accept a revision in that practice only when we can see that an appropriate representation will not be forthcoming. Dummett's revisionary view about inferential practice stems from his insistence that we provide a semantic validation for logic. We rehearsed and defended his argument that a semantic validation of logic will not be vacuously circular. In fact, it is rather strange that this accusation was ever levelled against Dummett: how could he base a revisionary view on a vacuous requirement? The defence noted that the justifications offered will not be blatantly but only pragmatically circular and went on to point out that an explanatory justification, in contrast to a suasive justification, may permit pragmatic circularity. The justification is, in addition, *semantic*, so it will make use of certain semantic notions, pre-eminently, that of truth. There is no guarantee that a given notion of truth will issue in a justification of the rules of inference that we happen to accept. So the justification can motivate a revision in inferential practice: it is certainly not nugatory.

Having defended the general business of offering semantic justifications of logic, we went on to question whether this is a legitimate anti-realist enterprise. For Wright argues that the normative role of inferential practice entails that the non-conservativeness of an inferential practice relative to a first-order practice cannot be recognized, so, by anti-realist standards, must be declared a vacuous demand. However, the argument that Wright gives focuses on the possibility of arriving at this recognition in a single instance. His underlying thought, which motivates this focus, seems to be that we should be able to *force* a practitioner of a non-conservative inferential practice to recognize this fault. But what we can recognize need not coincide with what we can be forced to recognize.

Lastly we examined Edgington's attempt to justify classical logic working within Dummett's constraints on a meaning-theory. I claimed that the attempt fails because it amounts to an adoption of a policy which assumes the truth of realism or which assumes that all propositions are decidable. Edgington wants to harness her justification of classical logic to an acceptance of the equivalence principle to justify a realist notion of truth. I faulted this strategy on the grounds that it cannot always be correct to employ the equivalence principle in this way – it cannot be correct where vague predicates are concerned – and Edgington fails to justify her particular employment of it.

The discussion has had a limited focus in that we have concerned ourselves with inferential practice. Another sphere of revisionary anti-realist activity concerns traditional mathematics and its use of non-constructive methods and impredicative definitions. Here we now have programmes of developing constructive analogues of portions of classical mathematics. An important contribution in this field is Dummett's own *Elements of Intuitionism*. The issues and material here are complex and technical and would take us well beyond the scope of this book. Part of the reason for this difficulty is that aspects of classical mathematics are vexed, even from a realist perspective, because of the set-theoretical paradoxes.[18] Dummett thinks that realism is part of the problem here and that a constructive view of mathematics will lead to a natural resolution of the paradoxes. In support of this view he has argued that many of the fundamental concepts of mathematics are not completely definite so they do not have extensions which are settled once and for all, rather they are indefinitely extensible. A significant body of literature has arisen in response to this idea.[19]

A second consequence of our limited focus is that the question of revising whole regions of language has been pushed to the side. We have only been concerned with revising at most a limited aspect of inferential practice: for instance, adherence to the law of excluded middle. In Chapter 7 we will look at two cases – mathematics[20] and the past – where it seems anti-realist arguments force a much more radical revisionary stance.

Chapter 7

Two case studies: the past and mathematics

In this final chapter we look at the application of anti-realist ideas in two particular cases, that of the past and that of mathematics. Both provide potentially favourable ground for a Dummettian approach since the anti-realist in either case is unlikely to adopt a reductionist view. The anti-realist about the past doesn't think that there's a class of statements which is both distinct from past-tense statements and such that the truth of any past-tense statement consists in the truth of some statement or statements of this class. For an anti-realist understanding of past-tense statements will consist in an appropriate sensitivity to evidence. But at least some evidence will consist in the deliverances of memory, that is, remembering that such and such occurred. There won't be any characterizing the content of the memory independently of the past tense itself. Also an attempt to construe realism or anti-realism about the past as views about a range of entities is completely counter-intuitive.

In the mathematical case it seems far more natural to think of the realism debate as a debate about a range of entities. But Dummett argues (in "The Philosophical Basis of Intuitionistic Logic", T&OE: essay 14) that the clearest, most plausible form of anti-realism here too relates primarily not to matters ontological but to the manner in which the meanings of mathematical statements are given. The anti-realist once again will characterize those meanings in terms of what counts as establishing the truth of a sentence, namely, proof. And there won't be any characterizing what counts as a proof of, say, the fundamental theorem of arithmetic by means of vocabulary which is independent of that of the theorem. So the anti-realist theory of meaning won't be reductive.

Michael Dummett

Thus in each case we have a debate which promises to fit well into Dummett's framework. Both, however, throw up interesting and particular difficulties for anti-realism. In the case of the past tense the, so-called, truth-value links seem to offer a means of justifying a realist notion of truth. If this is indeed so, then the anti-realist must either acknowledge defeat or accept, what at first sight seems to be, an absurdly revisionary stance. In the case of mathematics the anti-realist's arguments seem to apply to her own favoured semantics, forcing her into incoherence or adoption of a finitistic position, which, again, seems to be absurdly revisionary. How do these arguments against anti-realism run? And what defences can the anti-realist summon?

Anti-realism and the past

Statements about the past are made on the basis of currently available evidence: memories, documentary evidence and traces. However, in many cases – for example, "The archaeopteryx with the greatest life span was a female" – the evidence we currently possess won't justify either asserting or denying the statement. Nor have we any method for putting ourselves in touch with evidence which would justify a verdict on the statement. So by anti-realist lights we cannot assume that the statement has a determinate truth-value.

In "The Reality of the Past" (T&OE: essay 21) Dummett focuses on the truth-value links as offering a potentially potent challenge to this application of anti-realism. For, using the truth-value links, one seems to be able to argue that past-tense statements are determinately either true or false, even though we may have no means available for deciding their truth-value.

The truth-value links are systematic linkages between the truth-values of statements made by uttering differently tensed sentences at different times. So, for instance,

"It was raining yesterday" is true today iff "It is raining today" was true yesterday.

In general (for a truth-value link of this form) a past-tense sentence is currently true just in case a present-tense sentence was true at some earlier time. We might, semi-formally, represent the link as follows:

[$Past(S)$] is true iff [$Pres(S)$] was true[1]

144

Similarly we also have links of the following forms:[2]

[*Fut*(*S*)] is true iff [*Pres*(*S*)] will be true
[*Pres*(*S*)] is true iff [*Past*(*S*)] will be true
[*Pres*(*S*)] is true iff [*Fut*(*S*)] was true

Why does the presence of these truth-value links provide a source of difficulty for anti-realism? It will take a little work to make the supposed difficulty clear. However a first thought might run as follows. Let's suppose I'm wandering through a meadow and notice a clump of snakeshead fritillaries. So the sentence "There is a clump of fritillaries at such and such a spot" is now true. Now it's possible that in a year's time the meadow is ploughed over and I forget having seen the fritillaries – unlikely given their beauty and rarity – and, if this did happen, then in a year's time there won't be anything to warrant asserting the sentence "A year ago there was a clump of fritillaries at such and such a spot." However that sentence will nonetheless be true; its truth is guaranteed by the truth-value links and the present truth of "There is a clump of fritillaries at such and such a spot." So it is possible for a sentence to be true in the absence of all evidence; in other words, truth outruns verification. The general point is that the anti-realist must admit that we assert sentences in the present on the basis of warrants that may leave no trace. So she seems forced to admit, by the truth-value links, that in the future a past-tense sentence will be true although entirely lacking in evidence. Thus truth is not constrained by the obtainability of evidence.

Thus far the argument has an undoubted intuitive pull but is by no means conclusive. The reason for this is that the argument doesn't simply concern truth but involves the truth predicate occurring with a significant tense. Now the anti-realist would find it hard to deny the truth-value links since these seem to be embedded in the way we learn to use the tenses. More than this though, from her own perspective, the anti-realist will find the truth-value links irresistible. On an anti-realist reading of the biconditional, a biconditional will hold just in case a warrant for the assertion of the sentence on the right-hand side can be transformed into one for the assertion of the sentence on the left-hand side and vice versa. So the truth of the following biconditional will be guaranteed just in case a warrant for the assertion of either side can be transformed into a warrant for the assertion of the other:

"There is a clump of fritillaries at such and such a spot" is true iff "A year ago there was a clump of fritillaries at such and such a spot" will be true in a year's time.

But the transformation is easy since a warrant for the assertion of "There is a clump of fritillaries at such and such a spot' just *is* a warrant for the assertion of "'A year ago there was a clump of fritillaries at such and such a spot' will be true in a year's time" and vice versa. So from an anti-realist perspective the truth-value links seem bound to hold. And now the anti-realist can respond that the realist line of thought gains credibility only because it makes an illicit appeal to a spurious realist picture. From the anti-realist perspective we need only account consistently for our assignments of past, present and future truth in time. And this she can do. If one bears in mind the reason the anti-realist will give for accepting the truth-value links it is quite evident that she can never be faced with an instance of a sentence which is true though unverifiable. When the realist talks about a past-tense sentence which will be true she mistakenly takes herself to be considering a conferral of truth on a sentence at some future time by a currently available (but then past) fact. That is, she seems to envision a timeless series of temporally situated facts that make our tensed statements true independently of our access to them. From the anti-realist perspective talking about a past-tense sentence which will be true is something we do *now* and so is subject to the present availability of warrants. So once we take our use of tenses in time seriously and eschew the realist's alluring but otiose metaphysical picture the problem vanishes.

Not unsurprisingly, the realist has a response to this rebuttal of her challenge. Now it's true, the realist might admit, that she cannot use the truth-value links to bring the anti-realist to acknowledge an instance of a sentence which is true but unverifiable. Thus the anti-realist may be able to offer a coherent account of our use of the tenses and the tensed truth predicates. However, the realist goes on to point out that the anti-realist's general account of meaning and understanding is in tension with her acknowledgement of the truth-value links. Anti-realism espouses a philosophical view which, if it is worth taking seriously, must be applicable at all times, not just in the specious present. Given her account of meaning and understanding, the anti-realist is committed to holding that, if a sentence is true, then it is true in virtue of an available warrant. But the stability[3] of that view entails that significantly tensed versions of that claim must hold too. So the anti-realist must also think that if a sentence was true then it was true in virtue of a warrant then available and that if a sentence will be true then it will be true in virtue of a warrant then available. And now she has a problem since she's admitted that "A year ago there was a clump of fritillaries at such and such a spot" might be true in a year's time only in virtue of a warrant *now* available, since, in a year's time, all trace of the fritillaries might have disappeared. So the realist's challenge is premised not on an objectionable metaphysical picture but on the anti-realist's ascription of past, present and future truth as these would be informed by the stability of her philosophical view.

The argument just given is effective only against an anti-realist who is prepared to affirm that truth must coincide with the availability of a warrant. But an anti-realist might resist making this forthright assertion, restricting herself simply to a refusal to assume that truth transcends the availability of a warrant. That is, she may be agnostic rather than forthright. The following argument (courtesy of Wright 1993: 189–90) has the agnostic anti-realist in its sights. At the time I wandered through the meadow, the sentence "There is a clump of fritillaries at such and such a spot" was decidable. So, using the equivalence schema and truth-value links, we have:

> "'There is a clump of fritillaries at such and such a spot' is decidable" was true.

So (since LEM applies to decidable sentences),

> "There is a clump of fritillaries at such and such a spot or there isn't a clump of fritillaries at that spot" was true.

So (by truth-value links),

> "There was a clump of fritillaries at such and such a spot or there wasn't a clump of fritillaries at that spot" is true.

So (since LEM applies only to decidable sentences),

> "There was a clump of fritillaries at such and such a spot" is decidable.

Thus the anti-realist is committed to an absurdity: any past-tense sentence whose present-tense analogue was decidable is itself decidable. That is, the past tense is not a sentential operator that produces undecidability: no statement becomes undecidable as a result of the passage of time.

Dummett acknowledges these difficulties and his final suggestion carries further the idea that the problem here emerges from not taking seriously enough our use of language in time. His thought is that in making an assertion we make a claim of truth. That is, we claim that *there is something* in virtue of which our assertion is true. So asserting implicitly involves an unrestricted quantification. The range of this quantification is, according to realist lights, static. But for the anti-realist the range of quantification is temporally determined: we can only quantify over currently available facts. So the *content* of an act of assertion cannot remain invariant across time since the content is, in part, determined by the range of the quantifier. In other words, when I assert something I hold my assertion responsible to a range of facts. For two assertions to carry the same import they must be responsible to the same range of facts. Similarly apparent conflicts between assertions are not genuine if each is responsible to a different range of facts.[4] Dummett now points out that the range of facts is not invariant across time and thus the import of assertions made at different times will differ. Therefore, in admitting that $Past(S)$ may in a year's time be (absolutely) true in virtue of present (but non-enduring) evidence for S, the anti-realist contends that "he will not in a year's time mean the same by 'absolutely true' as he now means by it: indeed, he cannot by any means at all now express the meaning which he will then attach to the phrase in a year's time" (T&OE: 373). So he accepts the truth-value link but also insists that in a year's time the claim that $Past(S)$ is true will be responsible to a different range of facts and in this way he preserves the stability of his philosophical view.

Similarly when we come to the argument framed in terms of decidability, we begin from a point where we imagine a certain sentence to have been decidable. But here we mean decidable in relation to a range of facts then available. Since those facts are no longer available, we cannot now express that relation of decidability by any claim we can make now. For such a claim will be responsible to currently available facts.

To this Wright objects[5] that "the threatened cost is an inability to explain how there can be such a thing as conflicting views held by protagonists who are sufficiently separated in time" (1993: 194).[6] The anti-realist, according to this view, prevents herself from agreeing or disagreeing with her earlier and later selves. In attempting to explain away the appearance of a conflict in the anti-realist's view Dummett has ruled out the possibility of a conflict. A kind of stability is ensured but only at the cost of a much more radical and thoroughly implausible instability.

In addition, Dummett insists that in thinking of the range of quantification as altering we must not be thinking of a range of things which pass out of existence but can still be referred to. No, the range of quantification is completely unrestricted; what lies outside this range is beyond the reach of reference. But that means that it makes no sense to speak of the range of facts available at some other time: we cannot by any means talk about these facts. How then are we to understand Dummett's explanation of why it is that in a year's time we cannot mean the same by "true" as we now mean by it? If we are to understand the claim that what we mean by "true" will vary from one time to another as more than mere dogmatic insistence we must have some notion of alteration in the range of quantification. But I don't see how we win through to that realization without forming some idea about different, and so other than currently available, such ranges.

So has anti-realism met its nemesis in the truth-value links? Consider a truth-value link:

[S] is true iff [*Past*(S)] will be true.

The link is compelling for an anti-realist since a warrant for asserting the left-hand side just is a warrant for asserting the right-hand side and vice versa. But we have a problem when we then conjoin this thought with these two ideas: (i) the warrant we now have for asserting S may be lost and; (ii) for an anti-realist truth must coincide with the availability of a warrant. For then it seems that the link commits us to the future truth of [*Past*(S)], that is, to the future availability of a warrant for [*Past*(S)], contradicting the transience of warrants – contradicting (i).

Let us retreat for a moment from our problem. When a speaker makes an assertion she asserts something about the world – she makes a statement – but she also makes a claim about what she can achieve. That is, she both intends to convey a piece of information and takes on a certain commitment, namely, she claims to be in possession of, or that she (or another, on her behalf) is able to furnish, an appropriate warrant for her assertion. What, I suggest, we need to think about is the way the tensed truth predicates function in relation to these dual aspects of assertions. On the one hand they seem to function as a way of talking about the past or the future. So, for instance, "[S] will be true" is a way of talking about the future which we might take to be a mere stylistic variant of "*Fut*(S)". On the other hand we think that if, say, [*Past*(S)] will be true at some future time then the *claim* made by asserting [*Past*(S)] at that time will hold. So at that future time it should be possible to furnish an appropriate warrant for asserting $[Past(S)]$. In other words, we think of the tensed truth predicates as applying to the claim made in asserting a sentence. So on the first interpretation the tensed truth predicates apply to the statement made, on the second they apply to the claim made. Let's call the former the statement-reading and the latter the claim-reading.

It is clear that a realist can afford to see more of a gap between the content of an assertion (the statement made) and what counts as a warrant for an assertion. In contrast, the anti-realist takes a characterization of content to be given in terms of (something like) warrants for assertion. So it might appear odd that we should introduce a separation here as a way of helping the anti-realist. However, the distinction persists even on an assertibility-conditions account of meaning. The meaning of, say, "The dog is barking" is characterized by means of its assertion-conditions. But when one asserts that the dog is barking one does not assert that the relevant assertion-conditions obtain. So the specification of meaning is not direct: there need be no informative clause of the form "The dog is barking" means that . . .. When we form an understanding of the past tense we grasp the assertion-conditions of past-tense sentences as functions of the past-tense operator and the meaning of the original sentence. So the assertion-conditions of "The dog was barking" are a product of the meaning of the past-tense operator and the meaning of "The dog is barking". The past-tense sentence thus acquires assertion-conditions that are distinct (though possibly related) to those for asserting that the assertion-conditions for "The dog is barking" were available. Thus, if we treat "was true" ("will be true") as a way of forming the past (future) tense – if we adopt the statement-reading – it will be inappropriate to think of it as asserting the past (future) availability of a warrant, that is, to identify it with the claim-reading.

On the statement-reading the link "$[S]$ will be true iff $Fut(S)$ is true" is trivial: one side of the biconditional is a mere stylistic variation of the other. In addition the modality of a truth predicate may "counter-act" the modality of a sentence. So, for example, the future tense of the truth predicate would expunge the past tense of a sentence: "$[Past(S)]$ will be true" says the same thing as does "S".[7]

Now, in considering the truth-value link a few paragraphs ago, we noted how obvious the link is apt to appear but how problematic it is when we bring its validity together with thoughts about the obtainability of warrants. So a plausible thought is thus that the anti-realist is led into difficulties because she brings herself to accept the truth-value links by adopting the statement-reading of the truth predicates but goes on to interpret them according to the claim-reading. If she separates these two readings her problems might thus dissolve. This, however, is only to gesture at a resolution; we need to see how the suggestion delivers a response to our problematic arguments.

Before we do so, I want to consider an objection to the account. Arguably, we are inclined to think that a warrant for asserting either "*Past*(S)" or "[S] was true" must be related to there having been a warrant for S, in which case the two readings seem dangerously close to collapsing into one another. Presumably, insofar as this thought is indeed attractive, its pull derives from supposing that the best time to observe an event is when it is happening. After this time, evidence of the event can only decay, and evidence which survives to a future time must be causally related to the original event and so must have been available (in some sense) at intervening times. It is by no means clear that such thoughts are always moot but that need not concern us here.[8] Rather what needs to be made clear is that they pose no problem to the present approach. But that should quickly be apparent, for the application of these ideas is only to genuine past-tense sentences: sentences of the form, "*Past*(S)" or "[S] was true" where S is not significantly tensed. But the problematic cases were those in which we were led, by the truth-value links, to acknowledge (say) the *future* truth of a *past*-tense sentence. (Recall that our problems emerged from thinking about the statement "There was a clump of fritillaries at such and such a spot" made a year's hence.)

Where have we arrived? The truth-value links have been admitted as truistic on a reading of the tensed truth predicates as modes of transforming the tense of a sentence, that is, on the statement-reading. Given this, and given too that the truth-value links seem so intuitively compelling, I shall recommend the statement-reading.[9] What we have to do now is to bring this thought together in some coherent fashion with that of the stability of the anti-realist position. Consider once again the forthright anti-realist and her claim that if a sentence is true then it is true in virtue of an available warrant, that is, if [S] is true then there is a warrant for asserting [S]. If this view is stable then we seem to be committed to a claim such as the following: if [S] was true then there was a warrant for asserting [S]. And, since (unlike in the case discussed in the previous paragraph) substitutions for S are unrestricted, we might have: if [*Fut*(S)] was true then there was a warrant for asserting [*Fut*(S)]. This is clearly problematic in cases where we have a sentence S which is currently assertible, since then "[*Fut(S)*]] was true" will be assertible, on the statement-reading, and we shall be committed to the consequent, which would be absurd.

However, notice that on the statement-reading of the tensed truth predicates the original conditional is equivalent to: if *Past(S)* then there was a warrant for asserting *S*. And we've just noted that this (though arguably supportable in some cases) is *not* a general consequence of anti-realist views. So the correct conclusion seems to be, not that this reading of the tensed truth predicate is problematic in itself, but that, in the context of this reading, the conditional gives the wrong expression to the stability of anti-realism. How then are we to express that stability? Surely there's no significant problem here. We cannot, on the statement-reading, use the tensed truth predicates to capture the appropriate thought but we can use a truth predicate which isn't significantly tensed, so we might, for instance, say that whenever a sentence is true it is then assertible. Or we can focus on the meaning of the original conditional which in anti-realist ears doesn't say anything very controversial since it holds just in case we can convert a warrant for asserting "[*S*] is true" into a warrant for asserting "[*S*] is assertible". And this we can do on the basis of the simplest reflection. Now the stability we require can be established by noting that this reflective ability is temporally stable.

Let us return to the argument framed in terms of decidability. A step in that argument takes us from something of the form, "[[*S*] is decidable] was true" to something of the form "[*S* ∨ −*S*] was true". The inference depends upon the equivalence: [*S*] is decidable iff *S* ∨ −*S*. We then substitute one equivalent statement for another within the context of the predicate "was true". Now "was true" on the statement-reading is being read as a past-tense operator, so what we have is an instance of the, generally invalid, schema:

Past(*S*)
S iff *T*
Past(*T*)[10]

The schema won't in general hold since it may be the case, for instance, that Chad was happy and that Chad is happy iff Pepper is. Still it would not follow from this that Pepper was happy. Being happy just in case Pepper is, is an accidental property of Chad which he may not have possessed at the earlier time when he was happy (when, perhaps, he had not yet met Pepper). But do we, in the present case, have a reason for rejecting the inference?

Let's try to mimic this reasoning as far as possible. We assume that S was decidable. We also know that S has the property of being decidable just in case it or its negation holds. That is a property we currently ascribe. It is not an accidental property so at this point our reasoning must part company with that just rehearsed. The question is, does S possess the property of having been decidable just in case it or its negation held, that is, just in case $Past(S \lor \neg S)$? To claim that a sentence was decidable is to claim that we possessed a decision procedure. If we currently possess a decision procedure we assume[11] it has a determinate outcome. And this justifies our use of LEM here. But when we transpose this into the past we cannot assume that it is now determinate what the determinate outcome would have been or was (assuming that the decision procedure was implemented), for that is to assume determinacy where we have no decision procedure. We would be ignoring the fact that the past tense gives rise to undecidability. Now it is, of course, true that the realist will not be persuaded by this reasoning; for her the inference is likely to seem solid enough. But, given that the anti-realist was supposedly faced with an incoherence in her own position, it is enough for her to voice distinctively anti-realist objections to the inference.

Does this solve the problem for the anti-realist? I think it deals with the problem posed by the truth-value links. But lurking in the wings of this discussion is a more difficult and more general problem. Let's assume that we have a score card from a tennis match which informs us that on a certain point the first serve was good but the point went against serve. We infer that, since the receiver returned the serve, the return shot was either a forehand or a backhand,[12] although, to be sure, there is now no knowing which. So it seems we have a case of a sentence which is true but not verifiable: the shot was a forehand but this is not verifiable, or the shot was a backhand but this is not verifiable. But this is a little too quick. At present we cannot exclude the possibility of a verification since we don't know what future evidence may come to light: an enthusiast may dig up a photograph which, fortuitously, settles the question. So what we have is: the shot was a forehand but this is not verified, or the shot was a backhand but this is not verified. Thus since one or other disjunct must be true, there is a sentence which is true and unverified but for which we lack a means of decision. So we cannot exclude the *possibility* of unverifiable truths: since the sentences are undecidable we cannot exclude the possibility that they cannot be decided, in which case one of the sentences is true but unverifiable. Thus it would seem that only agnostic anti-realism is viable.

However, more than this, what we've been given is an argument for the application of LEM[13] to a sentence which is not decidable. Let's reconsider the form of that argument. We reason from a fact about the past, namely, the truth of "The serve was returned", to the truth of the disjunction, "The return shot was a forehand or it was a backhand." So we combine a particular piece of knowledge about the past with a general knowledge of tennis (its rules and how it is played) to yield the disjunctive truth. That is, we assume that our knowledge about tennis extends unproblematically to this (past) case. In other words, we take a kind of stability to be in place here. Given this stability, we find ourselves committed to a disjunction where, problematically for the anti-realist, we have no warrant (nor any means of obtaining a warrant) for either disjunct.[14]

It is not clear quite what the consequences of this position are for anti-realism. Certainly, they are not immediately damning since the argument doesn't appeal to a notion of truth. When we give a semantic justification of LEM we make use of a notion of truth which transcends verification (in the presence of undecidable sentences no other notion of truth will yield a validation of LEM[15]). But here the argument doesn't appeal to a notion of truth so the question is rather the reverse: are we committed by the argument to an anti-realistically repugnant notion of truth? Clearly some liberalization of the notion of truth beyond that of the forthright anti-realist is called for. But what liberalizations are consistent with anti-realist scruples?

I want, for the moment, to leave that question hanging. We shall return to it after considering the case of mathematics.

Anti-realism and mathematics

In Chapter 6 we looked at some of Dummett's thoughts on the justification of deduction. There we saw that he tries to defend the project as possible; there is, he claims, no crippling circularity in the enterprise. But the idea of a justification of deduction can appear problematic from a rather different angle. On the one hand, we want our account of deduction to show that the inferential steps are, in some sense, *legitimate*. On the other hand, we also want to be able to explain how it is that inference is *useful* to us: how is it that inference enables us to make epistemic progress, to move from the known to the unknown?

If you were a realist these two aspects of deduction would not give rise to a worrisome tension. An inferential step is valid just in case it is guaranteed to take us from truths only to truths. That is, inference is valid just in case it is truth preserving. Inference is epistemically useful because it takes us from truths which we have acknowledged to truths which we haven't acknowledged: it provides a means of acknowledging these truths.

The anti-realist has a more difficult time in reconciling these two aspects of inference. She won't help herself to a notion of truth in explicating the validity of inference but rather will fix on the way inference preserves some epistemic pedigree, or, equivalently, she will think of truth in epistemic terms and thus will think of validity as the preservation of an epistemic property. So, for her, an inference will be valid just in case it is guaranteed to take us from premises for which we possess warrants to a conclusion for which we possess a warrant. Thus, it seems that the validity of the inference renders the warrant it provides otiose; the inferential warrant is valid just in case we "already" possess a (non-inferential) warrant for the conclusion, that is, just in case the inferential warrant is redundant. The only solution for the anti-realist is, Dummett admits, to make a concession to the realist and to allow that truth might transcend our possession of a warrant. In this case the inference will be truth preserving (and so valid) when it takes us from premises for which we possess warrants to a conclusion for which we *could* possess a (non-inferential) warrant. It is epistemically productive because it provides us with a warrant where otherwise we would not have one, even though we would have been able, in some sense, to obtain one. We might put the point in terms of direct or canonical means of establishing a proposition and indirect means of so doing. Inference need provide no more than an indirect means of establishing the truth of a proposition. Since it constitutes a genuine establishment of the proposition's truth we thereby make epistemic progress. The indirect means of establishing a proposition as true shows the availability of a way, effective in practice or, perhaps, only in principle, of obtaining a direct warrant for the truth of a proposition. So we can view truth as the availability, in some sense, of a warrant and see inference as truth preserving.

An instance of this syndrome emerged in Chapter 5 in the discussion of the distinction between canonical proofs and proofs as more generally conceived. There we noted that if we were to have any use for disjunctions we should see ourselves as entitled to assert them on grounds other than the possession of a (canonical) proof of one or other disjunct. Thus a proof of a disjunction was taken to be a construction of which it could be recognized that it yields a (canonical) proof of one or other disjunct (without us necessarily knowing which). Since proofs are truth conferring the truth of the disjunction (and hence of other statements) could not be held to consist in the possession of a canonical proof: truth only coincides with the availability, in some sense, of a canonical proof.

Let us focus for a moment on what sense of availability we need here. One thought would be that we insist that obtaining the canonical proof or direct warrant be something which we are actually capable of achieving: a proof would establish that we are actually capable of achieving a canonical proof of its conclusion. So its value in epistemic terms would be purely pragmatic: it would save us the expense of time and effort involved in actually constructing the canonical proof. On the other hand we might think that the indirect warrant or proof provides a means that is only effective in principle of achieving a direct warrant or canonical proof. Thus we would take a proposition to be true just in case we could see that, abstracting from our contingent cognitive limitations, or, alternatively, imagining those cognitive capacities to be extended by arbitrary finite amounts, we could envisage the production of canonical proofs or direct warrants. But this provision won't be possible for us. For instance, the anti-realist thinks that it is decidable whether any given finite number is prime even though the number may be so large as to render it impossible for anyone or for the human race collectively to determine whether or not it is prime. On this reading inference would have very real epistemic value since it would provide us with a way of establishing the truth of propositions which otherwise we would have no way of establishing. Thus it seems that the anti-realist has some work for a notion of truth which equates with the availability in principle of a warrant. But is she entitled to such a notion?

The problem is that she seems to be helping herself here to a notion which suffers from the same defects as the realist's notion of truth does. The realist assumes that any sentence has a determinate truth-value irrespective of our ability to determine that value and the anti-realist complains that there is nothing a speaker is able to do by means of an exercise of recognitional capacities which shows that she has succeeded in conferring such a meaning on her sentences. Now the anti-realist assumes that any sentence has a determinate truth-value just in case we have a means, effective only in principle, for determining that value. But since the means of determining the truth-value is effective only in principle there is nothing *we* can do by means of an exercise of *our* recognitional capacities which shows that we have succeeded in conferring such a meaning on our sentences. To put the point slightly differently, if the assumption that a sentence has a determinate truth-value must be justified by appeal to the way we are able to employ it in response to recognizable circumstances, then there is nothing we are able to do with a sentence which demonstrates its possession of a determinate truth-value unless we are *actually* capable of determining that value. What we might be able to do were we quicker, more acute, more sensitive, longer lived, more robust and so on, is irrelevant to the question of what we are able to do. And to assume determinacy of truth-value under these hypothesized circumstances is to assume that the meaning of a sentence transcends the use we are capable of making of it. So the broad form of the challenge is that the anti-realist's notion of truth (linked to decidability in principle) is susceptible to precisely the same form of attack that she launches against the realist. Thus, to have a consistent and motivated position, the anti-realist should adopt a more extreme notion of truth linked to decidability in *practice*. We will call this form of anti-realism "strict finitism", to be distinguished from the less extreme form which we will call "intuitionism". The terms derive from the philosophy of mathematics and are apt since we shall pursue the discussion with particular reference to mathematics.

In "Wang's Paradox" (T&OE: essay 15) Dummett begins by giving voice to this threatened instability in the intuitionist's position and he then goes on to argue that strict finitism is itself incoherent. Thus, unless we are to be forced to conclude that there is something amiss with the anti-realist challenge, we had better find a suitable disanalogy between the intuitionist and the realist. I shan't go into the question of the incoherence of strict finitism. Rather I want simply to focus on the question of whether there is an appropriate disanalogy.[16]

A position that linked truth to what has actually been verified would clearly be absurd and unmotivated. It would be absurd since it could find no room for the usefulness of deductive inference; to be truth preserving, all indirect means of establishing the truth of a sentence would have to coincide not merely with the availability of a direct means of verification but with the actual existence of a direct verification. The indirect method would then be redundant. The position would be unmotivated since the manifestation constraint is itself framed in modal terms. It does not insist that every aspect of a speaker's understanding of an expression be manifested in her use of it but only that it be so manifest*able*. One may, of course, grasp the meaning of an expression without having a need or encountering the opportunity to use it. But one understands the expression because one could use it appropriately were such circumstances to present themselves. Indeed it is hard otherwise to see how we could come to understand novel utterances for, presumably, that understanding accrues from a prior understanding of the component expressions and their mode of combination. But then that aspect of our understanding of the components must have been present but unmanifested, though clearly manifestable.

Understanding an expression is to be in a certain state, it is possession of a (certain sort of) capacity. Possession of that capacity is not compromised by the mistakes one makes due to tiredness, lack of attention or forgetfulness. Nor does one necessarily cease to be in that state when asleep or gravely ill. So possession of the capacity is manifested only when conditions are suitably favourable.[17] But what capacity or capacities does one manifest possession of in performing a certain action? Let's say Archie runs 100 m in 11.2 seconds after little or no preparation. Thereby he certainly demonstrates a capacity to run 100 m in less than 11.5 seconds. Perhaps too (to the trained eye of a coach) he demonstrates a capacity to run 100 m in less than 10 seconds (after suitable training and preparation). But certainly he fails to manifest a capacity to run 100 m in less than 9 seconds.

Now we can think of the debate between the intuitionist and strict finitist in these terms. The strict finitist will limit talk of capacities to what, at most, the experienced coach will be prepared to ascribe. The intuitionist, however, wants to say that the runner's performance warrants ascription to him of the capacity-in-principle to run any finite distance in any finite time. We need to think both about what warrants ascriptions of capacities-in-principle and what is warranted given an ascription of a capacity-in-principle. On the one hand, we might think of capacities-in-principle in terms of subjunctive conditionals involving capacities. So the runner would have the capacity-in-principle to run any given finite distance in any given finite time since were his actual capacities to be appropriately finitely extended he would be able to run that distance in that time. It then seems reasonably clear that exhibition of the runner's capacity enables ascription to him of the capacity-in-principle. But, returning to the original debate, we would then want to know why possession of a capacity-in-principle to decide a sentence's truth-value justifies belief that that truth-value is determinate.

We might press this point by constructing another position: ideal verificationism, which hinges on the possession of ideal capacities.

Then we might say that the runner has the ideal-capacity to run infinitely far infinitely quickly since an infinite extension of his actual capacities would result in his so doing. But why would possession of an ideal-capacity (like a capacity-in-principle) justify belief in bivalence?

A rather different tactic would be to eschew the subjunctive conditional explanation of capacities-in-principle (which anyway, in its use of the notion of finitude, runs into problems of circularity[18]) and instead to attempt to assimilate ascription of capacities-in-principle to that of capacities. Let us say that I have a life-threatening heart condition. I am, indeed, about to die. However, I am as mentally alert and active as I always have been. If I am confronted by a problem whose solution involves tediously long but quite straightforward working out, so much so that I am bound to have shuffled off my mortal coil before completing it, then (questions of consciousness after death aside) there is a sense in which I am unable to solve the problem. But, equally, there is a sense in which I am as able as ever I was to solve the problem. In the relevant intellectual sense I still possess the capacity to solve the problem. Now this, no doubt, raises a significant difficulty: that of explaining the sense of "relevant". I shall delay briefly addressing that question, and, when I do so, I shan't be offering a solution to it. Rather I shall attempt to relate that question to one about the correct interpretation of intuitionistic negation. But first I want to pursue our original question a little further.

Our problem was that the strict finitist cannot understand why possession of a capacity-in-principle to decide a sentence justifies believing that it has a determinate truth-value. The answer is to point out that the strict finitist believes that possession of the relevant capacity (no matter whether or not it is exercised) does justify that belief and then to insist that in the cases that matter to the intuitionist we do possess the relevant capacity. We possess the relevant capacity because whatever it is that bars us exercising the capacity is extraneous: to borrow from Russell, it *is* a mere medical impossibility to determine the primality of some enormously large number. For here we are concerned with intellectual capacities. In contrast, Archie doesn't manifest possession of the capacity to run any finite distance in any finite time because here the physical bar to his completion of these tasks is relevant to his possession of what is a physical capacity. So, far from there being a slide from intuitionism into strict finitism, there is, provided an apt notion of relevance can be made out, no stable strict finitist position which doesn't inflate into intuitionism.[19]

The contrast between this strategy and that involving subjunctive (or counterfactual) conditionals needs to be clarified. It isn't that those conditional claims cease to be warranted. Rather those claims are substantiated by the present way of looking at capacities (ascription of relevant capacities becomes the categorical base for the conditional assertions). In focusing on our practice of ascribing capacities we avoid three problems: (i) that of explaining what warrants the subjunctive conditional; (ii) that of explaining the notion of finitude used in the conditionals; and (iii) that of explaining why the truth of the conditional warrants belief in determinacy of truth-value. However, as already remarked, we conjure up another problem: that of explaining the notion of relevance. Let's consider that problem now.

For an intuitionist warrant for asserting $-P$ is a warrant for asserting that it is impossible to obtain a warrant for P. But then it seems that once the four-minute warning has been issued we should be entitled to assert the negation of any unsolved (moderately difficult) mathematical problem.[20] Clearly what we want to say here is that imminent consumption in a nuclear conflagration[21] is not relevant to our capacities to solve mathematical problems. Dummett himself is unhappy with this somewhat pat formulation and prefers instead to think of the negation of P as a conditional: "If P then Q", in which, in order to guarantee the law of *ex falso quodlibet*, Q is taken to be the infinite product of atomic sentences in the language (here, the language of mathematics).[22] So, on this account, relevance would be determined by circumscribing the language to that of the relevant region of language. Now, whether or not Dummett's account is to be adopted, the upshot will be that announcement of the four-minute warning won't provide grounds for denying an unsolved mathematical problem (for that knowledge won't enable us to infer the truth of each atomic mathematical sentence). In general the point is that to arrive at a conception of intuitionistic negation we need to be able to deal with conditions which, although they render provision of a proof of P impossible, don't justify asserting $-P$. These, precisely, are conditions that place a bar on an exercise of our capacities. So *if* we can form a conception of intuitionistic negation then we can form a conception of relevant capacities which will justify the intuitionistic conception of truth.

Truth and verification

We have extended the notion of truth, first, beyond mere possession of a warrant (or verification) to the availability of a warrant (or verification). Without such an extension the usefulness of inference becomes impossible to explain. A second phase of extension was then called for in order to avoid strict finitism. For an intuitionist the availability of a warrant must be interpreted as a warrant which *could* be obtained by an exercise of the relevant capacity, or, as it is more usually put, which could, in principle, be obtained. The second phase of extension has not been fully justified. Rather I've simply pointed out how deeply the relevant notions are embedded in the intuitionistic point of view, suggesting too that they coincide with our usual practices of ascribing capacities. So, although it doesn't coincide with possession of a warrant, truth is reducible to, or is explained in terms of, possession of a warrant.

I want now to close this discussion by returning to the problem posed at the end of the discussion of the past. There we found that we could use the temporal stability of certain of our views[23] combined with knowledge of particular past facts to infer other truths about the past. Those truths seem to hold yet are not connected (even in the comparatively etiolated sense admitted by the intuitionist) with a capacity to furnish warrants. So, for instance, in the example we were discussing, we infer that a shot must have been a forehand or a backhand but have no capacity to determine which (unless, absurdly, you allow a capacity to travel back in time). Similarly we might endorse a statement such as "All Fs are Gs" yet not have a capacity to verify of every F that it is a G. For it may be that there are Fs that we cannot be presented with (Fs which have ceased to be or which inhabit far-flung reaches of the universe), or there may be Fs that we cannot guarantee to recognize as such or, finally, even if we recognize something as an F we may not be able to recognize that it is a G since the relevant portion of F's career may now be history. The point is that, since the scope of the universal quantifier will include non-observables and/or partially observables, its truth won't be linked to a capacity to verify each of its instances. So these instances must be true independently of our ability to verify them. Now, on many occasions, the universal generalization will be held on inductive grounds. In such cases the inference will be ampliative (not guaranteed to be truth preserving) and, although we shall want some story from the anti-realist, the issue isn't pressing and is linked to more general questions about inductive support. But clearly there will be other cases where the generalization isn't held on inductive grounds. To use an, admittedly somewhat contrived, example, the generalization "All spotted things are of more than one colour" is guaranteed to be true (so is not an inductive generalization) and includes within its scope objects which we are incapable of observing appropriately. So there are instances of the generalization which *must* be true but cannot be observed to be so. The temporal stability of many of our views, which underpins so much of the syndrome surrounding the truth-value links, provides just one means of extending the scope of generalizations in this way. Similarly, Dummett points out that in our application of the results of inference to the past we shall very often be forced to admit the truth of statements not because we can verify them but because we *could have* verified them. The example he uses is that of Euler's Königsberg bridge theorem. The theorem states that, if on a journey around Königsberg one crosses every bridge at least once, then one will have crossed at least one bridge more than once. The theorem is convincing because it enables one to convert (an appropriate) set of observations which establish that one crossed every bridge at least once into a set of observations establishing that one crossed at least one bridge more than once. But naturally we think that the theorem applies to historical cases of having crossed the bridges of Königsberg and in these cases we obviously cannot transform the one set of observations into the other. What we are inclined to say is that the theorem still applies, not because we are able to observe a crossing of a bridge twice, but because we *could have observed* this. If we admit this much then anti-realism about the past is indeed dead: the past is as determinate as the present is.[24]

One tempting line of thought is thus to reject any constraint on truth which is based simply on our current epistemic capacities. Rather truth will be constrained by what could be observed were we appropriately situated either in space or in time. The questions then are: (i) what is left as a focus of disagreement between realist and anti-realist? and (ii) is this concession to realism compatible with the basis of (Dummettian) anti-realism?

I shall look at each question in turn. However, before doing so it is worth noting one position which fails to discern any concession to realism here. On this approach we simply allow a notion of truth to be characterized in terms of our inferential practices (including, perhaps, principles such as the truth-value links). In this case we couldn't invoke the notion of truth in justifying those practices, which would be self-standing, responsible to nothing. Dummett[25] takes this to be Wittgenstein's approach and he condemns it as a nihilistic view. Truth, on this account, is a mere human construct, a product of what we agree to say is true.

Let's consider our first question. The dispute between realist and anti-realist centres on their respective treatments of undecidable sentences. The sources of undecidability are our use of tense operators, quantification over unsurveyable domains and subjunctive conditionalization. (Perhaps we should also add to this our talk of the very distant and our talk of the microscopic.) The concession to realism forces us to abandon any dispute over the past. However, it is not at all clear that realism about the future is forced on us.[26] And, though there might be reasons for saying that the instances of a quantified statement are determinate in truth-value, there is no argument from there to a position which takes the quantified statement itself to be determinate in truth-value, otherwise intuitionism trades on an incoherent notion of arithmetic truth. So the concession to realism doesn't abolish the possibility of focuses of disagreement. The real question is whether it undermines the basis for the anti-realist's dispute with the realist.

This is our second question. What it is asking is whether we can reconcile this new conception of truth with the supposed success of the anti-realist's challenge to the realist's conception of truth. That challenge was premised on a requirement that one's understanding be manifestable. Thus we can either argue that the new conception of truth is not challenged under the original interpretation of the manifestation requirement or that it calls for a different interpretation of the manifestation requirement but one on which realist truth is still ruled out. I shall consider both sorts of argument, each in turn.

One might argue that the concession to realism does not run into tension with the manifestation requirement since we can supply an anti-realistically acceptable account of understanding. To be sure there won't be any grounds provided by that account of understanding for supposing that truth has the properties that we now attribute to it. Rather we are forced to make those attributions in order to make sense of aspects of our practice. And here we shall need to point to a disanalogy between these aspects of our practice and our use of LEM. In the latter case revision is a feasible (though perhaps unpalatable) option: we need simply to revise an element of inferential practice. But in the present case the expense of spurning the new conception of truth is to give up making sense of whole regions of our language: our talk of the past and the practice of inference itself. Here a revisionary stance just is not an option.[27] This position involves a rejection of Fregeanism[28] since it recognizes semantic facts which aren't justified by appeal to the theory of understanding. However, an obvious route to full-fledged realism doesn't emerge because we have only admitted that we can make use of a semantic notion which is justified by the character of speakers' understanding or which is required to make sense of whole regions of our practice. It isn't evident that a realist notion of truth is needed or is available in either of these capacities.

Another sort of argument would be to retain the Fregean assumption but to reinterpret the manifestation requirement. The point might be that speakers manifest (implicit) grasp of a given semantic concept if that concept is required to make sense of an irrevisable aspect of their practice. Thus in talking about the past a speaker manifests grasp of the new notion of truth because it is impossible to make sense of such talk without appealing to such a notion of truth. Again, given this notion of irrevisability, the very same point as made in the last paragraph shows that we do not immediately usher in a realist notion of truth.[29]

Difficulties attend either strategy. Both place a great deal of weight on the notions of irrevisability and of making sense of a practice. It is far from clear that we can firm up these notions sufficiently to support the weight placed on them. The decision between the strategies will hinge on whether we should relinquish the Fregean assumption or revise the manifestation requirement. Dummett never seriously questions and so never argues substantially for the Fregean assumption.[30] In presenting himself with the problem posed by adoption of the new notion of truth he returns to the meaning-theoretic view that spawned the challenge for the realist notion of truth. He notes that it consists in a principle – "that meaning is encapsulated in what we learn when we learn to use statements of that form" (1998: 137) – and an ancillary thesis – "all that we learn, when we learn the use of a given form of statement, was what constitutes the verification of a statement of that form, or what establishes its truth and hence conclusively warrants an assertion of it" (*ibid.*). The principle he regards as unassailable but he questions the ancillary thesis. In other words, he insists on the manifestation requirement but considers how best it should be interpreted. One of his most recent statements on the matter remains inconclusive and, perhaps, his words are best left to speak for themselves.

I regret that I do not feel able at present to offer a clear formulation of the necessary qualification; but it surely involves a fairly substantial concession to realism. We must concede that our understanding of statements about the past incorporates, not merely a knowledge of the grounds for asserting them, but a grasp of how they represent reality: how acceptance of them contributes to the picture which we form of the world we inhabit and with which we operate to guide our actions. I am aware that this is intolerably vague. Our acquisition of the concept of the past, and our resulting grasp of the past tense, are from any standpoint, things of which it is exceedingly difficult to give a satisfactory account. To do so must result in a modification, and a deepening, of the way in which a constructivist conception of meaning is presented and defended.   (1998: 137–8)

Summary

We've looked in this final chapter at two hard cases for anti-realism. In the case of the past the problem arose from an acceptance of the truth-value links. When we combine these with an acceptance of the stability of the anti-realist's views and of the transience of warrants then we seem able to force the anti-realist into incoherence. Dummett's solution to the case of the past is, as he admits, hardly a solution at all. It saves the position from incoherence but only by sacrificing almost all claims to any plausibility. I have tried to do a little better on the anti-realist's behalf by offering what is, in effect, a deflationary account of the tensed truth predicates. The solution, if it is one, enables the anti-realist to accept the truth-value links but then defuses the consequences of that acceptance by showing that, so construed, the tensed truth predicates are inapt for expression of the stability of the anti-realist's views. Dummett won't be happy with my solution because he thinks it can only find a proper home in a general deflationary account of truth, and this he rejects.

In a similar vein, Dummett's discussion of the mathematical case left the anti-realist position in some difficulties. Here the threat was that the anti-realist's argument against realism can be recycled as an argument against intuitionism. The upshot seems to be a slide for the anti-realist into a seemingly incoherent strict finitism. Again I've offered some thoughts which might help the anti-realist but these thoughts were a long way short of conclusive. I suggested that a notion of relevance is in operation in our ordinary ascription of capacities and used this suggestion to argue that *in the relevant sense* we possess the capacities required to justify the intuitionist's notion of truth. This, however, left it obscure how the requisite notion of relevance is to be cashed. I left that question hanging but hung it together with a question about the intuitionistic notion of negation.

The final part of the chapter developed a more general worry about the anti-realist's notion of truth. The upshot of this discussion was that if we accept the obligation to justify our practices (in particular, our inferential practices) then we shall be forced to adopt a notion of truth which goes well beyond what can be justified within the framework of the original argument for anti-realism. So either we shall have to concede the realist's position or we shall have to reconsider that framework. I've sketched some directions in which that framework might be modified. The crucial idea here is that we find some way to legitimate semantic concepts which are required to make sense of an irrevisable aspect of our practice. The notions of *being-required-to-make-sense* and of *irrevisability* were, however, left thoroughly vague. There may be some grounds here for anti-realist hope that we can revise the framework in a manner that doesn't play completely into the realist's hands. But equally the nature of that revision is still radically unclear; the questions in this area of philosophy are as pressing and as intriguing as ever.

Conclusion

This conclusion, and indeed this book, are not a summation of Dummett's major contributions to philosophy. I am not in a position to offer such a summary, not having an encompassing view of his work. But neither is anyone else in such a position. Dummett is an active philosopher who is temperamentally disposed to question and rethink many of his most basic assumptions and views. It would take an unholy alliance of arrogance and recklessness to anticipate the future direction his philosophy might take. So, more modestly, what are some of the broader lessons of this book's engagement with his philosophy?

Dummett's approach to philosophy is both distinctive and, in some respects, out of vogue. Although he is a theoretical philosopher he is acutely aware of the dangers of vacuously theorizing in philosophy and he sees philosophical theorizing as quite distinct from scientific theorizing. Dummett's philosophy is an attempt to understand ourselves and the way we represent the world. We aim at uncovering a certain class of truths and thus employ the most powerful elements of our cognitive architecture: for instance, systematic theory building and the techniques of mathematical logic. But we aim to understand ourselves from our own point of view; we don't seek an understanding of ourselves as natural phenomena. Moreover the *philosophical* attempt to understand is not a self-contained, purely reflective business. It emerges from, and, in some ways, is continuous with, an essential feature of normal human life, namely, the way we reflectively engage with one another and with our practices. The philosopher is not alienated from her mundane self, rather she pushes elements of that self further than her mundane necessities invite her to.

Perhaps the one element of Dummett's thought that most clearly exhibits these aspects of his philosophical approach is his insistence on molecularity. That requirement emerged again and again as informing aspects of his theorizing. Although motivated by considerations about the nature of language and of linguistic understanding, Dummett thinks that we would be failing to make matters intelligible were we to lose sight of the requirement. His revisionism, an element in his thinking that sets him apart from so many of his contemporaries, would evaporate were it not infused with the substance of the molecularity requirement.

Of course it would be absurd to claim that Dummett's approach and view have broadly been vindicated. They are still too contentious and too unclear for any claim of that sort. Let me select, what I take to be, some of the most pressing difficulties.

In the theory of meaning the character of speakers' knowledge of language is, perhaps, the most crucial and vexed question. It is crucial because so many issues pivot on how it is answered. The manifestation requirement is motivated by a constraint on what it is to make ascriptions of knowledge. What counts as an adequate manifestation of a piece of knowledge will depend on the character of the piece of knowledge we are ascribing. At many points, we found that a reason for insisting on molecularity derived from a need to ascribe knowledge, in the sense of an awareness, of meanings to speakers. Full-bloodedness relates to the question of how, in what terms, we are to characterize speakers' knowledge of language. Despite this, the question is thoroughly vexed, as Dummett admits. To see this we might begin from, what seems at first to be, a surprising feature of Dummett's work, namely, the comparatively scant attention he devotes to Wittgenstein's considerations about following a rule. But his discussion of knowledge of language is plausibly a recapitulation in Dummettian terms of Wittgenstein's worry: knowledge of language cannot be purely practical since this leaves out of the picture the way use is guided by knowledge of meaning but neither can it be wholly explicit since this is question begging or regressive.[1]

Dummett's characterization of realism is often confused with a rejection of the particular brand of anti-realism he is, again confusedly, often seen as espousing. When perceived in this way his characterization of realism is apt to seem too narrow. However even if we appreciate the full scope of his recommendation it may well be that there are focuses of the debate to which Dummett's semantic approach is blind. Nonetheless I find it difficult to deny that Dummett has succeeded in capturing an important and general element in the realist outlook. But it is worth being clear that the *point* of his characterization cannot be divorced from his views about the relation between the semantic theory and the meaning-theory for a region of language. If Dummett's Fregean assumption is wrong then it is simply not clear that the role of a semantic theory is to form the base of a meaning-theory. In which case our choice of semantic theory won't be dictated by general considerations about the nature of meaning and understanding. Dummett's thought that the latter provide a principled way of deciding between semantic theories, and thus of resolving the metaphysical dispute, would then falter; the point of his characterization of realism would, at the very least, be threatened. Fregeanism is not current philosophical orthodoxy and, although it is an assumption which he has defended, Dummett hasn't provided a clear argument in its favour.

The theory of meaning can only be used to resolve the metaphysical dispute (identified with adoption of a particular semantic theory) if the theory of meaning is itself metaphysically neutral. It is far from clear that this is true. An adequate theory of meaning must cohere with a view about the conditions in which it makes sense to ascribe understanding. But can we arrive at such a view without taking on metaphysical commitments? It may well seem that statements which make ascriptions of understanding are as metaphysically challenging as any other to which we have turned our attention.

In the final stages of the book we seemed to have uncovered a tension relating to the notion of truth. The notion which we arrive at when we work up from what is needed in order to make sense of a practice, or to which a practice seems to commit us, seems to go beyond what we arrive at when we work down from our general considerations about the nature of meaning and understanding. The downward approach is driven by an insistence on the publicity of meaning, given content in the form of the manifestation constraint. The manifestation constraint is, however, imprecise and it is not clear whether and how it can be liberalized so as to chime with the notion of truth delivered by the upward approach.

Let me leave matters here, with this series of questions. Dummett's work may not have settled these questions (and others) but this doesn't undermine the value of his philosophy. These all seem to be good questions to be asking and – although I am mystified by those who claim that it is philosophy's questions that matter, not its answers – the value of Dummett's philosophy lies, at least in part, in the way it has raised and connected a set of crucial philosophical problems.

Appendix 1

Mood, force and convention

Let's consider Davidson's argument against any attempt to base an account of force on mood. His first step is to pull apart mood and force by highlighting the obvious fact that an utterance of one or another force can be made by uttering a sentence in a number of different moods. An assertion may be made by uttering an interrogative ("Did you notice that Joan was wearing her purple hat again?"), an enquiry may be made by uttering an imperative ("Tell me who won the third race"), and so on.[1] Now Davidson's commonplace observation won't come as news to anyone who wants to base force on mood. Rather they will insist on the connection but explain away Davidson's cases as somehow deviant, either because they diverge from the normal or because they diverge from the conventionally established link between mood and force. Davidson finds the first thought muddled since it either fails to explain why a command issued by means of an indicative is abnormal or involves a spurious appeal to statistical regularities.

The appeal to convention is more interesting but ultimately, he claims, just as spurious. Although he allows that there may be conditions that guarantee that an utterance is, say, an assertion, Davidson doesn't think that these conditions are conventional in character. If there were such conventions then we should be able to say what they are. But any such conventions could be exploited by a prankster or actor in conjuring the (false) appearance of having made an assertion. Also, if such conventions operated, we shouldn't be in doubt (as we often are) over whether an assertion has indeed been made.

Davidson's fundamental point is that conventions cannot determine the interpretation of an utterance since these conventions can always be used to serve different extra-linguistic ends. To know what sort of utterance is being made we need to know what its purpose is and the (conventionally established) mood of the sentence is no guide to that. Or, rather, the latter may, in fact, be a guide to the former but its being so is not a product of what it is to make an assertion, issue a command, and so on. There is no set of conventions that are constitutive of these linguistic acts.

Dummett denies this.[2] His denial, of course, doesn't involve a rejection of the phenomena, which initiate Davidson's argument, but it does reject Davidson's description of them. Davidson points out that the force of an utterance of an imperative (e.g. "Give me your phone number") may be that of asking a question. This enables him to pull apart mood and force and thus to go on to point out that any conventional feature of language can subserve quite different extra-linguistic ends. Dummett objects by redescribing the case and introducing a distinction in order to do so. The utterance "Give me your phone number" is indeed an issue of a command but its being so does not mean that, in the circumstances, it cannot serve the same function as the request "What is your phone number?" Dummett wants to distinguish what is said from the point of saying it. A command uttered in an obviously non-authoritative tone or with an unlikely content for a command (e.g. "Have a good day") may serve the same function as a request or an expression of a wish. But these facts shouldn't confuse us into thinking that the utterance was not a command, it is simply that, in these cases, in order fully to understand the utterance we have to answer the further question of what the point of issuing a command with that content in these circumstances is. The conventional significance of the utterance is not undermined by this further (extra-linguistic) process of interpretation; rather it provides the basis for such interpretation of the point of the utterance. Or, better, Dummett's view is that what makes an utterance an assertion or command is its role within a certain conventionally determined practice of making assertions and issuing commands. A relevant feature that determines when an utterance is an assertion, say, will be the intention with which it is uttered. Dummett goes on to note that for most utterances this intentional aspect is not crucial (no specific intention need accompany the making of a bet or the issuing of a command) but assertions and requests are linked to the possession of beliefs and desires respectively. So an assertion has only been made when a speaker has the appropriate belief (note: a consequence is that, in lying, one is not asserting). In order to avoid, what Dummett takes to be, a circular appeal to the content of a belief he explains a speaker's belief in terms of her holding a certain sentence to be true. Thus we must attribute to speakers a grasp of what it is for a sentence to be true, a grasp that is ultimately displayed in their ability to engage in the conventionally determined practice of making assertions.

Appendix 2

Truth-conditional accounts of meaning

Davidson's guiding thought is that we can reverse the Tarskian procedure so that rather than define truth we instead presuppose it and use the theory of truth to deliver an account of meaning.

A simple reconstruction of the train of thought might proceed as follows. A theory of meaning might enable us to form clauses of the following form:

(i) *S* means that *P*

That is, on the left-hand side we have a name of a sentence in the language while on the right-hand side we have a clause specifying its content. Now, one way of thinking of what a theory of meaning is about is to think of it as about some relation that can replace the *means that* relation while preserving the pairings of sentences with content specifications. Now the content specification can, undoubtedly, be used to specify the truth-condition of the sentence. So if (i) holds then the following clause,

(ii) *S* is true iff *P*

is guaranteed to be correct. But what we want is rather the reverse. We want to be able to move from the specification of truth-conditions (from a clause of the form (ii)) to a specification of meaning (to a clause of the form (i)). So what we need to do is to place conditions on the specification of truth-conditions in clauses of the form (ii), which will entitle us to treat these effectively as meaning specifications. So the thought is that a theory of meaning becomes a theory of truth that satisfies certain further constraints.[1]

The theory of truth will generate acceptable clauses of the form (ii) for each sentence of the language from a finite base of clauses specifying the references of primitive expressions of the language. Crudely, the thought is that the truth-condition of "Fred is red" is determined by the referent of "Fred" and the satisfaction conditions of the predicate "is red". Thus the theory of sense is based on a theory of reference.

Appendix 3

Decidability

Although the notion of decidability has been used somewhat uncritically in the preceding chapter, it is by no means an uncontroversial notion. Dummett's use of it is clearly heavily influenced by an idea which applies most naturally to mathematical sentences but it is quite different to the usual notion found in mathematical logic. There one speaks of a *set* of sentences as being decidable just when there is an effective procedure for determining whether any particular sentence is a member of that set or one talks of a sentence as being decidable *in a given formal system* just when there is a proof or disproof of the sentence in that system. Dummett's use of the notion is similar in some respects to the latter notion but is importantly different in others. First, and most obviously, Dummett is not concerned about decidability in a particular formal system. But secondly, Dummett's notion concerns a subject's epistemic position (it isn't simply a relational property holding between a sentence and a formal system). For Dummett a sentence is decidable just in case we can guarantee to be able to furnish a proof or a disproof of it. So any sentence which can be proved or disproved by instituting a mechanical procedure or algorithm – one which is certain to terminate after a finite number of steps – is decidable. But also any sentence for which we possess a proof (even if that proof wasn't the result of implementing a mechanical procedure: it took ingenuity to find) is decidable. So a sentence may become decidable when we find a proof of it and thus extend our epistemic position: the notion of decidability concerns what we are able to guarantee in a given epistemic state.[1]

The notion does not easily generalize beyond the mathematical realm since, in the empirical case, we do not, in general, have procedures which deliver *conclusive* verdicts on truth-value. So the notion must be weakened: a statement is decidable if we possess a method which is guaranteed to issue in best possible evidence either in its favour or against it.[2] The paradigm examples that Dummett gives of the operations in language which enable the expression of undecidable statements are use of the past and future tenses, quantification over unsurveyable domains and subjunctive conditionalization. By means of these operations we can construct sentences that express statements for which we have no guaranteed means of uncovering best possible evidence either for or against. This is not to say that we shouldn't find ourselves in such a fortunate position, just that we have no guarantee of achieving it. Now the notion of best possible evidence is itself unclear: it can perhaps be explained in terms of that of canonical warrant, a notion which is crucial to anti-realist theories of meaning (see Chapter 5). However, since that notion may well be distinctively anti-realist and so unfit for employment in a characterization of the dispute between realist and anti-realist, it is best to stick with the less committing notion of best possible evidence, evidence of a kind which cannot be improved upon by addition of evidence of another kind. Now this is to leave matters vague indeed, but they are not, I think, intolerably vague. The debate can be pursued and issues tackled even allowing for a vagueness in the notion of decidablity. This, of course, is not to say that a complete resolution can be achieved in the absence of a clarification of decidability.

Notes

Introduction

1. "Southall 23 April 1979: The Report of the Unofficial Committee of Enquiry". London: National Council for Civil Liberties, 1980.
2. "The Death of Blair Peach: Supplementary Report of the Unofficial Committee of Enquiry". London: National Council for Civil Liberties, 1980.
3. *Frege: Philosophy of Language, The Interpretation of Frege's Philosophy, Frege: Philosophy of Mathematics, Frege and Other Philosophers.*
4. *Origins of Analytical Philosophy.*
5. So Dummett is wont to lambaste the Wittgensteinian position as one which simply amounts to saying "This is what we do" and as being nihilist in its resistance to *explaining* or *justifying* what we do.
6. Caused, at least in part, by a craving for generality or systematicity.
7. This is not to quibble with Diamond's contention that we cannot circumscribe the form in which illumination might come, but it is emphatically to reject the view that we cannot ever or for any reason adopt such a circumscription.

Chapter 1: What is a theory of meaning?

1. A terminological nicety: in his later work Dummett comes to call any philosophical investigation into meaning part of the theory of meaning; a theory of meaning for a particular language is, then, termed a "meaning-theory". Dummett's proposal is then that theory of meaning should be pursued by considering the form that a meaning-theory should take (see LBoM: 22).
2. It might well seem that the last step of the argument has involved a slide from generally applicable adequacy conditions on specifications to adequacy conditions on a global specification of meanings. But I don't think that the slide matters unless we presuppose something about the form of the meaning-theory: that is, the shape of a global specification of meanings. And, although the theory has been conceived of as systematic, this presupposition is, as yet, vague and, when made precise, will need to be argued for (see "Systematicity, compositionality and meaning-theories", p. 12).

3. In fact, Davidson's interest is to offer an explanation of mood from within a theory of interpretation which takes the form of a theory of truth (modelled on a definition of truth à la Tarski). His solution is an extension of his paratactic analysis of saying that.
4. For more detailed discussion of this difficult but important debate, see Appendix 1.
5. Although the discussion has focused on imperatives the point should be general and is perhaps even clearer for interrogatives.
6. See T&OE: essay 9.
7. See Chapter 2 for further discussion of this.
8. We return to this in Chapter 4.
9. See SoL (pp. 24–5). Also FPL: "we *say* what the reference of a word is and thereby *show* what its sense is" (p. 227).
10. In Chapter 2 we will look at the question of whether this embedding must be holistic or molecular.

Chapter 2: Knowledge of the meaning-theory

1. We can only regret this lack of elaboration since the relation between Dummett's requirement of publicity and the rule-following considerations is somewhat vexed. See below (discussion of McDowell). (Cf. LBoM: 106.)
2. Dummett does, however, seem to be on firmer ground in arguing against meaning as an inner process (psychologism) from an insistence on publicity. (See SoL: 102.)
3. See SoL (pp. 34–8).
4. In his "What is a Theory of Meaning? II" (SoL).
5. Compare this with Dummett's remarks about implicit knowledge of truth-conditions (of, especially, undecidable sentences) and exercise of recognitional capacities – see below.
6. See SoL (essay 3).
7. So it would be wrong to conceive of knowledge in general as consisting of the polar extremes of practical and theoretical knowledge.
8. Dummett later replaces talk of "full-blooded meaning-theories" with talk of "robust meaning-theories".
9. The finitude of one's use is, in fact, a red herring. The point concerns continuing to use an expression in the *same* way in a *new* case and that difficulty, so far as I can see, is untouched by allowing infinite samples of use.
10. And Dummett importantly wants to distinguish this from the following piece of knowledge: S knows that "'x is red' is true iff x is red" is true. This knowledge accrues simply on the basis of a grasp of the syntax of the predicate "red" and, to move from this to the knowledge specified in the text, what one needs is, precisely, an understanding of that predicate. This is why Dummett thinks that modest theories of meaning are an abnegation of one's intellectual responsibility.
11. Indeed, as we shall come to see, Dummett has attracted considerable attention not merely for contemplating philosophically inspired revision of this sort but for recommending that we revise our logic from classical to intuitionistic logic.
12. Matar (1997) makes this insistence on obtaining a clear view a fundamental element in Dummett's philosophical view. Although it is undoubtedly an

important aspect of Dummett's thinking I suspect that Matar overplays its role.

13. The question is very complex since molecularity must be explained by reference to a certain conception of the nature of understanding: what can be described in compositional terms on a truth-conditional conception of understanding might not be so describable on an assertibility conditions construal. So one might hang on to molecularity and alter one's conception of the nature of understanding.

14. We return to these questions when we discuss the form of an anti-realist theory of meaning in Chapter 4 and when we discuss the revisionary implications of anti-realism in Chapter 5.

15. This notion of a theory is very general, amounting to little more than that of a set of sentences held true.

16. See Chapter 5 for more discussion of molecularity.

Chapter 3: The characterization of realism

1. The most important piece to consult is Dummett's second "Realism" paper (SoL: essay 11) but see also essays 2 and 20 (SoL) and essay 10 and the preface of T&OE.

2. See Appendix 3 for a slightly fuller discussion of the notion.

3. For an excellent illustration of this see "The Philosophical Basis of Intuitionistic Logic" (T&OE, essay 14). There Dummett shows that on the meaning-theoretic approach a plausible anti-realism, namely, intuitionism, results while on the ontological approach the opposition to realism collapses into a form of scepticism.

4. See Chapter 1.

5. This description, in fact, presupposes that indeterminacy should not itself be characterized in epistemic terms: an interesting issue in itself.

6. See Chapter 5.

7. Because the plausibility of a truth-conditional account of the meaning of basic sentences will depend upon whether or not we can embrace modesty.

8. "Agnostic" because she refuses to accept a notion of truth which transcends verification rather than denies its possibility.

9. Which, otherwise, would be impossible without the (somewhat baroque) mechanics of substitutional quantification. Substitutional quantification is a method of forming general statements in which the variable position does not range over a domain of objects but marks a place into which expressions from a certain class can be substituted. The truth of the general statement will then depend on the truth-values of the statements formed by means of this process of substitution. An important feature of substitutional quantification is that it allows one to generalize over expressions which occur both as used and as mentioned.

10. This may also skew the debate against the anti-realist by supposing that she must deny factuality, offer a reductive thesis or embrace scepticism; Dummett's anti-realist does none of these.

11. Wright criticizes the Dummettian approach for these sorts of reason (1993: essay 15).

12. We will discuss this further in Chapter 5.

13. Similar thoughts motivate Wright's argument against minimalism or, as he prefers to call it, deflationism (1992: Ch. 1). He makes his point by contrast-

ing truth and positive normative force, showing that they are potentially extensionally divergent.

We return to the issue of defeasibility and Dummett's notion of ingredient sense (the contribution a sentence makes to the sense of more complex sentences of which it is a component) in Chapter 5.

Chapter 4: The challenge for realism

1. See Chapter 2.
2. See Chapter 2.
3. See Loar (1987).
4. See below.
5. The terminology comes from Wright (see, for example, 1993: essay 5).
6. For an anti-realist, the negation of a sentence is assertible just when an absurdity follows from supposing that we are in a position to assert the sentence.
7. We'll discuss this in Chapter 5.
8. Edgington's (1981) justification of classical reasoning in terms of probability perhaps simply provides a route for an anti-realist to endorse classical logic (see Chapter 5).
9. But note now that Horwich's point made in the context of vague statements (see Chapter 3) generalizes. Recall that his point was that, given an acceptance of classical logic for vague statements, we can justify applying bivalence to them but that this doesn't entitle us to believe that such statements are *determinately* either true or false. Here likewise we would again have no justification for thinking that either truth or falsity determinately applies to a statement.
10. Wright (1981) questions Dummett's (supposed) equation of realism with an acceptance of bivalence by noting just this point: *if* classical logic is deemed acceptable then there's no obvious distinction between an endorsement of LEM and of bivalence. But this neglects Dummett's later more nuanced view according to which realism is seen in terms of accepting a certain sort of semantic theory for a region of language. That is, realism involves use of semantic concepts in a justificatory (and not merely expressive) role.
11. Note that my bracketed comments indicate that the notions of a rigid and a flexible designator are to be explained in terms of that of scope. However, Kripke elucidates the notion through talk of possible worlds: a rigid designator designates the same object in each possible world, a flexible designator designates the unique satisfier of the description, if there is one, in each possible world. Dummett's claim is that the possible worlds mode of explanation is merely metaphorical elucidation whose content must be sought elsewhere, namely, in talk about scope.
12. Kripke wants to reject the account which focuses on scope. That might be an acceptable solution if what we were primarily concerned with was the behaviour of names and descriptions in modal contexts. But, according to Kripke, what he has shown is a difference in the behaviour of the truth-conditions of simple sentences involving names and definite descriptions in counterfactual situations. (Note that, although this has nothing to do with Kripke's motivation here, this view sits very well with a molecularist line of thought, which would attempt to explain the behaviour of a term in complex sentences on the basis only of its behaviour in simple sentences.) His point is

that "St Anne was virtuous" represents situations in which St Anne, that very person, is virtuous. "The mother of Mary was virtuous" does not; it represents situations in which whoever is the mother of Mary is virtuous. What is perplexing in Kripke's account is that he doesn't explain (except in metaphorical terms) the content of talk about the behaviour of truth-conditions in counterfactual situations which doesn't invoke the behaviour of simple sentences in more complex ones.

13. See below for explanation of this phrase (due to Putnam).

14. It is no part of the story that travel between Earth and Twin Earth is impossible.

15. It is a good question whether the issue of the semantics of natural kind terms can be decided independently of that of realism. (Putnam certainly thinks that a resistance to his account stems from a mistaken resistance to realism.) If it cannot then Dummett's approach faces considerable difficulties. For, although a given meaning-theory will certainly not be metaphysically innocent, the aptitude of the theory should be decidable independently of one's metaphysical leanings.

16. Wiggins (1994) pursues what might be a similar strategy, arguing that a Fregean might try to incorporate the lesson of Putnam's examples by employing a notion of sense according to which to form a conception of the relevant concept (in the Fregean sense of that term) the speaker must have encountered instances of the concept.

17. McGinn (1982a, 1982b) argues for such a notion of sense but then uses this to buttress realism by claiming that such a notion of sense shows the manifestation requirement to be misplaced.

18. This, of course, is a simplification, but is a harmless one.

19. This is, I think, the right question to press the non-Fregean on but not until a further tension has been brought out in her position. (See below.)

20. Model theory is a branch of mathematical logic. It examines the relations between language, presented as a formal structure, and another mathematical structure, usually a set-theoretic structure. Mathematicians are interested in model theory because they are interested in the nature of a linguistic structure needed to characterize a mathematical structure (usually up to isomorphism). Formal semanticians think of the mathematical structure as standing in for the world and are interested in possible semantic relations between language and "the world". Model theory has been exploited in attempting to define notions of logical consequence and validity. Putnam argued that, given plausible constraints on the acceptability of a model for an ideal theory, there will be an indefinite number of apparently acceptable models. So, if we see the process of fixing an intended interpretation for our language as analogous to determining the intended model for our theory, then that task is impossible. We cannot therefore think of ourselves as talking about anything in particular. Clearly to appraise the argument we need to know why we should think the analogy is good and whether Putnam moots the right constraints and applies them well. These largely are questions for another occasion (but see the text for a little on the first question and the next note for something on the second).

21. Dummett's question (see note 13) now becomes moot. For the point of the indeterminacy argument is that the non-Fregean must offer an argument for identifying her preferred relation with reference. However, given the indeterminacy results, she is unable to do this. To be very brief, the point would be that the non-Fregean faces a sceptical challenge to her notion of

reference. To rebut the challenge she appeals to a naturalistic account of reference. The response accepts that this naturalistic account spells out a relation of words to worldly items but asks for a reason to accept this relation as the reference relation. That reason must depend upon knowing something about reference. But what might this be? Three sorts of knowledge suggest themselves. First, there is specific knowledge of the references of terms in the language but this, given the sceptical challenge, begs the question. Secondly, there is knowledge about the relation of truth to reference but the indeterminacy results precisely show that we can fix facts about truth-conditions without thereby fixing reference relations. Thirdly, there are platitudes about the relation of reference; however, whatever these might be, they seem insufficiently strong to fix a relation of reference. So no sort of knowledge is available by means of which to justify an identification of a relation with reference: Dummett's pert criticism is, ultimately, telling.

Chapter 5: What is anti-realism?

1. Tarski gave us the machinery to define truth in a formal language, assuming a scheme of translating sentences of that language into sentences of the theory, that is, in effect assuming that meaning is given.
2. Dummett suggests the first alternative in "Truth" (T&OE: 17–18) and the second in the Preface (T&OE: xxii). Of course, neither alternative need deny that the knowledge which the theory attributes to speakers *amounts to* knowledge of truth-conditions. The difference is whether we characterize truth and then employ this notion in an account of knowledge of truth-conditions or whether we characterize understanding and then identify this with knowledge of truth-conditions.
3. *Pace* fictionalists about mathematics, who think that mathematics is false.
4. A construction is simply a chain of mathematical reasoning.
5. The problem is moot partly because of worries about circularity but partly also because it is not clear whether or not the existential quantifier should be interpreted classically.
6. More strictly, this is so if the deduction is supposed to have no premises. Here we can confine our attention to such deductions.
7. Similar remarks will apply to universal quantification where, in proving the universal statement, we are led to make assumptions about the manner of specification, or mode of presentation of elements in the domain. Thus, for the intuitionist, grasp of a certain domain will not consist purely in an understanding of what qualifies an object for inclusion in that domain (together with a criterion of identity applicable to members of the domain) but will also involve knowledge of a canonical means of specifying objects in the domain. This, surely, is the root of the intuitionist's objection to impredicative specifications (specifications of elements in a domain which themselves quantify over that domain). For then, to grasp an impredicative specification, one needs to understand quantification over the domain and that requires grasp of how elements in the domain may legitimately be specified. But if that in turn includes grasp of impredicative specifications we presuppose a grasp of the domain. It is hard to see how one could ever gain ingress to this circle.
8. See my 1997 for a more complete discussion.
9. Note that this presupposes that informal sentences have formal analogues

and that there is no formal proof where there isn't a corresponding informal one.

10. See T&OE (essay 12: 194–201).

11. Actually Dummett requires the stronger condition of stability. Stability obtains when, if we start the justification procedure in one direction and then return in the opposite direction, we end up justifying the original conditions. We shall skirt these technicalities here and stick with our informal characterization of harmony.

12. We discuss this further in Chapter 6.

13. Again, see Chapter 6 for more discussion of this issue.

14. But see Rumfitt (2000) for criticism of Dummett's argument. His point is that if we include denial in our considerations then each of correctness and incorrectness conditions may have a substantial role to play.

15. That is, warrants for assertion.

16. See Wright (1993: essay 14) and Brandom (1976; 1994: 116–31) for further discussion of this problem.

17. See the close of Chapter 3.

18. Dummett wants to reply to Kripke (see Chapter 4) that the respective sentences containing a proper name and its reference-fixing definite description agree in content sense but differ in ingredient sense (as shown by their behaviour in modal contexts). But I argued that, to adhere to his molecularity requirement, Dummett had better say that here we have a convention governing our use and so understanding of modal operators in application to sentences involving names and descriptions.

19. Brandom (1994: 125–30) makes a similar proposal but is unconcerned with issues to do with molecularism.

20. Ironically, Dummett's accusation of holism is apt to seem plausible given (and, perhaps, *only* given) a prior commitment to seeing the inferential passage encapsulated in an assertion as logically valid. For, if we accept that constraint, we shall only be able to preserve logical validity by admitting a change in meaning in the original class of sentences. So introduction of the new region of language fails to be conservative with respect to those meanings. In contrast, it seems that we can precisely insist on conservativeness here, provided we accept that the inference is only materially valid.

21. I do not, in any case, see any way of making out a notion of canonical conditions of use without an appeal to the basis on which ascriptions of understanding are made.

22. Here's a lesson Wittgenstein drew from his discussion of following a rule.

23. But see Wright's "Can a Davidsonian Meaning-theory be Construed in Terms of Assertibility?" (1986) for a proposal which gives an anti-realist account of truth and then uses this in a theory of meaning.

Chapter 6: The revisionary implications of anti-realism

1. And this concern may well be a positivistic inheritance.

2. "Part" because positions may agree in their revisionary implications yet still differ in the way they justify first-order practice.

3. I use square brackets to indicate quotation marks around sentential variables.

4. Horwich (1990: section 25) argues from the circularity of these justifications

against the idea that truth has a substantive role to play in them. So the deflationist can, as she must, eschew the need for semantic validations of logic. But that gets things the wrong way around. The justifications are circular if only a minimal conception of truth is available; they aren't obviously circular if we have a more substantial notion. So we cannot argue from the supposed circularity of the justifications to the deflationary view: making clear the circularity presupposes the deflationary view.

5. Technically our justification of a system of logic will take the form of a soundness and completeness proof, the former showing that all syntactic consequence relations coincide with semantic consequence relations and the latter showing the reverse: that all semantic consequence relations coincide with syntactic consequence relations. Soundness proofs are more crucial because unsoundness, unlike incompleteness, is a crippling defect in a logical system. Here I've kept the discussion on the informal level. That shouldn't be problematic in itself but one may think that the notions of syntactic and semantic consequence collapse into one another once we identify truth with provability. But they don't. The notion of provability is characterized relative to a set of rules of inference. However, as we come to see, this still leaves room for the "semantic" question of whether these rules can be reconciled with an identification of truth with provability. Technically, we would pursue these informal questions by constructing a formal semantics which models this identification. Beth trees are intended to play just this role. But we don't need to follow that route to make the point at issue here.

6. We might think we could reason from not-not-P to not-not-($[P]$is true) and then use double negation elimination in the meta-language to infer $[P]$ is true. But the first step fails since "not" (unlike "–") is a meta-linguistic connective, so cannot be applied to P.

7. Of course, *given* a certain deflationary or minimal conception of truth there may be no substantive justificatory project here.

8. Dummett (Taylor 1987: 254) makes a similar point focusing on formal semantic theories. He points out that if we adopt a semantic theory such as Beth trees for intuitionistic logic or ortholattices for quantum logic then, even if we reason classically in the meta-language, we shall be able to see that classical principles (LEM and the distributive law, respectively) fail to hold in the object language. If, therefore, we think that these formal semantics offer a good model for an informal conception of truth we shall be led to a general rejection of classical logic. The point about having a substantial conception of truth then becomes one of rejecting a purely homophonic semantics.

9. See Chapter 2 and Chapter 5.

10. Assume that there are no dogs but terriers and poodles. Of course, no terrier is a poodle.

11. See my (1992) for a more careful development of this argument.

12. But see below.

13. See Tennant (1997: section 6.6.2) for further discussion.

14. This issue will crop up again in Chapter 7.

15. If the equivalence schema holds then truth distributes over the disjunction (simply substituting equivalents involving the truth predicate in "$P \vee Q$"). So if we deny the latter we must deny the former.

16. Note that, although this must be the right interpretation of degrees of justification, it sits a little oddly in the setting of an argument for realism – which is where Edgington places it. How, for instance, are subjective assignments of degrees of justification related to objective truth?

17. Peter Milne suggests the following defence of Edgington. Even in intuitionistic logic $-(P \vee -P)$ is conclusively refuted. So $J(-(P \vee -P)) = 0$. From which we infer that $J(P \vee -P) = 1$. He points out, however, that it is unclear whether we can assume the logical result. Although the issue warrants more thought, Edgington offers her account, first, as one which applies to ordinary empirical statements not to those of logic and mathematics and, secondly, as an account of the meanings of the logical constants, and for both of these reasons it seems reasonable to restrict our attention to rules of inference which can be justified by constraining P to be logically simple.

18. Russell's paradox was an early, and is a good illustrative, example. Any definite condition defines a set over the domain of objects. Sets themselves are part of the domain of objects. So some sets, for example, the set of sets containing more than three members, contain sets as members and indeed contain themselves as members. So the condition of being a set which does not contain itself should define a set: the set of sets which do not contain themselves. Now if this set is a member of itself then it satisfies its defining condition: it does not contain itself. So it seems that the set must not be a member of itself. But that is to satisfy its membership condition so it is a member of itself. Thus the set both is and is not a member of itself.

19. See Dummett (FPM: Ch. 24); Heck (1993); Oliver (1994, 1998).

20. The issue we shall discuss is rather different to the complex of problems gestured at in the previous paragraph.

Chapter 7: Two case studies: the past and mathematics

1. Here *"Past"*, *"Pres"* and *"Fut"* are operators transforming the tenseless sentence S into a past, present and future tense sentence, respectively. Strictly we should have time indices in place – as we had "yesterday", "today" and "tomorrow" in the informal example – but, since these aren't essential for the point at issue, I have omitted them for the sake of simplicity.

2. To offer an illustrative but inexhaustive list.

3. Not to be confused with the notion of stability mentioned in connection with that of harmony (Ch. 5).

4. Obviously, if I said that Amanda was the tallest girl and then that Jessie was the tallest girl I would not have contradicted myself were it clear that the range of girls in each case differed.

5. Although the objection is well taken, one shouldn't be deceived about Dummett's commitment to its target. In his paper, Dummett was investigating whether the past posed an irresolvable problem for the anti-realist. His conclusion was that the problem was not conclusive but that the resulting anti-realist position was so implausible as to be scarcely credible.

6. Wright goes on to offer his own solution on behalf of the anti-realist. It depends on a notion of double indexing: the truth predicates are taken to apply to statements which are characterized by referring to what a sentence expresses at a certain time of utterance. So they're indexed by the tense-modality of the sentence and the tense-modality of the verb "to express". For instance we might have the following link:

What $[Past(S, t)]$ expresses is true iff what $[S]$ expressed at t is true.

Wright's strategy is now to arrive at new versions of the truth-value links, which won't sustain the problematic inferences. However, I argue (1996) that since the original links can be deduced from Wright's surrogates no progress has been made.

7. Here, clearly, the time indices would have to match appropriately.

8. A similar train of thought might be developed in the case of the future. But here the general thought, although suggestive, is not as persuasive, perhaps because the evidence for the truth of a future-tense sentence is not caused by the event it is about.

9. I'm doubtful that anything of substance hangs on this recommendation.

10. Taking "*S*" to be "[*S*] is decidable" and "*T*" to be "*S* ∨ –*S*".

11. But see below for more discussion of this.

12. Undoubtedly we are making a simplifying assumption here that all tennis shots are easily and exhaustively so classified. (I know that some of mine aren't.)

13. Since "The shot was a backhand" entails "The shot was not a forehand."

14. Dummett (see LBoM: 179; *Theoria* 1998) offers an argument roughly to the same effect, focusing on the application of inferential reasoning to past-tense sentences. We shall return to this below.

15. This will hold when we insist that truth distributes over disjunction.

16. There are a number of issues in this region which we shan't be able to investigate. Among them are the following: what form would a strict finitist position take? and is the notion of decidability legitimate when extended beyond the mathematical realm? (See Wright (1980) and "Strict Finitism" in Wright (1993) for the most thorough extant discussion of these topics.)

17. Although, of course, there may be no non-trivial specification of conditions sufficient for a successful exercise of the capacity.

18. See Wright (1980) and George (1988).

19. The reasons why the position doesn't inflate into ideal verificationism would have to hinge on features of our ascriptions of capacities. The point would have to be either that arriving at an end of a decision after a finite number of steps is part of the concept of a decision procedure (that an infinite decision procedure is an incoherent notion because it doesn't incorporate a description of the end of the procedure) or that limitations on capacities due to finitude of one or another form are not extraneous.

20. The example is Wright's (see Taylor 1987).

21. Intuitionistic logic is patently no subject for the faint-hearted.

22. See LBoM (p. 295).

23. Meaning, of course, not that the relevant views aren't subject to revision but that when held they are held to apply across time.

24. Dummett connects this position with the truth-value links. I cannot concur; it seems both independent of and more general than any lesson that might be drawn from them.

25. *Theoria* 1998.

26. Indeed in his unpublished Gifford Lectures Dummett experiments with a view that is realist about the past but strictly anti-realist about the future: reality is, as he says, cumulative. I find this asymmetry with respect to past and future hard to reconcile with his stress on the truth-value links, which are symmetrical with respect to past and future.

27. Of course this raises a weighty question about just when revision is and is not an option.

28. See Chapter 3.

29. Incidentally, if either of these approaches is successful then we might have a quick way with the problem posed by strict finitism. For then the incoherence of strict finitism will function to show that we need a notion of truth that goes beyond that of being decidable in practice. The intuitionistic notion of *decidability in principle* might then be justified as the least metaphysically committed notion of truth needed to account for arithmetic practice.
30. We noted this already in Chapter 3.

Conclusion

1. I owe this observation to Nils Kurbis.

Appendix 1: Mood, force and convention

1. The examples are Davidson's.
2. See his "Mood, Force and Convention' (SoL: Ch. 9).

Appendix 2: Truth-conditional accounts of meaning

1. We don't need to go into these here. See "Truth and Meaning" in Davidson (1984), McDowell (1976) and Wiggins (1997).

Appendix 3: Decidability

1. See Shieh (1998), George (1993) and Tennant (1987: Ch. 15; 1997: sections 6.2, 6.5) for much more discussion of issues surrounding this theme.
2. One might weaken this even further by eschewing the notion of best possible evidence and concentrating on that of evidence sufficient for a justified verdict on truth-value.

Bibliography

Works by Dummett

Books

1973. *Frege: Philosophy of Language*. London: Duckworth (2nd edition 1981).
1977. *Elements of Intuitionism*. Oxford: Oxford University Press (2nd edition 2000).
1978. *Truth and Other Enigmas*. London: Duckworth.
1981. *The Interpretation of Frege's Philosophy*. London: Duckworth.
1991. *Frege and Other Philosophers*. Oxford: Oxford University Press.
1991. *Frege: Philosophy of Mathematics*. London: Duckworth.
1991. *The Logical Basis of Metaphysics*. London: Duckworth.
1993. *Origins of Analytical Philosophy*. London: Duckworth.
1993. *The Seas of Language*. Oxford: Oxford University Press.

Papers

1979. Reply to Putnam. In *Meaning and Use*, A. Margalit (ed.). Dordrecht: Reidel.
1986. "'A Nice Derangement of Epitaphs': Some Comments on Davidson and Hacking". In *Truth and Interpretation: Perspectives on the Philosophy of Donald Davidson*, E. LePore (ed.), 459–76. Oxford: Blackwell.
1987. Replies. In *Michael Dummett: Contributions to Philosophy*, B. Taylor (ed.). Dordrecht: Nijhoff.
1994. "Wittgenstein on Necessity: Some Reflections". In *Reading Putnam*, P. Clark & Bob Hale (eds), 49–65. Oxford: Blackwell.
1995. "Bivalence and Vagueness", *Theoria* **61**: 201–16.
1998. "Truth from the Constructive Standpoint", *Theoria* **64**: 122–38.

Michael Dummett

Collections of papers on Dummett

1987. *Michael Dummett: Contributions to Philosophy*, B. Taylor (ed.). Dordrecht: Nijhoff.
1994. *The Philosophy of Michael Dummett*, B. McGuiness & G. Oliveri (eds). Dordrecht: Kluwer.
1997. *Language, Thought and Logic: Essays in Honour of Michael Dummett*, R. Heck (ed.). Oxford: Oxford University Press.
1998. *New Essays on the Philosophy of Michael Dummett*, J. Brandl & P. Sullivan (eds). Rodopi.

Works by other authors

Appiah, A. 1986. *For Truth in Semantics*. Oxford: Blackwell.
Brandom, R. 1976. "Truth and Assertibility", *Journal of Philosophy* **83**: 137–49.
Brandom, R. 1994. *Making it Explicit*. Cambridge, Mass.: Harvard University Press.
Davidson, D. 1984. *Inquiries into Truth and Interpretation*. Oxford: Oxford University Press.
Davidson, D. 1986. "A Nice Derangement of Epitaphs". In *Truth and Interpretation: Perspectives on the Philosophy of Donald Davidson*, E. LePore (ed.), 433–46. Oxford: Blackwell.
Devitt, M. 1983. "Dummett's Anti-realism", *Journal of Philosophy* **80**: 73–99.
Devitt, M. 1984. *Realism and Truth*. Oxford: Blackwell (2nd edition 1991).
Edgington, D. 1981. "Meaning, Bivalence and Realism", *Proceedings of the Aristotelian Society*: 153–73.
Evans, G. & J. McDowell (eds) 1976. *Truth and Meaning*. Oxford: Oxford University Press.
Evans, G. 1985. *Collected Papers*. Oxford: Oxford University Press.
Frege, G. 1950. *The Foundations of Arithmetic*, J. L. Austin (trans.). Oxford: Blackwell.
Frege, G. 1952. *Translations from the Philosophical Writings of Gottlob Frege*, P. Geach & M. Black (eds). Oxford: Blackwell.
George, A. 1988. "The Conveyability of Intuitionism: An Essay on Mathematical Cognition", *Journal of Philosophical Logic* **17**: 133–56.
George, A. 1993. "How not to Refute Realism", *The Journal of Philosophy* **2**: 53–72.
Haack, S. 1982. "Dummett's Justification of Deduction", *Mind* **91**: 216–39.
Heck, R. 1993. "Critical Notice of M. Dummett, *Frege: Philosophy of Mathematics*", *Philosophical Quarterly* **43**: 223–33.
Heck, R. (ed.) 1997. *Language, Thought and Logic: Essays in Honour of Michael Dummett*. Oxford: Oxford University Press.
Heyting, A. 1971. *Intuitionism: An Introduction*. Amsterdam: North Holland.
Horwich, P. 1990. *Truth*. Oxford: Blackwell.
Kripke, S. 1980. *Naming and Necessity*. Oxford: Blackwell.
Kripke, S. 1982. *Wittgenstein on Rules and Private Langauge*. Oxford: Blackwell.
Lewis, D. 1984. "Putnam's Paradox", *Australasian Journal of Philosophy* **62**: 221–36.
Loar, B. 1987. "Truth Beyond all Verification". See Taylor (1987), pp. 81–117.

Luntley, M. 1988. *Language, Logic and Experience: The Case for Anti-realism*. London: Duckworth.

McDowell, J. 1976. "Truth Conditions, Bivalence and Verificationism". See Evans and McDowell (1976), pp. 42–66.

McDowell, J. 1981. "Anti-realism and the Epistemology of Understanding". In *Meaning and Understanding*, H. Parret & B. Bouveresse (eds), 225–48. Berlin: de Gruyter.

McDowell, J. 1982. "Criteria, Defeasibility and Knowledge. In *Proceedings of the British Academy*, **LXVIII**, 455–79. Oxford: Oxford University Press.

McDowell, J. 1987. "In Defence of Modesty". See Taylor (1987), pp. 59–80.

McDowell, J. 1997. "Another Plea for Modesty". See Heck (1997).

McGinn, C. 1982a. "The Structure of Content". In *Thought and Object*, A. Woodfield (ed.), 207–58. Oxford: Clarendon Press.

McGinn, C. 1982b. "Realist Semantics and Content-ascription", *Synthese* **52**: 113–34.

Margalit, A. 1979. *Meaning and Use*. Dordrecht: Reidel.

Matar, A. 1997. *From Dummett's Philosophical Perspective*. Berlin: de Gruyter.

Millikan, R. 1984. *Language, Thought and Other Biological Categories*. Cambridge, Mass.: MIT Press.

Oliver, A. 1994. "Dummett and Frege on the Philosophy of Mathematics", *Inquiry* **37**: 349–92.

Oliver, A. 1998. "Hazy Totalities and Indefinitely Extensible Concepts", *Grazer Philosophische Studien* **55**: 25–50.

Papineau, D. 1987. *Reality and Representation*. Oxford: Blackwell.

Putnam, H. 1975. "The Meaning of 'Meaning'". In *Mind, Language and Reality: Philosophical Papers Volume 2*, 215–71. Cambridge: Cambridge University Press.

Putnam, H. 1979a. "Reference and Understanding". See Margalit (1979), pp. 199–216.

Putnam, H. 1979b. "Reply to Dummett;s Comment". See Margalit (1979), pp. 226–8.

Putnam, H. 1981. *Reason, Truth and History*. Cambridge: Cambridge University Press.

Putnam, H. 1983. "Models and Reality". In *Realism and Reason: Philosophical Papers, Volume 3*, 1–26. Cambridge: Cambridge University Press.

Quine, W. V. O. 1953. "Two Dogmas of Empiricism". In *From a Logical Point of View*, 20–46. Cambridge, Mass.: Harvard University Press.

Rosen, G. 1995. "The Shoals of Language", *Mind* **104**(415): 599–609.

Rumfitt, I. 2000. "'Yes' and 'No'", *Mind* **109**(436): 781–824.

Shieh, S. 1998. "Undecidability in Anti-realism", *Philosophia Mathematica* **6**(3): 324–33.

Taylor, B. (ed.) 1987. *Michael Dummett: Contributions to Philosophy*. Dordrecht: Nijhoff.

Tennant, N. 1987. *Anti-realism and Logic: Truth as Eternal*. Oxford: Clarendon.

Tennant, N. 1997. *The Taming of the True*. Oxford: Oxford University Press.

Tennant, N. 2000. "Anti-realist Aporias", *Mind* **109**(436): 825–55.

Weiss, B. 1992. "Can an Anti-realist be Revisionary about Deductive Inference?", *Analysis* **52**(4): 216–24.

Weiss, B. 1996. "Anti-realism, Truth-value Links and Tensed Truth Predicates", *Mind* **105**(420): 577–602.

Weiss, B. 1997. "Proof and Canonical Proof", *Synthese* **113**: 265–84.

Wiggins, D. 1994. "Putnam's Doctrine of Natural Kind Words and Frege's

Doctrine of Sense, Reference and Extension: Can they Cohere?". In *Reading Putnam*, P. Clark & B. Hale (eds), 201–15. Oxford: Blackwell.

Wiggins, D. 1997. "Meaning and Truth Conditions: from Frege's Grand Design to Davidson's". In *A Companion to the Philosophy of Language*, R. Hale & C. Wright (eds), 3–28. Oxford: Blackwell.

Wittgenstein, L. 1958. *Philosophical Investigations*, G. E. M. Anscombe (trans.). Oxford: Blackwell.

Wright, C. 1980. *Wittgenstein on the Foundations of Mathematics*. London: Duckworth.

Wright, C. 1981. "Anti-realism and Revisionism". Reprinted as essay 15 in Wright (1993).

Wright, C. 1987. "Dummett and Revisionism". See Taylor (1987), pp. 1–30.

Wright, C. 1992. *Truth and Objectivity*. Cambridge, Mass.: Harvard University Press.

Wright, C. 1993. *Realism, Meaning and Truth*. Oxford: Blackwell (1st edition 1986).

Index

Michael Dummett